WORLD BEATS

University of Hertfordshire UH

College Lane, Hatfield, Herts, AL10 9AB

This item must be returned if reserved.

Fines are charged for the late return of reserved items.

Helpdesk@herts.ac.uk +44(0)1707 284678

RE-MAPPING THE TRANSNATIONAL
A Dartmouth Series in American Studies

SERIES EDITOR
Donald E. Pease
Avalon Foundation Chair of Humanities
Founding Director of the Futures of American Studies Institute
Dartmouth College

The emergence of Transnational American Studies in the wake of the Cold War marks the most significant reconfiguration of American Studies since its inception. The shock waves generated by a newly globalized world order demanded an understanding of America's embeddedness within global and local processes rather than scholarly reaffirmations of its splendid isolation. The series Re-Mapping the Transnational seeks to foster the cross-national dialogues needed to sustain the vitality of this emergent field. To advance a truly comparativist understanding of this scholarly endeavor, Dartmouth College Press welcomes monographs from scholars both inside and outside the United States.

For a complete list of books available in this series, see www.upne.com.

JIMMY FAZZINO

WORLD BEATS

Beat Generation Writing
and the Worlding
of U.S. Literature

DARTMOUTH COLLEGE PRESS
HANOVER, NEW HAMPSHIRE

Dartmouth College Press
An imprint of University Press of New England
www.upne.com
© 2016 Trustees of Dartmouth College
Manufactured in the United States of America
Typeset in Sabon and Scala Sans by Integrated Publishing Solutions

For permission to reproduce any of the material in this book,
contact Permissions, University Press of New England, One Court
Street, Suite 250, Lebanon NH 03766; or visit www.upne.com

Page 247 constitutes a continuation of this copyright page.

Library of Congress Cataloging-in-Publication Data

Names: Fazzino, Jimmy, 1981–
Title: World Beats: Beat Generation writing and the worlding of U.S.
literature / Jimmy Fazzino.
Description: Hanover, New Hampshire: Dartmouth College Press, 2016.
| Series: Re-mapping the transnational: a Dartmouth series in American
studies | Includes bibliographical references and index. | Description
based on print version record and CIP data provided by publisher;
resource not viewed.
Identifiers: LCCN 2015040764 (print) | LCCN 2015035037 (ebook) |
ISBN 9781611689471 (epub, pdf & mobi) | ISBN 9781611688979
(cloth: alk. paper) | ISBN 9781611688986 (pbk.: alk. paper) | ISBN
9781611689471 (ebook)
Subjects: LCSH: Beat generation. | American literature—20th century—
History and criticism. | Literature and transnationalism.
Classification: LCC PS228.B6 (print) | LCC PS228.B6 F39 2016 (ebook) |
DDC 810.9/0054—dc23
LC record available at http://lccn.loc.gov/2015040764

5 4 3 2 1

for Suzanne and Olive

NO ONE WAY WORKS, it will take all of us
shoving at the thing from all sides
to bring it down.
—Diane di Prima, *Revolutionary Letters*

CONTENTS

WORLD BEATS

IN THE EARLY 1960S Allen Ginsberg spent fifteen months traveling around India with partner Peter Orlovsky. They were joined for a spell by Gary Snyder and Joanne Kyger visiting from Japan, where Snyder had been studying Zen Buddhism. While in Kolkata, Ginsberg was naturally drawn to Sunil Gangopadhyay and the group of dissident Bengali poets known as the "Hungryalists," or, in a clearer echo of Ginsberg and his Beat comrades, the "Hungry Generation," who felt disaffected by the fervent nationalism they saw all around them in a still newly independent India and were dismayed by the escalating militarism that followed the 1962 war with China.[1] Like the Beats, the Hungry Generation poets would be censored and even jailed for their literary licentiousness and antinomian views. They discussed with Ginsberg the need to break free from the stifling legacy of Nobel laureate Rabindranath Tagore—to them what T. S. Eliot had been to Ginsberg and so many others—and Ginsberg urged them to write in Bengali and abandon Western models in favor of a renewed and native spiritualism. In particular, his new friends in Kolkata were searching for a way beyond both colonialism and a nationalism that did not, they believed, truly serve India's needs, and their example highlights the multivalent legacies of European imperialism, the complexities of decolonization, and, to a much greater extent than has been acknowledged, the interest of Beat Generation writers in such matters.

The tensions within Bengali intellectual life and among Kolkata's *adda* poets: between the past and the present, colonial rule and national independence, "their gods" and "the gods of modernism," as Deborah Baker puts it, mean that India for Ginsberg is not timeless or unchanging or utterly exotic (hallmarks of orientalist thinking) but vital and dynamic; it retains the specificity of its historical moment and engages with the poet on its own terms.[2] To grasp the nature and significance of this engagement requires a transnational perspective on Beat writing. The Beats were prolific travelers, and the fact that they produced some of their most significant and enduring works abroad—including Ginsberg's *Kaddish*, Jack Kerouac's *Mexico City Blues*, William Burroughs's *Naked Lunch*, and Gregory Corso's *Happy Birthday of Death*, just to name a few—suggests that their calling as writers was somehow predicated upon their leaving the United States behind. This distance from home is what opens up a space for all sorts of unexpected connections and crossings to arise in their work. Beat Generation writers were profoundly engaged with the world at large, particularly colonial and postcolonial spaces in what was then called the third world. Living and writing abroad at the great moment of decolonization across the globe, the Beats were more than just tourists (as more than a few critics have asserted), that is to say, unconcerned or altogether unaware of the immediate and usually fraught political situations unfolding around them. They could in fact be very attuned to local struggles and local histories, although it can take a certain kind of *worlded* reading practice to unearth these histories in their work.

Every travelogue is, at some level, a comment on home, and the worlded and worldly view gained by Beat writers abroad often involved a new perspective on the United States as well. When Amiri Baraka, for instance, visited Cuba in 1960 along with a delegation of African American artists and activists under the banner of the Fair Play for Cuba Committee, his experiences there marked a real shift in consciousness for him.[3] Among other things, Baraka's time in Cuba gave him a different point of view on the U.S. civil rights movement, which was then in full swing. He saw firsthand how incredibly overdetermined and far from universal the discourse on race had become in the United States and how limited the solutions offered by the mainstream protest movement. He became open to the possibilities of a broader, more radical conception of political struggle and social change; as Todd Tietchen has argued, Baraka's experience of Cuba was the first step on a path that would lead him to black nationalism and then third world Marxism.[4] He was deeply affected by the presence of fellow traveler Robert Williams. As an NAACP chapter head in North Carolina, Williams had recently made waves by arming the local African American community against the Klan. Williams, who would return to Cuba in 1961, wanted by the FBI, represented a more militant wing of the civil rights movement. He would inspire the future Black Panthers, and his philosophy was something that Baraka began to find more and more appealing as the 1960s wore on.

Even Gregory Corso, seemingly the most apolitical of Beat poets, has something to say about the global affairs of the day. Barry Miles, writing specifically about William Burroughs but expressing a more general sentiment about the Beats in Paris and elsewhere abroad, argues that Burroughs's "experience was much more internal; his was more a landscape of ideas, and in many ways he could have been living anywhere."[5] Yet Corso, however committed to the lyrical and averse to the earthbound, did not remain unaffected while in Paris by the tense political situation that existed there during the final months of the Fourth Republic—driven largely by the turmoil of the Algerian War. And he cannot help but figure these issues into his poetry, notably in "The Sacré-Coeur Café" and in "Bomb" (the centerpiece of his 1960 volume of Paris poems, *The Happy Birthday of Death*), where Corso makes his immediate political and historical context quite visible. On the surface, "The Sacré-Coeur Café" is a standard lament for a romanticized Paris of yore, no longer available to an artist and dreamer like Corso. The city's literary past colors the poet's perceptions of it in the present, and much of the poem deals with the gap between his expectations of Paris and the workaday reality he finds there. But the past Corso longs for is specifically a revolutionary past. The opening image:

> The fierce girls in the Sacré-Coeur Café
> bang their wines on the table
> screaming Danton triumphed having denied liberty
> While the garçon demands Murat triumph on all that triumphs

gets utterly transformed by the poem's end:

> Ah but there are plastic tables in the Sacré-Coeur Café
> The fierce girls all work in the Post Office
> The proprietors have no Cosette but a big fat son
> who sits dunking croissants.[6]

"Cosette" appears because in the poem's middle section the speaker imagines himself in the world of *Les Misérables* (which Victor Hugo wrote in exile following Louis-Napoléon's 1851 coup d'état and which dramatizes the 1832 republican uprising against the July Monarchy), playing the role of fellow "ex-convict" Jean Valjean and rescuing "little Cosette— the size of eternity."[7] Most striking in Corso's poem, however, are the ways in which it registers the situation in Algeria. After invoking Danton and Murat, Corso writes, "The bombed Algerians observe each others' burning teeth / A scarey café the Sacré-Coeur Café." And the poem ends,

"And the Algerians / they don't go to the Sacré-Coeur Café." Their conspicuous absence from the scene makes the Algerians' presence all the more palpable, and the poem implies that it is those currently engaged in armed insurrection against France itself who are the rightful inheritors of that nation's revolutionary history. It is the "Algerian question," along with the dying colonialism it comes to stand in for, that converts Corso's quaint Parisian scene from make believe to reality.

World Beats arrives at the convergence of two developments: (1) the flowering in recent years of critically capacious, theoretically informed scholarship on Beat Generation literature and (2) the concurrent shift in U.S. literary studies toward a transnational understanding of cultural production. Though long regarded as quintessentially "American," the mid-twentieth-century countercultural phenomenon known as the Beat Generation is not only what we would now recognize as a transnational literary movement par excellence but is thoroughly worlded in all the ways that I attempt to describe in this book. Situating my work in relation to the burgeoning field of Beat studies as well as the much broader zone defined by the transnational turn in the humanities, I argue that the study of Beat writing offers new approaches for transnationally minded criticism in the twenty-first century.

As approaches to Beat Generation writing become more theoretically capacious, and as the study of the Beats seems to be increasingly legitimated within the academy, critics reach a point where merely reflecting on what it means to be "Beat," asking who was or was not a Beat, or calculating when the Beat movement can be said to have begun or ended will no longer suffice. A collections of essays edited by Jennie Skerl and published in 2004, *Reconstructing the Beats*, called attention to the limitations of Beat scholarship and began to challenge the adulatory mythography that has characterized the study of Beat writing. The volume's goal, as Skerl states in her introduction, was "to provide a scholarly reassessment that will chart new directions for criticism and teaching at the beginning of the twenty-first century." Her elaboration of this mission neatly summarized the state of Beat studies: "This collection has several purposes: to re-vision the Beats from contemporary critical perspectives, to reassess their place in mid-century American history and literature, to recontextualize Beat writers within the larger arts community of which they were a part, to recover marginalized figures and expand the restricted canon of three to six major figures established from 1956 to 1970, and to critique media stereotypes and popular clichés that influence both academic and popular discourse about the Beats."[8]

The dozen or so essays in *Reconstructing the Beats* make progress in all of those areas Skerl delineates, especially where they are concerned with expanding the Beat canon to make room for female and minority voices like those of Kyger, Lenore Kandel, Ted Joans, and Bob Kaufman, each of whom has made significant contributions. Their emphasis on Beat interactions with other artistic, cultural, and historical developments also points the way to future work on the Beats, which must always insist on looking to and for the margins of Beat writing. The "new directions" that Skerl and others have begun to chart reorient scholarly attention toward a number of potential outsides—those of the nation and national identity, along with those of period, genre, gender, race, and ethnicity— that require a willingness to cross borders and transgress boundaries that have long served to isolate Beat studies by keeping it tethered to a single postwar countercultural moment. Skerl's 2012 follow-up collection, *The Transnational Beat Generation*, coedited with Nancy M. Grace, represents the next step in the evolutionary process of scholarly work on the Beats, now with an explicitly stated interest in wresting Beat writing away from the immediate U.S. contexts that have dominated prior understandings of the Beats and their significance. In their introduction Grace and Skerl write, "When viewed through the lens of transnationalism, with its many complicated and contradictory definitions and interpretations, the Beat Generation emerges as a global configuration of artists whose work in total resists the simplistic binaries of square versus hip 1950s culture and the equally simplistic binary of bad nationalism versus good transnationalism."[9] The study of transnational Beat literature, in other words, has as much to say about transnationalism as it does about the Beats themselves.

Charting the transnational dimensions of the Beat Generation requires an equally timely expansion of the Beat canon, not least because Beat transnationalism involves important contributions from "minor" figures who bring Beat writing into contact with a diversity of cultural and sociopolitical formations. While most scholars and critics have traditionally focused their attention on the major figures of Kerouac, Ginsberg, and Burroughs at the expense of other voices within the movement, particularly those of women, African Americans, and other minorities, Ronna Johnson and Nancy Grace have done pioneering work on questions of the Beats and gender, and A. Robert Lee and Aldon Nielsen have written on the intersection of race and Beat Generation writing. *World Beats* continues along these important trajectories and moves between major figures like Kerouac and Burroughs and those, like Philip Lamantia and

Brion Gysin, who are less well known but deserve greater attention. I devote chapters to African American Beat writing and—pushing temporal as well as spatial boundaries—to Chinese American novelist Maxine Hong Kingston and a group of primarily women "post-Beat" writers working today. Writing from the "margins" (to borrow Maria Damon's term), they have been central to shaping and defining the Beat movement as a whole.[10]

Two recent books on the Beat movement as such that have managed to escape being circumscribed by the domestic scene are Baker's *A Blue Hand: The Beats in India* and Todd Tietchen's *The Cubalogues: Beat Writers in Revolutionary Havana*. Baker's group portrait is an exemplary work of rhizomic Beat criticism whose thematic and narrative complexity mirrors the Beats' own entanglements with India. She dispenses with the usual Beat historiography by making the heretofore largely unknown Hope Savage a central figure in her book, along with Sunil Gangopadhyay and the Bengali poets Ginsberg befriends in Kolkata. Baker has taken material from an array of journals, letters, and other published and unpublished accounts and reassembled it in a manner that allows submerged indigenous and minority voices to enter into her densely polyvocal narrative web. And Tietchen, whose work on Amiri Baraka, Lawrence Ferlinghetti, and others in *The Cubalogues* resonates strongly with my own, does much to revitalize a politically minded understanding of the Beats, although his book (like Baker's) is necessarily limited in terms of geographic coverage. I have drawn on their insights to speak about an even larger cast of characters and to begin theorizing Beat travel and Beat geography to an even greater degree.

In this task I am indebted to two additional works that bridge the gap between transnationalist criticism and Beat Generation writing with great insight: Brian Edwards's *Morocco Bound: Disorienting America's Maghreb, from Casablanca to the Marrakech Express* and Rachel Adams's *Continental Divides: Remapping the Cultures of North America*. Edwards works through the thorny topic of Beat orientalism by placing Beat writing (through Burroughs in particular) within a persistent set of tropes surrounding Arab North Africa, and Adams has demonstrated the usefulness of applying a specific outernational model (the continent) to the work of Jack Kerouac. Also useful has been Jahan Ramazani's *A Transnational Poetics*, which brings a transnational and translocal method to bear on the poetry of Amiri Baraka, as well as analogous work, such as Vera Kutzinski's *The Worlds of Langston Hughes: Modernism and Translation in the Americas*, published in other areas of U.S. literary studies. It is alongside such perspicacious studies that I hope *World Beats* is read, as like-minded scholars continue to forge a new, worlded vision of U.S. literature today.

The language of *worlding* marks the point of contact between my work on the Beats and current discourses on transnationalism. Over the past two decades transnationally oriented criticism has become a dominant force in the humanities, with scholars across the disciplines recognizing the need to look beyond a strictly nation-based paradigm of human culture. In American studies and U.S. literary studies in particular, the transnational turn has led to new habits of thought and new modes of reading whose implications continue to be vigorously debated today. New works by prominent Americanists (e.g., Donald Pease, Paul Giles, Caroline Levander, José David Saldívar) make it clear that the borders of U.S. literature remain hotly contested and its terrain insufficiently surveyed. They challenge the field as a whole to keep refining its methods and scope—while remaining mindful of the blind spots inherent in any critical approach—to apprehend the multivalent, polycentric realities of cultural production in the era of globalization.

It is onto this still-unsettled landscape that I wish to project an image of the world as such, not as one term among many in the proliferating series of descriptors that has come to define transnational criticism (hemispheric, transatlantic, diasporic, and so on) but as a critical concept that gathers together the most productive elements of these various models. The world therefore denotes a set of attributes as much as it does a physical place. First and foremost, it becomes an oppositional term that upholds the local and the contingent in the face of the deracinating transcendence of the global. Rob Wilson and Chris Connery have traced the world as a model back to an ensemble of thinkers that includes Jameson, Said, and Spivak, hence its deep resonances with Marxist and postcolonial theory and its kinship with the ethical, even utopian, dimensions of Spivak's "planetarity."[11] The world, like the planet, is an image of totality, and a worlded critical method is informed by Marxian conceptions of time and space (in particular, the radical articulations of "social space" from Henri Lefebvre and Pierre Bourdieu to David Harvey and Kristin Ross). Alternately a critical method, a reading practice, and a habit of mind, worlding is the self-criticism of transnationalism.

In the domain of transnational theory, several notable volumes have emerged from the fields of American studies, cultural studies, and U.S. literary studies in recent years. These include *Re-framing the Transnational Turn in American Studies*, edited by Winfried Fluck, Donald Pease, and

John Carlos Rowe; *Globalizing American Studies*, edited by Brian Edwards and Dilip Parameshwar Gaonkar; *Hemispheric American Studies*, edited by Caroline Levander and Robert Levine; *The Worlding Project: Doing Cultural Studies in the Era of Globalization*, edited by Connery and Wilson; and *Shades of the Planet: American Literature as World Literature*, edited by Wai Chee Dimock and Lawrence Buell. These collections are wide-ranging by design and serve as provocations to future, more in-depth research. Recent monographs by Pease, Giles, Levander, Amy Kaplan, and John Muthyala have been similarly broad, often with the whole sweep of U.S. literary history as the object of inquiry. These field statements are, in a sense, what I take as a starting point—choosing rather to concentrate on a single moment (i.e., the Beat Generation) along with its broader implications for the study of U.S. literature.

The debates surrounding the transnational turn in the humanities are far too numerous and extensive to rehearse here, but I do want to highlight some approaches that can be brought to bear most usefully on the transnationalism of Beat Generation writing. Among these are Susan Gillman and Kirsten Silva Gruesz's "hemispheric text-network," especially its manner of thinking beyond traditional notions of literary influence. Like Adams's continental approach—which she stages as a response to a mere comparativism that, in the case of North America, "has often proceeded in terms of bilateral conversations between the United States and its neighbors, rather than an equitable dialogue involving many different parties"—Gillman and Gruesz likewise position their text-network as a critique of comparativism as such: "It is not mere semantic fussiness to begin by ruminating on how we talk about the United States in relation to the world."[12] In an overview of recent developments in transnationalist literary scholarship, they set comparative literature's obstinately U.S.-centric understanding of comparativism in opposition to more capacious and fluid paradigms such as those of Micol Seigel and Wai Chee Dimock.

Gillman and Gruesz envision a "transnational analysis [that] would draw multiple circles, replanting the foot of the drawing-compass in different, central points, moving across different scales of observation. In so doing, it aims to avoid what is all too frequently, as Seigel demonstrates, the outcome of comparative analysis: a patronizing affirmation that the Other is different, but essentially just like Us."[13] Their title alone—"Worlding America: The Hemispheric Text-Network"—registers multiple levels of analysis: nation, hemisphere, and world, and within this productive slippage of terms lies the recognition that the hemisphere, like the nation, is not a hermetic system. Or perhaps its critical enclosure as hemisphere is what makes the world visible as the world. In any case, Gillman and Gruesz, both identified with the "hemispheric turn" in U.S. literary and cultural studies, are now engaged in what John Muthyala calls "re-worlding" the hemisphere and the Americas: to use Muthyala's formulation, they are interested in revealing the "cultural, political, economic, and social processes that bring the world into [the] America[s] and [the] America[s] into the world."[14]

In *A Transnational Poetics* Ramazani employs two terms that also capture the in-betweenness of worlded thought, lest transnationalism itself become just one more of the "geographically inchoate rubrics" Adams cautions against. Very early on Ramazani introduces James Clifford's concept of the "translocal" along with an account of Gayatri Spivak's "planetarity," which in his words is a necessary "distinction between the abstract geometry of the global and the lived history of the planetary." The planet, like the rhizome, is fundamentally an ecological image of the world as organism: earth as *ecos* (home) and lived space. Clifford's translocalism is similar to Rob Wilson's "local/global" or his image of the "world-horizon come near."[15] In opposition to globalization's transcendent abstractions—for example, the market—these authors speak the language of transgression, contamination, hybridity, mapping, and movement.

Worlding entails a crucial dialectic of near and far that is at the core of thinking transnationally. In this regard, it too draws on Clifford's translocal sense of cultural adaptation. Buell associates these shifting spatial scales with the planetary "ecoglobalism" of environmental activists and writers.[16] In the Beat ecopoetics of Gary Snyder—to take a case from my own area of emphasis—the etymology of "eco-" as *oikos* (house, family) is made worldly and worlded in *Earth House Hold*, Snyder's 1969 collection of *Technical Notes and Queries to Fellow Dharma Revolutionaries*. That is to say, the lived, material experience of the near-at-hand (one's "household") is, in Snyder's conception, the necessary ground on which one might imagine communal ties that run much deeper than the nation (oikos as earth/planet). The world, then, becomes a necessary "third term," preserving the local within the global as it navigates the nefarious logic of East-West, colonialism-nationalism, communism-capitalism, and, finally, self-other.[17]

Manifestations of the near-far dialectic—"making the world-horizon come near and become local and informed," as Wilson puts it—arise again and again in Beat Generation writing, but these expansive gestures on the part of Beat writers can bring new dangers, such as a too-easy identification with the Other or the elision of cultural difference altogether.[18] The latter appears in Kerouac as the "worldwide fellahin," the notion of entire peoples existing somehow outside of history, timeless and utterly essentialized, which Kerouac and others adopted so enthusiastically from Oswald Spengler's *The Decline of the West*. This mindset has generally gone by the name "orientalism," and my work is ever mindful of what Brian Edwards has called "the orientalist trap" as it pertains to Beat writing.[19] As Snyder's *Earth House Hold* suggests, a worlded view can emerge only through a meaningful, material engagement with local histories and a good-faith reckoning with alterity, and I argue that Beat writers (even Kerouac) can be read as interrogating and problematizing the same orientalist discourses they appear to recapitulate in their work.

For Ramazani, the translocal and the planetary are versions of a middle path between what Clifford calls "the excessive localism of particularist cultural relativism" and "the overly global vision of a capitalist or technocratic monoculture," and Ramazani borrows from Spivak an emphasis on lived experience and local histories while also recognizing "the widening, deepening and speeding up of world wide interconnectedness" in the twenty-first century.[20] But in *Death of a Discipline*, Spivak sends out a warning: "To talk planet-talk by way of an unexamined environmentalism, referring to an undivided 'natural' space rather than a differentiated political space, can work in the interest of this globalization in the mode of the abstract as such. . . . The planet is in the species of alterity, belonging to another system; and yet we inhabit it, on loan." The planet is thus associated with the Other and with the uncanny (*unheimlich*, or "unhomely," which brings us closer to Snyder's *ecos* and Heidegger's *weltende Welt*, or "worlding world"). Spivak's final injunction to the reader in *Death of a Discipline* to "keep responsibility alive" in "this era of globalism triumphant" makes planetarity an ethics rather than an ontology and points to the productively irresolvable tension between the world or planet's physical and figural dimensions.[21]

Donald Pease argues that in its rise to become a dominant paradigm within the humanities, transnationalism writ large "has exercised a monopoly of assimilative power that has enabled it to subsume and replace competing spatial and temporal orientations to the object of study—including multicultural American studies, borderlands critique, postcolonial American studies, and the more general turn to American cultural studies—within an encompassing geopolitics of knowledge." Worse yet, this shift toward the "unmarked" space of the transnational recapitulates and mirrors the same global flows of capital and corporate power that transnationalist critics want to interrogate. I wish to posit, however, that transnationalism as *worlding*, with its counterhegemonic animus, its emphasis on materiality and historicity, and its attention to the always uneven encounter between the local and the global, is particularly well suited to retain the lessons of older critical formations, especially postcolonial theory. With roots in Spivak's planetarity and Said's global-materialist outlook, worlding privileges precisely those "peripheralized geographies and diasporized populations" that, for Pease, have been marked and marginalized by the transnational.[22] The idea, finally, is that a worlded reading of Beat Generation literature can help navigate some of the impasses that still surround the so-called transnational turn in the humanities and help clarify what a materially grounded, transnationally minded criticism can look like.

In their shared emphasis on worlded reading practices, Spivak is in conversation with Dimock, another important theorist of planetarity, whose work charts the spatiotemporal coordinates of literary inspiration and influence across the structures of what she calls "deep time." She writes, "Instead of upholding territorial sovereignty and enforcing a regime of simultaneity, literature . . . unsettles both." For Dimock, these structures of deep time are transgressive and transnational and effect a literary becoming-other of the individual as well as the collective:

> Reading ushers in a continuum that mocks the form of any finite entity. It mocks the borders of the nation, just as it mocks the life span of the individual. As a global process of extension, elaboration, and randomization, reading turns literature into the collective life of the planet. Coextensive neither with the territorial regime of the nation nor with the biological regime of a single human being, this life derives its morphology instead from the motion of words: motion effected when borders are crossed, when a new frame of reference is mixed with an old, when foreign languages turn a native tongue into a hybrid.[23]

Dimock has been especially interested in the expansive intimacies of writers reading other writers' work—radically transformative events that leave even the most iconic and canonical texts permeated by diverse elements and energies. Within the U.S. canon, this applies to Emerson and Thoreau perhaps above all. In her "Deep Time" essay, Dimock writes,

> The Transcendentalists were avid readers. Comparative philology and comparative religion—two newly minted disciplines of the nineteenth century— were high on their reading lists. The relative claims of various civilizations

were hot topics for them. Henry David Thoreau, immersing himself in a translation of Manu's Sanskrit text, the *Institutes of Hindu Law* (1825), was as elated as Malcolm X would be by ancient Islam: "I cannot read a sentence in the book of the Hindoos without being elevated as upon the tableland of the Ghauts. It has such a rhythm as the winds of the desert, such a tide as the Ganges, and seems as superior to criticism as the Himmaleh Mounts. Even at this late hour, unworn by time, with a native and inherent dignity it wears the English dress as indifferently as the Sanscrit." The Ganges and the Himalayas easily dwarf the landscape around Concord; they put America in perspective.[24]

Ultimately, in the work of Thoreau and Emerson, and also Whitman, the worlded view does not just put the United States "into perspective"; it unmakes the nation. Dimock concludes her essay with the bold claim: "Going back hundreds of years, triangulating at every step, reading the Koran by way of German, and looking forward to Malcolm X and James Baldwin by way of Goethe and Hafiz, Emerson is *American* only in caricature."[25] Paul Giles is similarly interested in the spatiotemporality of literature and the "deterritorializing" effects of time on the nation. Giles makes the point that when Emerson or Whitman write about "America" (or when we today call them "American" writers), the term accrues very different meanings then and now, not least simply because the nation as a physical entity was very different then; it was a "conception . . . that had not yet received any firm sense of territorial grounding or enclosure."[26]

The bottom line for Giles, Dimock, and like-minded critics and theorists is the transnationalism that exists at the core of the U.S. canon, and here is where the Beats are useful. It has been well remarked that Whitman, Emerson, and Thoreau all exerted a major influence on Beat Generation writers, yet this influence usually gets talked about in terms of Emersonian individualism or Whitmanian democracy; what they have most in common, in other words, is their Americanness. This manner of linking the Beat movement and the American Renaissance is not without merit, but it tends to ignore the complexity of the relationship. Instead, I want to argue that the Beats' inheritance from U.S. literary history, and from American Renaissance writers in particular, lies not just in their transnationalist dimensions but, more precisely, in their worldedness. Through an act of critical triangulation, then, a worlded Beat Generation can be used to survey the broader contours of U.S. literature and history.

The American experiment, from the "Pilgrim Fathers" onward, has been predicated on actual movement and very specific ideas about place.

As Sacvan Bercovitch and others have argued, America as the "New Jerusalem" or "New Canaan" has always represented the dislocation that precedes a new rootedness. Significantly for Bercovitch, Puritan ideology does not revolve around the old forms of family or nationality; rather, "they invented themselves . . . as God's people in America, meaning by this a community in process, and therefore released from the usual national restrictions of genealogy, territory, and tradition."[27] This curiously postnational formulation of Puritan identity is perhaps more closely allied with later expressions of the transnational than one might have expected. The rhetoric of America as the New Jerusalem soon gives way to the logic of manifest destiny. Just over a century after Plymouth Rock, George Berkeley would write his "Verses on the Prospect of Planting Arts and Learning in America," which famously conclude,

> Westward the course of empire takes its way;
> The four first Acts already past,
> A fifth shall close the Drama with the day;
> Time's noblest offspring is the last.[28]

The purest expression of America as telos, Berkeley's lines will become the measure by which all other iterations of manifest destiny may be judged as we chart the global history of the U.S. imperium through the nineteenth and twentieth centuries. This is also an argument about U.S. *literary* history, tracing a different inheritance from the American Renaissance writers to the Beats. Emerson, Thoreau, and Whitman all, at times, produce their own versions of manifest destiny and thus reaffirm its logic (even if idiosyncratically). But the exact opposite is also true; at a time of massive territorial expansion in the 1840s and 1850s, some of the most canonical American Renaissance texts work to unwrite manifest destiny in complicated, often antinomian ways. It is their legacy of reimagining the United States' place in the world that the Beat writers would inherit and further transform.

Deborah Baker's study of the Beats in India refers at several points to what they were reading along the way. Rudyard Kipling's *Kim* was a torchbearer, but no text is more emblematic of their journey than Whitman's "Passage to India." What "redeems" Beat travel writing from being just another imaginative appropriation of the Other is that so many of their accounts center on failure (failure to communicate, failure to reach one another, failure to find a guru). These often become *productive* failures that lead to unexpected encounters and fortuitous crossings. In a sense, the Beats are continuously reenacting Columbus's originary failure to find the East, and perhaps no one in the U.S. literary tradition is more attuned to this ur-narrative of America as a journey gone awry than Walt Whitman. While it comes to dominate later poems like "Passage to India" and "Prayer of Columbus" and the prose work *Democratic Vistas* (notably, all three were composed after the Civil War), the specter of failure haunts the poet from the very first edition of *Leaves of Grass* (1855). It is a major theme of the 1860 *Calamus* poems, and in each successive case failure becomes a more pressing concern because the fate of Whitman's poetic project becomes increasingly tied in the poet's mind to the fate of the nation.

The Whitman who asks himself if he is the true embodiment of Emerson's Poet: a seer, prophet, and liberator, is the Whitman who resonates so strongly with Ginsberg, who wants to take up Whitman's mantle but feels a similarly pervasive sense of doubt. The result of this doubt, of course, is the grandiosity of their poems, and in "Passage to India" Whitman's concern for his project and his nation are inflated to worlded proportions. Composed in 1870, occasioned by the triple achievement of the Suez Canal, the transatlantic cable, and the transcontinental railroad, the poem opens on an accordingly triumphal note:

> Singing my days,
> Singing the great achievements of the present,
> Singing the strong light works of engineers,
> Our modern wonders, (the antique ponderous Seven outvied,)
> In the Old World the east the Suez canal,
> The New by its mighty railroad spann'd,
> The seas inlaid with eloquent gentle wires.[29]

In "Song of Myself" and elsewhere, Whitman praises science and progress per se; here, he singles out technology's ability to "span" the globe, to make "the distant brought near." The earth as "Rondure" could easily become an abstraction without the voluptuousness of the word to make it tangible. And as with Thoreau and Emerson, the physical always has its spiritual counterpart. The flight of the soul has it within its grasp to "Eclaircise the myths Asiatic," which become the necessary analogue of progress (paradoxically into the past). The poem declares, "Nor you alone ye facts of modern science, / But myths and fables of eld, Asia's, Africa's fables, / . . . / You too with joy I sing" (531). But as his song unfolds, the poet becomes plagued with doubt. What next? he asks. We've spanned the globe, but where has it gotten us except right back where we began? The speaker of "Facing West from California's Shores" faces a similar conundrum, and, in Whitman's view, it is the task of the poet to answer such questions, for the poet is set apart precisely in being able to comprehend a worlded *totality* or "ensemble" (to use Whitman's term). In "Passage to India," questions arise, one after another, as the speaker awaits "the poet worthy that name / The true son of God" and repeats "that sad incessant refrain, *Wherefore unsatisfied soul? and Whither O mocking life?*" (534). These same questions will haunt Ginsberg too, whose questing through India and all over the world became a means to face or, alternatively, to escape them.

Standing in stark contrast to the triumphalist rhetoric of U.S. expansion, Whitman's "Prayer of Columbus," published as a kind of addendum to "Passage to India," suggests to readers that the history of the nation, along with the entire colonial enterprise, has been a history of failure. His portrait of Columbus, whose own passage to India was cut exceedingly short, is not as hero but as "A batter'd, wreck'd old man, / . . . / Sore, stiff with many toils, sicken'd and nigh to death" (540). A similarly pessimistic, and undervalued, text is Whitman's *Democratic Vistas*. If the earlier *Calamus* poems were a record of failed connection and comradeship at the interpersonal level, then *Democratic Vistas* is a record of failed democracy, a failed union. In that very ambiguous work as well, Whitman engages with the discourse of expansion. He warns, "In vain do we march with unprecedented strides to empire so colossal," lamenting, "In vain have we annex'd Texas, California, Alaska, and reach north for Canada and south for Cuba. It is as if we were somehow being endow'd with a vast and more and more thoroughly-appointed body, and then left with little or no soul" (962).[30] And the very late poem "A Thought of Columbus," said to be Whitman's last, represents a final redemptive effort that merges the poet's imagined legacy with that of the nation.

Of Whitman, Emerson, and Thoreau, it is Thoreau who presents the most challenging attitude toward U.S. expansion. His act of "civil disobedience," refusing to pay his poll tax, was in protest of U.S. belligerence toward Mexico and its likely outcome: the annexation of new slave territories. Yet in his unremitting desire to slough off the dead weight of Europe, the poet-prophet of American individualism sometimes can sometimes sound a lot like Bishop Berkeley. Such contradictions are themselves a way for Thoreau to short-circuit the ideology of manifest destiny and to forge a new narrative of his nation's place in the wider world. "Resistance to Civil Government" and "Plea for John Brown," two of his most powerful and polemical pieces, are in explicit response to the most pressing issues of Thoreau's day, but even *Walden* shares in a worlded imaginary that unites Thoreau the polemicist, Thoreau the environmentalist, and Thoreau the transcendentalist. In various ways, the Beats will conjure all of these roles as they look to his polyvalent example.

Like Whitman, Thoreau is interested in the curious warp-zone effect produced by the mere fact that on a round planet, one can, as Columbus intended to show, go east by going west. Thoreau's most concise formulation of this appears in his first book, *A Week on the Concord and Merrimack Rivers* (self-published in 1849, not long before *Civil Disobedience*), where he writes, "As we have said, there is an orientalism in the most restless pioneer, and the farthest west is but the farthest east."[31] Exactly what kind of geography is being conjured here? It could simply be the relativism produced by Thoreau's awareness of the fundamental contingency of one's point of view—from Asia's perspective, after all, "the West" lies to the east—or the even more banal reminder that the earth is indeed round, and those who travel west long enough will eventually find themselves on Asian shores. But Thoreau's landscapes are always charged with spiritual and symbolic as well as topographical significance, so the question becomes, what is it about the West that for Thoreau is better expressed in terms of the East? If Thoreau figures the East, as he does in *A Week*, primarily as a frontier, then the pioneer becomes primarily a *seeker*. But a seeker after what? Later on in *A Week*, he seems ready to do away with (extensive) geography altogether, writing, "The frontiers are not east or west, north or south, but wherever a man *fronts* a fact" (198), a sentiment that he gives fuller expression to in this later passage:

> It is easier to discover another such a new world as Columbus did, than to go within one fold of this which we appear to know so well; the land is lost sight of, the compass varies, and mankind mutiny; and still history accumulates like rubbish before the portals of nature. But there is only necessary a moment's sanity and sound senses, to teach us that there is a nature behind the ordinary, in which we have only some vague preëmption right and western reserve as yet. We live on the outskirts of that region. (249)

In these lines, as elsewhere in Thoreau, nature becomes the mediating "third term" between East and West, self and other, known and unknown, and we seek our "western reserve" only in our blindness before nature's truths.

In the early essay "A Winter Walk" (1843) nature as reserve is further described in terms of a subterranean continuity; Thoreau writes, "There is a slumbering subterranean fire in nature which never goes out, and which no cold can chill" and reiterates the point: "as where we detect the vapor from a spring forming a cloud above the trees. What fine relations are established. . . . Such is the beginning of Rome, the establishment of the arts, and the foundation of empires, whether on the prairies of America or the steppes of Asia."[32] With Thoreau's worlded geography again in play, the "vapor from a spring" recalls a similar passage in *A Week* that F. O. Matthiessen singles out for praise and ends with the image of a clear, vaporous flame rising up in thin smoke to the sky above, a poignant formulation of cosmic connectedness.

To think of movement or exploration, whether in Thoreau's work or in Beat writing, always in terms of an internal process of *self*-discovery misses the point because, for Thoreau, actual, physical movement westward, away from Europe and toward the East, is absolutely essential. The late essay "Walking" is where he bestows the greatest significance upon the literal act of "going west," writing, "Eastward I go only by force; but westward I go free. . . . It is hard for me to believe that I shall find fair landscapes or sufficient wildness and freedom behind the eastern horizon . . . but I believe that the forest which I see in the western horizon stretches uninterruptedly toward the setting sun." And a bit later: "I must walk toward Oregon, and not toward Europe."[33] And considering that, for Thoreau, walking is intimately connected with *writing*—Matthiessen cites Emerson's "trenchant" observation that "the length of his walk uniformly made the length of his writing. If shut up in the house he did not write at all"—these lines become all the more important to the present discussion.[34] But here again one finds several points where Thoreau sounds less than critical about the then prevailing notions of manifest destiny and the fate of the nation. After a short space are these further assertions: "And that way [westward] the nation is moving, and I may say that mankind progresses from east to west. . . . The eastern Tartars think that there is nothing west beyond Thibet. 'The world ends there,' say they; 'beyond there is nothing but a shoreless sea.' It is unmitigated East where they live."[35] At crucial moments, Thoreau, who imagines that "Columbus felt the westward tendency more strongly than any before" (605) and that "to Americans I need hardly to say, 'Westward the star [*sic*] of empire takes its way'" (608) seems to view U.S. expansion as underwritten by nature's occulted pathways.[36]

In the telos and rhetoric of the "Walking" essay, the reader is presented with further world-visions that reverse anew the expected east-west binary to proclaim: "We go east to realize history and study the works of art and literature, retracing the steps of the race; we go westward as into the future." Here, the East is again the West (as Western civilization), and the West—now inevitably inflected by his "West as East" thinking—is associated with futurity instead of something like "irrevocable Asias of the past." Thoreau further complicates matters, however, when he proceeds to equate this futurity not with progress but with a kind of (mythic) forgetting. He continues, "The Atlantic is a Lethean stream, in our passage over which we have had an opportunity to forget the Old World and its institutions. If we do not succeed this time, there is perhaps one more chance for the race left before it arrives on the banks of the Styx; and that is in the Lethe of the Pacific, which is three times as wide" (604). In Thoreau's worlded tableau of space and time, Asia ultimately comes to stand not for the past, which one might expect from the terms of this equation, but rather for a new chance at the future. He concludes, leading up to those words so dear to environmentalists: "The West of which I speak" (*the East*, it turns out), "is but another name for the Wild; and what I have been preparing to say is, that in Wildness is the preservation of the World" (609).

Just as Kerouac will project his own world-visions from the depths of his darkest isolation in Mexico, Thoreau's vividest apprehension of a "world-horizon come near" is born of his solitude at Walden Pond. In one of the last chapters of *Walden*, "The Pond in Winter," Thoreau observes a team of ice-cutters extracting pond ice for sale across the United States and around the world and provides an occasion for us to connect Matthiessen's reading of Thoreau with several of our transnational approaches to both the American Renaissance and Beat writing. Musing on the implications of the ice company's trade at distant ports, Thoreau concludes,

> Thus it appears that the sweltering inhabitants of Charleston and New Orleans, of Madras and Bombay and Calcutta, drink at my well. In the morning I bathe my intellect in the stupendous and cosmogonal philosophy of the Bhagvat Geeta. . . . I lay down the book and go to my well for water, and lo! there I meet the servant of the Bramin, priest of Brahma and Vishnu and Indra, who still sits in his temple on the Ganges reading the Vedas, or dwells at the root of a tree with his crust and water jug. I meet his servant come to draw water for his master, and our buckets as it were grate together in the same well. The pure Walden water is mingled with the sacred water of the Ganges.[37]

Matthiessen, contrasting Thoreau with John Donne at one point, calls Thoreau's experience "inevitably more literary" and says that "one of his chief distinctions . . . is the infusion of his reading into his perceptions." Matthiessen's appeal to Thoreau's literariness should call to mind Dimock's emphasis on reading in her planetary conception of transnational literature. Matthiessen has to this say about Thoreau at Walden Pond: "The waters have become mingled in a double experience: as the ships of the ice company complete their route around Africa, a further chapter in the history of transportation, in the conquest of space which has been progressing since the Renaissance, Thoreau also affirms his conquest—that of time—which can empower the provincial New Englander, while firmly rooted by his own green pond, *to make the remote near*."[38]

If Matthiessen concludes that in this passage Thoreau is celebrating a personal conquest of time, which happens to run parallel to the whole history of Western imperialism, there is also a corrective to Matthiessen's reading—a *material* rather than an allegorical one—suggested by David Trotter's recent analysis of D. H. Lawrence's *Lady Chatterley's Lover*. Trotter's reading centers on the status of rubber as a hot commodity at the time of the novel's composition. This material approach to *Lady Chatterley* allows one to read it in terms of what Trotter calls "techno-primitivism" (with rubber its figure in the novel: a substance at once natural and, like its successor, plastic, endlessly manipulable through machinic technology) rather than a static or assumed primitiveness destroyed by modern conventionality.[39] Through a similar reading of *Walden*, we get from Thoreau the commodity's eye view of the situation and the transactional nature of his worlded experience is integral to the world-dynamics he tries to represent. He wishes to forge a living connection to India and the East.

Emerson is not as restless a thinker as Thoreau, but Emerson's transcendentalism—"East meets West" as Hinduism and Hegelianism—spatializes thought in equally complex ways. The transnational dimensions of Emerson's philosophy are not simply an appeal to syncretic spiritual traditions or the oneness of creation; even Emerson must acknowledge the historicity, contingency, and site specificity of all religions. And even Emerson intimates from time to time that the same world-historical forces that have opened up the world and allowed the wisdom traditions of the East to migrate along their uncertain and unpredictable routes have also brought domination and oppression. A poem in this direction—uncharacteristic in tone though not in sentiment—is Emerson's 1846 "Ode" to socialist clergyman William Henry Channing. The "Ode" is equivocal and contradictory, yet its startlingly poisonous sarcasm does give the poem a unity of voice. A few stanzas into the poem, the speaker asks, "But who is he that prates / Of the culture of mankind, / Of better arts and life?"

Could this refer to none other than Bishop Berkeley, whose "Verses on the Prospect of Planting Arts and Learning in America" is where he writes that "Westward the course of empire takes its way"? Emerson characterizes the march westward as the progress of a "blindworm," writing, "Go, blindworm, go, / Behold the famous States / Harrying Mexico / With rifle and with knife!" He then makes the connection explicit between the pioneering spirit of the American individualist and the enduring institution of slavery in a further question: "Or who, with accent bolder, / Dare praise the freedom-loving mountaineer? / I found by thee, O rushing Contoocook! / And in thy valleys, Agiochook! / The jackals of the negro-holder." The speaker's own "bold accent" is shaped by these indigenous references to the New England landscape. The poem's middle section ranges from growing national tensions over slavery to a more expansive meditation on reification and the commodity fetish ("Things are in the saddle / And ride mankind!").[40]

The polemical tone of the poem is out of the ordinary for Emerson, but most of its content is standard fare: the politics of a Northern reformer, the transcendentalist's protest against base materialism. With the final two stanzas, however, Emerson's poem leaps into a worlded critique of imperialist geopolitics—territory as worlded critique. The poem concludes with these lines:

The over-god
Who marries Right to Might,
Who peoples, unpeoples,—
He who exterminates
Races by stronger races,
Black by white faces,—
Knows to bring honey
Out of the lion;
Grafts gentlest scion
On pirate and Turk.

The Cossack eats Poland,
Like stolen fruit;
Her last noble is ruined,
Her last poet mute:
Straight, into double band
The victors divide;
Half for freedom strike and stand;—
The astonished Muse finds thousands at her side.[41]

Why does Emerson all of a sudden jump across the Atlantic to find an analogy for his nation's drive to annex Mexico? Who exactly are these "victors" who "strike and stand" for freedom? The "angry Muse" at the beginning of the poem is now the "astonished Muse"—astonished as those trying to make sense of this ending. Is this a deliberate echo of Berkeley's "Verses," which begins, "The Muse, disgusted at an age and clime / Barren of every glorious theme, / In distant lands now awaits a better time, / Producing subjects worthy fame"?[42] A provisional conclusion might be that just as Gregory Corso, that most lyrical of Beat poets, writing from Paris intuitively registers the Algerian War as the necessary corollary of his impossibly romanticized view of France—or as Walter Benjamin puts it in his "Theses on the Philosophy of History": "There is no document of civilization which is not at the same time a document of barbarism"—Emerson's "Ode" recognizes that the Polish nationalists rising up against imperialist Russia, like "harried" Mexico, like those at home suffering the torments of slavery's "jackals," like those everywhere alienated under the new hegemony of industrial capitalism, are all caught up in the same world-system.

The pathbreaking "world-systems analysis" pioneered by Immanuel Wallerstein has become part of a recognizable and increasingly consolidated canon of worlded thought among its practitioners. This canon includes Spivak and Said, both of whom point to worlding's postcolonial origins and its materialist bent. If globalization is top-down and transcendent, a view from above, then worlding is bottom-up and immanent, a view from below (or, from Wallerstein's perspective, the "periphery"). I want to hold on to these key characteristics and major thinkers even as I open up a more expansive genealogy that pushes into new domains: a discrepant tradition comprising metaphysics and phenomenology, and poetics and biology, in addition to literary and cultural theory and criticism. Sketching this larger field of play will help pull the conversation into a specifically Beat orbit; it will also help draw out certain aspects of the worlded world that are crucial to the story I want to tell about the Beats and about U.S. literature.

Wallerstein makes an important distinction when defining "world-system," writing that "a world-system is the system of *the* world, but a system *that is a* world and that can be, most often has been, located in an area less than the entire globe."[43] The world indicated by Wallerstein's world-system is neither identical to nor coterminous with the world as empirical object (he uses "globe"). It is thus a nontotalizing totality, a totality in the Marxian sense, that is to say, a critical concept that functions descriptively but also works to denaturalize what it describes, just as our "species-being" is determined by yet exceeds the "totality of social relations" under the prevailing economic system. For Marx, the totality serves a dialectical function; it is precisely the *universality* of capitalism that sets the stage for the universal liberation of proletarian revolution. (Transferring it from base to superstructure, Peter Bürger makes an analogous argument when he writes that it is only after the aestheticists declare the supremacy of "art for art's sake" that avant-garde movements like Dada can come along and attempt to negate *any* distinction between art and life.)[44]

The Marxian world-system as a nontotalizing totality means that civilization progresses, in dialectical fashion, from one world to the next (e.g., from the feudal world to the capitalist world). But what if multiple worlds, an infinite number of worlds, can exist simultaneously? This is the conclusion to draw from the work of biologist and proto-posthumanist Jakob von Uexküll, whose concept of Umwelt (environment, life-world) posits that each species' sensorium is fundamentally unique and constitutes a world unto itself. In Uexküll's most enduring work, *A Foray into the Worlds* (Umwelten) *of Animals and Humans*, he asks readers to take an imaginary stroll with him:

> We begin such a stroll on a sunny day before a flowering meadow in which insects buzz and butterflies flutter, and we make a bubble around each of the animals living in the meadow. The bubble represents each animal's environment and contains all the features accessible to the subject. As soon as we enter into one such bubble, the previous surroundings of the subject are completely reconfigured. Many qualities of the colorful meadow vanish completely, others lose their coherence with one another, and new connections are created. *A new world* [Eine neue Welt] *arises in each bubble.*

The author emphasizes the salutary estrangement involved in such a pursuit when he writes, "Only when we can vividly imagine this fact [of the "bubbles"] will we recognize in our own world the bubble that encloses each and every one of us on all sides."[45] Uexküll's perspective, which radically decenters human consciousness and imagines a dense, rhizomic web of inputs and interactions among all life forms, is picked up by Gilles Deleuze and Félix Guattari in *A Thousand Plateaus* and has come back to the fore in the field of animal studies and among today's theorists of posthuman biopolitics.

This talk of worlds and bubbles is strangely reminiscent of Leibniz even, whose rationalist abstractions seem miles away from Uexküll's empiricist phenomenology. Yet Leibniz's "monad" is but the metaphysical counterpart to Uexküll's model of ecological interdependence. On the surface, the self-sufficient monad—a substance without windows or doors, as Leibniz puts it—is an image of extreme isolation, but the exact opposite is true. The "monadology" works only because we live in a universe where everything is connected to everything else and everything affects everything else; transculturally speaking, it is a version of Indra's net. The philosopher writes, "This interconnection or accommodation of all created things to each other, and each to all the others, brings it about that each simple substance [i.e., monad] has relations that express all the others, and consequently, that each simple substance is a perpetual, living mirror of the universe." Leibniz also plays on the tension between singularity and multiplicity inherent in the monad, and like Uexküll he is interested in perspective, writing, "Just as the same city viewed from different directions appears entirely different and, as it were, multiplied perspectively, in just the same way it happens that, because of the infinite multitude of simple substances, there are, as it were, just as many different universes, which are, nevertheless, only perspectives on a single one, corresponding to the different points of view of each monad."[46]

Leibniz's monism offers a new way to read Beat writers and their supposed isolation from and indifference to the wider world—an antidote, in other words, to Barry Miles's claim that the Beats "could have been living anywhere." The common view of the Beat Generation as essentially isolationist is similar to what George Orwell once said about Beat precursor Henry Miller. Orwell's essay "Inside the Whale" centers on Miller as it contemplates the proper relationship between art and politics in an era of totalitarianism. He recalls the time in 1936 when he first met Miller. Orwell was on his way to Spain to serve the republican cause, an act that Miller told him was "sheer stupidity."[47] He comes to agree, arguing in the essay that a literature of utter passivity (e.g., Miller's *Tropic of Cancer*) is far preferable to the "committed" literature of the day (e.g., Auden, Spender), and more honest.

To capture the full extent of Miller's passivity and attitude of acceptance—the latter he shares with Whitman, according to Orwell—the author adapts an image that Miller himself uses to describe Anaïs Nin: he compares him to "Jonah in the whale's belly." Orwell writes,

And however it may be with Anaïs Nin, there is no question that Miller himself is inside the whale. All his best and most characteristic passages are written from the angle of Jonah, a willing Jonah. Not that he is especially introverted—quite the contrary. In his case the whale happens to be transparent. Only he feels no impulse to alter or control the process that he is undergoing. He has performed the essential Jonah act of allowing himself to be swallowed, remaining passive, *accepting.*

"Short of being dead," Orwell calls this "the final, unsurpassable stage of irresponsibility," but maybe irresponsibility is sometimes more principled than its opposite.[48] The ambivalence of Orwell's description is signaled by a central paradox: Miller is trapped in the belly of the whale, but "the whale happens to be transparent." Put another way, he is inside one of Uexküll's "bubbles"; only in Miller's case the bubble happens to contain the entire world.

Wallerstein's differentiation between a conceptual world and an empirical globe points to the dual nature of world as both physical and figural, topological and tropological. And the space opened up by the distinction is what makes possible the worlded imaginaries that are the subject of this book. In "Inside the Whale," Orwell ponders the idea of "books that 'create a world of their own,' as the saying goes"—books that, like *Tropic of Cancer* or *Ulysses,* "open up a new world not by revealing what is strange, but by revealing what is familiar."[49] (He uses "world" exactly two dozen times in the essay.) The book-as-world, alternately poem-as-world, is certainly an old and venerable trope. Often, the world of the poem is held in contrast to the "outside world," as in Donne's "The Canonization" (*We'll build sonnets in pretty rooms*), which is the source of the New Critics' much-loved "well-wrought urn" and the sentiment behind their nothing-outside-the-text philosophy. There are other times, though, when the text-world is what gives the poet privileged access to the world at large, such as Saint-John Perse's enigmatic *monde entier des choses* ("whole world of things") in *Vents,* which was a favorite of Burroughs.[50]

As similar examples proliferate, each draws out a different aspect of the worlded world: some its materiality, some its multiplicity and heterogeneity, others its oppositional force, and still others its yoking together of the near and the far. Fellow New Jersey native and mentor to Allen Ginsberg, William Carlos Williams mobilizes them all in his epic poem *Paterson,* where he proclaims,

The province of the poem is the world.
When the sun rises, it rises in the poem
and when it sets darkness comes down
and the poem is dark   .[51]

At the outset of book 2 Williams gears up for his meticulous description of a "Sunday in the Park" at Passaic Falls with these lines:

Outside
                    outside myself
                                        there is a world,
        he rumbled, subject to my incursions
        —a world
                    (to me) at rest,
                                which I approach
concretely—[52]

With this last word a play on the poem's emphatically urban setting, in addition to being a statement of purpose from Williams the "objectivist" poet, the speaker suggests that the world as such can be approached only locally, through its tangible specificity and nearness at hand. While always, and necessarily, in contact with the tangible and material—the poet's dictum: "No ideas but in things" becomes a refrain in *Paterson*—the many worlds of the poem are often associated with thought, memory, and the imagination, which stand in contrast to the corrupted and lamentable workaday world. Within the dialectical movement of the poem, one requires the other.

Paterson notably incorporates entire letters that Williams had received from friends and admirers. Three of those letters are from Ginsberg. In the first and longest, written before the two had met and when Ginsberg was but twenty-three years old, the younger poet hits on the great themes of Williams's epic. Ginsberg tells him, "I envision for myself some kind of new speech . . . out of the subjective wanderings through Paterson. This place is as I say my natural habitat by memory, and I am not following in your traces to be poetic: though I know you will be pleased to realize that at least one actual citizen of your community has inherited your experience in his struggle to love and know his own world-city." In book 5 Williams follows another letter from Ginsberg (enclosed with the poem "Sunflower Sutra") with these lines: "the virgin and the whore, which / most endures? the world / of the imagination most endures"—that is to say, it trumps dull binaries like virgin and whore and, ultimately, poem and world, art and life.[53]

Finally, essential for a worlded understanding of the global flows of cultural production and power has been the borderlands critique pioneered by Gloria Anzaldúa and José Saldívar. Thinking transnationally means thinking about and beyond borders of all kinds, and transnationalism as worlding keeps a concept of *transgression* front and center. Worlding is interested in transgressive acts, whether they involve borders internal or external, textual or otherwise; worlding seeks to *be* transgressive: that is to say, counterhegemonic, reading against the grain, writing against empire and globalization transcendent. The latter is tricky business, as Pease and others have shown, and a worlded critique needs to take into account its own entanglements within the always uneven interchange between the local and the global, core and periphery. Where transgression is concerned, the accounting has to involve asking who has the privilege, the authority, the power to transgress and who gets denied passage, whether the crossing is undertaken willingly and to what ends.

Anzaldúa's *Borderlands/La Frontera* is a classic that spans disciplinary boundaries (Latin American and Chicano/a studies, queer theory, and borderlands critique, among others). Her central insight that borders are not just lines on a map but something we carry inside ourselves means transgression is something lived and also something performed. Borders are multiple and overlapping, spatial and figural, and transgression is both an act and a state of being. One can think of a border zone of constantly shifting identifies and allegiances. In *Rogues*, Jacques Derrida points out that transgression and sovereignty are always linked: the sovereign proves its sovereignty precisely by being the exception to its own rule (giving rise to what Giorgio Agamben calls a "state of exception").[54] Angela Davis would argue that in the twenty-first century what is truly sovereign is capital. In this age of free trade on an increasingly global scale, capital is what is free to cross borders—factories, jobs, commodities, and natural resources also move from core to periphery and back again: everything but people, in other words.[55]

The caveats by Davis and Anzaldúa will serve as guardrails throughout this book, reminders that travel and movement, writing and representation, always involve relations of power. The Beats were primarily, though by no means exclusively, white and male with U.S. passports, which means they possessed an extraordinary freedom to move in the world. It becomes all the more important, then, to expand the Beat canon to include a larger, more diverse group of writers. As an African American, Ted Joans's experience of Morocco is likely to be different from that of William Burroughs; Japan and India are bound to make different impressions on Kyger than they do her husband and traveling companion, Gary Snyder, although while in India, they were both uncomfortably aware of the luxuries afforded them as white and Western. By and large the Beats are hip to such dynamics and use their privilege strategically to thematize both cultural difference and Cold War geopolitics, as when Burroughs, traveling in Colombia, let himself be mistaken as a representative of the Texas Oil Company, which got him better accommodations, yes, but also gave his writing a greater critical purchase on U.S.–Latin American economic relations and their effects at home and abroad.

Burroughs the oilman is a great example of how the Beats were constantly *performing* transgression, so to speak. Such performances often began with the particular locales Beat writers were drawn to. To visit Castro's Cuba (Baraka, Ginsberg, Ferlinghetti) or Nicaragua under the Sandinistas (Ginsberg, Ferlinghetti) was to make a political statement. Even if that statement is equivocal: Ginsberg was famously expelled from Cuba and then Czechoslovakia in the space of a few months, both times under murky circumstances having something to do with Ginsberg's homosexuality (transgression upon transgression). The transnational geographies of Beat travel writing notably include Latin America, India, and North Africa, parts of the world that were supremely affordable and usually offered easy access to drugs, sex, and a sense of permissiveness that comes with being in an alien culture. There is something predictably exoticist and undeniably exploitative about such an arrangement that needs to be reckoned with. Thinking back to Burroughs and Texas Oil, a slightly different way of phrasing the question could be, how is transgression represented in Beat writing? More often that not, it is about making connections, or "contacting," as Burroughs would say, with local histories and ways of being (e.g., Lamantia's participation in native Cora ceremonies in Mexico, Ginsberg's *ayahuasca* cure session in Peru), which Beat writing consistently figures as subversive and disruptive of established power structures. The Beats abroad, and especially in the third world or Global South, bring into sharpest relief the legacies of Western imperialism as well as the United States' expanding footprint internationally after World War II.

The most profound forms of transgression in Beat writing, however, are textual: the Beats share with their modernist precursors and postmodernist contemporaries a perfect willingness to blur the boundaries of genre and form. Genre has long been notoriously tricky in the study of Beat writing. *On the Road* . . . is it fiction or memoir? That question has vexed readers for decades, and the failure to attend to it properly has led to some fairly reductive readings of Kerouac's work. In 2007 the Library of America published its first volume of Beat Generation writing: *Jack Kerouac: Road Novels, 1957–1960*, an evocative title that goes some way to describing a distinctive genre, one that bridges the gap, uncovers a hidden dialectic, between memoir and fiction in Kerouac's oeuvre. A transgressive genre in and of itself, the road novel is akin to the travelogue, which has long functioned as a form of social critique. Travel writing in the West came into its own during the age of discovery and is thus linked to colonialism and the modern world-system. It was during the Enlightenment that Denis Diderot and the philosophes began to see the critical potential of the travelogue. Diderot's *Supplément au voyage de Bougainville* (1772) "supplements" the just-published *Voyage autour du monde* by Louis-Antoine de Bougainville, the first Frenchman to circumnavigate the globe. Diderot's satirical version is sharply critical of colonialism and missionary activity, and he uses the handy (because new at the time) trope of the noble savage to decry European decadence and heavy-handed morality.

Accounts by Bougainville and fellow explorers to document "primitive" societies resemble early attempts at ethnography. When Antonin Artaud alludes to Diderot in his 1945 "Supplément au voyage au pays des Tarahumaras"—one of a series of texts by Artaud documenting and reflecting on his peyote quest in Mexico (published in English as *The Peyote Dance*)—he does so in regard to a voyage that was itself undertaken in a quasi-anthropological manner.[56] And when Burroughs, who had pursued graduate work in anthropology at Harvard, travels to the Amazon in search of the mythical hallucinogen ayahuasca, or *yagé*, the resulting *Yage Letters* read even more like ethnography, but a satirical ethnography that complicates in canny ways the power and the privileged knowledge of the scientist. As the title suggests, the *Yage Letters* also plainly involves an epistolary element: an opportunity for more genre bending on Burroughs's part but also a mark of the interpersonal dimension in Beat writing and the strongly collaborative nature of Beat Generation literature.

The essential point about Beat transgression is the extent to which crossing textual boundaries is activated by, and in many cases predicated on, first crossing physical borders. Accordingly, the following chapters are organized around particular writers and texts but also around specific locations. Geography thus acts as a cohesive force across chapters. Prominent locales are Latin America (Colombia, Peru, and especially Mexico) and North Africa (chiefly Morocco but also Algeria and Mali), which in the Beats' transnational imaginary become radically transformed, or deterritorialized, and linked textually to the United States, Europe, the Pacific Rim, and so on. An additional structuring principle is the overlapping formal and rhetorical tactics by which Beat writers engage with the world, and the book's recursive structure allows writers to speak to one another across chapters in mutually illuminating ways: Joans and Lamantia through their shared commitment to surrealism, Burroughs and Gysin through their mutual development of the cut-up technique, Kerouac and Kingston through the character of Wittman Ah Sing in Kingston's novel *Tripmaster Monkey*. Underlying all of this, however, is a desire not merely to apply transnational theory to Beat Generation writing but to demonstrate that Beat writing can help advance a vision of what a truly worlded literary criticism might look like.

Most of the following chapters center on single authors, while always looking outward to the broader contexts and text-networks that shape that author's work. Chapter 1 focuses on Kerouac, presenting Dean Moriarty's ecstatic "It's the world!" (uttered just after he and Sal Paradise cross the border into Mexico in the final section of *On the Road*) as the zero degree formula for worlded Beat writing. Chapter 1 also opens up a discussion of the "subterranean" in Beat literature. A central Beat trope, an image of rhizomic connection, and a reading practice, subterranean thought is an important corollary of worlded thought, and Kerouac's practice of using travel and immersion in one location to construct radically expansive textual landscapes becomes a template for other Beat writers to follow.

Chapter 2 explores the transnational assemblages of influence integral to the work of African American Beat writers Amiri Baraka, Ted Joans, and Bob Kaufman. Joans, for example, wrote jazz- and Beat-inflected verse animated in equal parts by the avant-garde legacies of surrealism and by the Pan-Africanist rhetoric of black nationalism. He believed these disparate interests were fully compatible, and through the lens of his poetry, Beat writing becomes a swirling matrix of transgressive energies. Chapter 2 places the Beat movement within the venerable tradition of avant-garde art and literature that includes the Dadaists, the futurists, and especially the surrealists. Lamantia, at the center of chapter 3, was likewise influenced by the international avant-garde. Next to Joans's playfully idiosyncratic, politically canny poems, Lamantia's hermetic verse reads as very purely surrealist, yet his writing is also quite porous, shot through with competing interests and obsessions. Lamantia's career bridges the gap between avant-garde New York in the 1940s (where many European artists and writers had sought refuge during World War II) and the San Francisco Renaissance a decade later.

While the first half of the book fleshes out the various world-conjuring tactics employed by Beat writers, the next two chapters present extended readings of key texts. In a variation on Dimock's deep time, chapter 4 argues that William Burroughs's breakthroughs in *Naked Lunch* are the result of a collaborative process spanning several continents. A worlded reading of Burroughs's novel ultimately reveals its Latin American origins, for the seeds of *Naked Lunch* were planted in the less well-known *Yage Letters*, where his dream of a great "Composite City" projects a utopian vision of a transgressive community and worlded connectivity. Chapter 5 focuses on Gysin's 1969 novel *The Process*, which I read as an exemplary work of postcolonial Beat fiction. Set during the tumultuous years preceding national independence in the French Maghreb, Gysin's novel dramatizes the events in Morocco and Algeria in a kaleidoscopic manner that allows him to imagine alternative histories and inhabit a variety of subject positions. The plot unfolds around protagonist Ulys O. Hanson, an African American professor of history traveling through North Africa to research his book on the "future of slavery." For much of the novel, Hanson (aka Hassan Merikani) passes as African and Muslim, a situation that raises important questions of racial, religious, and ethnic difference, testing the limits of narrative identification while suggesting new possibilities for community building within a postcolonial—even postnational—framework.

Finally, chapter 6 loops back around to Kerouac by way of Maxine Hong Kingston's *Tripmaster Monkey: His Fake Book*, taking seriously the notion of post-Beat writing that signifies both rupture and continuity with regard to the Beat canon. Kingston is best known as the author of *Woman Warrior*; in *Tripmaster Monkey*, she dramatizes her own deeply ambivalent alliance with the Beats. Kingston's protagonist, Wittman Ah Sing, is a Chinese American beatnik (the novel is set in San Francisco in the mid-1960s) who wrestles with Kerouac's ghost and rewrites the Beat mythos in more inclusive terms. Kingston presents Wittman as a kind of latter-day flaneur, whose wanderings across San Francisco trace a subversive geography in the mode of the lettrist/situationist *dérive*. I use these concepts together with other models of "social space" to emphasize the point that post-Beat writing likewise engages an active process of world making, or worlding. I also point to the emergence of a cluster of contemporary Bay Area writers and activists whose work unites language, landscape, and political struggle in ways that further transform the tactics and traditions of worlded Beat writing.

1

A WORLD, A SWEET ATTENTION: JACK KEROUAC'S SUBTERRANEAN ITINERARIES

Kerouac and the Transnational Turn

In the final journey of *On the Road*, Sal Paradise and Dean Moriarty drive down at last to Mexico, and not long after crossing the border, Dean cries, "It's the world. . . . My God! . . . It's the world! We can go right on to South America if the road goes. Think of it! Son-of-a-*bitch*! Gawd-*damn*!"[1] Dean's exclamation is characteristic of the wide-eyed exuberance celebrated in Kerouac's novel. His telescopic vision of space and motion, in which *some*where becomes *every*where, also provides a formula of sorts for understanding the meaning of Beat travel more generally. Beat travel writing comprises a large and significant subset of the Beat corpus. Rob Wilson speaks of a "world-horizon come near," and this is what Beat writers bring into view again and again in their travel writing; Dean's ecstatic "It's the world!" is but the pure form of the "world-horizon come near." This chapter gathers together the various world-making tactics in Kerouac's prose and poetry, which is the point of departure for a worlded analysis of a whole series of Beat writers in subsequent chapters.

It is only after Dean and Sal leave the United States behind that Dean can apprehend "the world" as such. Yet Kerouac's own travels abroad (primarily to Mexico, but also Tangier, London, and France) provide him with new perspectives on the United States as well. A few pages after Dean's "It's the world!" Sal offers to drive (a rare occurrence) while Dean sleeps (also a rare occurrence). Sal soon finds himself dreaming his own world-vision:

> I was alone in my eternity at the wheel, and the road ran straight as an arrow. Not like driving across Carolina, or Texas, or Arizona, or Illinois; but like driving across the world and into the places where we would finally

learn ourselves among the Fellahin Indians of the world, the essential strain of the basic primitive, wailing humanity that stretches in a belt across the equatorial belly of the world from Malaya (the long fingernail of China) to India the great subcontinent to Arabia to Morocco to the selfsame deserts and jungles of Mexico and over the waves to Polynesia to mystic Siam of the Yellow Robe and on around, on around, so that you hear the same mournful wail by the rotted walls of Cádiz, Spain, that you hear 12,000 miles around in the depths of Benares the Capital of the World. (280)

These lines are the expression of a foundational moment in Kerouac's transnational imaginary, precipitated by and dependent on crossing the border into Mexico. Readers encounter various iterations of this "fellahin" dream throughout Kerouac's corpus, especially his writings from and about Mexico. Kerouac's reference to "the Fellahin Indians of the world"—in the famous scroll version of the novel, it's the even more crazed "worldwide fellaheen people of the world"—is straight out of Oswald Spengler's *Decline of the West*, whose influence on Kerouac (through Burroughs) cannot be overstated.[2]

It is possible to oversimplify his influence, however. Kerouac knew his Spengler well, writing about his 1957 trip to Morocco in *Desolation Angels*, for example: "In fact [Tangier is] exactly like Mexico, the Fellaheen world, that is, the world that's not making History in the present: *making* History, manufacturing it, shooting it up in H bombs and Rockets, reaching for the grand conceptual finale of Highest Achievement (in our times the 'Faustian' West of America, Britain and Germany high and low)."[3] Spengler's conception of history, and specifically his concept of the fellahin who live *outside* of history, retains its critical function in Kerouac's rendering, which pits the "Fellaheen world" squarely against the grasping "Faustian" West with its imperialist and militarist aims. But the real force of this passage lies in Kerouac's characteristic wordplay: the West's "H bombs" are "shot up" like the H of heroin (its "*Highest* Achievement"—Kerouac was staying with Burroughs at the time). In other words, he adapts Spengler to suit his purposes, which were aesthetic as well as philosophical. Discussing Kerouac's posthumous *Some of the Dharma* (composed in the mid-1950s, much of it in Mexico), Nancy Grace adds another twist, suggesting that "*Dharma* repudiates Spengler's mindset as . . . preoccupied with a falsely detailed view of history. Spengler, he concluded, failed to understand Eastern thought or the nature of the universe."[4]

Spengler's History with a capital H is strangely echoed in *Lonesome Traveler*, in the "Fellaheen Mexico" chapter, where Kerouac's "guide and

buddy," Enrique, "couldnt say 'H' but had to say 'K'—because his na-
tivity was not buried in the Spanish name of Vera Cruz his hometown,
in the Mixtecan Tongue instead.—On buses joggling in eternity he kept
yelling at me 'HK-o-t? HK-o-t? Is means *caliente*. Unnerstan?'"[5] Kerouac,
a French Canadian who grew up speaking *joual* in working-class New
England, is always attentive to the power dynamics inscribed within linguistic difference. Enrique the indigenous subaltern cannot even utter the
word "History," let alone possess one. In general, what makes Kerouac's
use of the fellahin concept irreducible to a mere orientalist othering is
the redemptive freedom of language it enables, not at the expense of the
Other but as a means of giving voice to the Other (however fraught that
becoming-other of the self might be). Such linguistic experimentation is
perhaps most evident in the poems of *Mexico City Blues*, but manifests
itself wherever the fellahin appear in Kerouac's work. Finally, it is not
inconceivable that Burroughs and Kerouac were familiar with the German title of Spengler's *Decline of the West*—which is *Der Untergang des
Abendlandes*. Alternatively rendered as *The Setting of the Eveninglands*
(as of the sun in the west—*Abendland* the German equivalent of "oc-
cident"), Spengler's title calls to mind the planetary dimensions of his
grand historical drama.

Kerouac's many references and allusions to a distinctly Spenglerian
view of history, it must be said, do also point to the dangers lurking
within Kerouac's conception of a worldwide communion of beatific
souls. Taking seriously the dangers of Brian Edwards's "orientalist trap,"
what I want to emphasize, however, is the fact that even with something
like "the worldwide fellaheen" bearing all the hallmarks of orientalism—
the East (which in Kerouac's case becomes the Global South) as timeless,
unchanging, essential, primitive, and all the rest—given the problematic
choice between depicting total alterity or total identification ("going native"), Kerouac consistently tends to the latter. What Wilson has aptly
called Kerouac's "fellaheen orientalism" always involves an expression
of felt solidarity and mutual understanding. Wilson sums up both the
possibilities and the pitfalls of such a gesture: On one hand, he praises
Kerouac, "whose language of maximal openness to sites such as Mexico
City, San Francisco, and Tangier was invaded by cultural otherness, by
what Gilles Deleuze would call the *third worlding* of his own language
and tactics." But on the other hand, Wilson concedes, "However multiple,
impure, or compassionate, fellaheen orientalism is still an orientalism as
such doing discursive work in and upon the world: its language works
to circulate, cite, and reiterate typifying representations of binary other-

ness that can occlude, distort, convert into metaphor, and romanticize the peoples and places of the worlds Kerouac's open roads would embrace."[6]

Only through this double lens of a strategic orientalism—a double move caught between identification and otherness—does a scene like the one in *On the Road*, where Sal has spent the day picking cotton with Teri (his Mexican lover) and her family of migrant farmworkers, gain any critical purchase whatsoever. Sal, nervous about recent violence committed against a worker in their party, says, "They thought I was a Mexican, of course; and in a way I am."[7] His boundless identificatory impulse leaves a bad taste in many readers' mouths. There are limits, after all. D. H. Lawrence lampoons the same impulse to "merge" in Whitman's poetry: "oozing into the universe," as Lawrence calls it.[8] (Doris Sommer calls it an imperialist gesture on Whitman's part.)[9] To many, the most outrageous instance of the always fraught relationship with otherness in Kerouac's fiction also appears in *On the Road*: "At lilac evening . . . in the Denver colored section, wishing I were a Negro, feeling that the best the white world had offered was not enough ecstasy for me, not enough life" (180). (Sal Paradise's Denver doldrums are reminiscent of Whitman's "I am the hounded slave" in "Song of Myself.") Unlike Teri and her family, Sal possesses the privilege of crossing borders, of wearing disguises. But at the very same time, this kind of *transgression*, or willful alienation from a hegemonic U.S. culture at home and dominance abroad, also makes visible and contests the underlying structures of dominance and hegemony that Beat writers are themselves able to profit from.

It is certainly ironic that the author of *On the Road* traveled much less extensively abroad than his Beat Generation peers. But Kerouac did spend a good deal of time in Mexico at several points throughout the 1950s. His first trip there was the one referred to in the passages from *On the Road* quoted earlier. He stayed with Burroughs in Mexico City in the spring of 1952 and composed *Dr. Sax* at that time; the fact that Kerouac's most intimate and idiosyncratic portrayal of his Lowell childhood should be written from Mexico is exemplary of the temporal and especially the geographic displacements and layering so characteristic of Kerouac's writing. Kerouac wrote *Mexico City Blues* in his rooftop abode at 210 calle Orizaba in the summer of 1955 and stayed there again in the fall of 1956. (Both stays are dramatized in the short novel *Tristessa*.) Apart from Mexico, Kerouac visited Burroughs in Tangier in 1957 while Burroughs was assembling what would become *Naked Lunch*. But as the story goes, he began to long for the comfort and routine of life with his Memère and left Morocco after only a few weeks. While Burroughs,

Ginsberg, and Gregory Corso were living it up in Paris at the famous "Beat Hotel," while Ginsberg searched India for a guru, and while Gary Snyder, Joanne Kyger, and later Philip Whalen studied Zen in Japan (and so on and so forth), Kerouac chose to remain stateside and dispatch letters of grim forbearance to his more worldly friends.

Nonetheless, Kerouac's writing has proven to be fertile ground for a number of critics interested in literary transnationalism. Rachel Adams refers to Kerouac as a paradigmatically "continental" writer, and Hassan Melehy discusses the significance of the author's Quebecois roots, theorizing Kerouac as a diasporic and nomadic writer and creator of a "minor literature" à la Deleuze. Kerouac has also provided a model for the kind of worlded writing that I am most interested in. At first glance, Kerouac may seem out of place in Adams's study, with its strong emphasis on indigenous and women writers and artists, as well as the U.S. expatriates of the 1930s, who, as Adams points out, had traveled to Mexico to take part in revolutionary history. So how, exactly, does Kerouac fit into a project that "grants new centrality to people and places that have been marginalized by official histories of conquest and nation building," especially given the fact that Kerouac's writings on Mexico so often get read as blindly appropriative and orientalizing?[10] Adams's study moves beyond such a reading, although she too poses the familiar critique of Beat writing, and Beat travel writing in particular, as narcissistic and apolitical. Ultimately, Kerouac figures in Adams's conception of continental literature not simply because he is someone who, with his Canuck background and formative experiences in Mexico, truly does span the continent but also, and more important, because he is able to translate (a key term for Adams as well as Susan Gillman and Kirsten Silva Gruesz in their formulation of a transnational or hemispheric "text-network") so many different kinds of continental flows and energies.

Adams asserts that Kerouac "is one of a very select group of authors who could be described as genuinely continental in scope," a transnationally minded writer "who crossed multiple borders of class, language, and nation." Yet Kerouac's work, according to Adams, has not been sufficiently well understood in its extranational contexts:

Whereas Kerouac has come to assume canonical status as a U.S. American author, I show the importance of his French Canadian background and his Mexican travels to his influential "visions of America." As much as we associate Kerouac with the Beat subcultures of New York and San Francisco, I argue that we must also recognize the profound impact of French

Canadian Lowell and Mexico City on the form and content of his writing
. . . paying particular attention to his status as a theorist of language, an
author concerned with the possibilities of translingual communication as
well as the problem of untranslatability.[11]

Kerouac's primary importance to Adams is precisely as a "theorist of language," and the texts she chooses to focus her attention on, those which
most fully disclose the transnational poetics of Kerouac's writing, include
Lonesome Traveler and *Desolation Angels*, with their transcontinental
itineraries, and *Mexico City Blues*, where Kerouac's language is most experimental and discernibly rhizomic. Moving away from the usual emphasis on his so-called bop prosody and the rhetoric of "spontaneous
prose," Adams underscores instead Kerouac's *minor* use of the English
language.

For Adams, as for Hassan Melehy, a good deal of what makes Kerouac's writing distinctive and significant is linked to Kerouac's upbringing
in the working-class French Canadian community of Lowell, Massachu-
setts. Kerouac would often point out that English was not his first language; Adams cites an early passage in *The Subterraneans*—where he
writes "confession after confession, I am a Canuck, I could not speak
English till I was 5 or 6, at 16 I spoke with a halting accent and was a
big blue baby in school"—as one example among others in Kerouac's
work of the link between language and otherness.[12] With moments like
these in mind, Melehy argues that "Kerouac explicitly raises the question of identity through a thoroughgoing exploration of the relationships
among *québécité* or Québec-ness, Frenchness, and provincial versus met-
ropolitan identity in France, and indeed of the fleeting, nomadic nature
of cultural identity itself."[13] But while his linguistic background, as he
illustrates poignantly in *The Subterraneans*, certainly contributes to Kerouac's shy awkwardness, he also understood his "halting accent" to be a
source of strength (as does Deleuze when he refers to *minor language* as
language that productively "stammers"[14]) and something to be turned to
his advantage as a writer. Kerouac composed an early sketch of *On the
Road* in French—it turns out that what some consider the "great American novel" was originally penned in a language other than English—and
snatches of French dialogue and description can be found in nearly all of
his published works.

There is a crucial distinction to make between the standard French
that, by all accounts, Kerouac could speak and write, and the French that
most often appears in his oeuvre: a transcription of the French Canadian

dialect *joual*, a patois with no written form. Adams explains that, for Kerouac, *joual* is closely allied with not just the past (familial and cultural history) but also linguistic and cultural vitality in the present; he often equates the language of his youth with musicality, rhythm, breath, and performance. Within this fruitful yet admittedly logocentric paradigm, it becomes easy to see how the method and ideal of "spontaneous prose" arose in part from the linguistic milieu of Kerouac's Lowell. Throughout his work, linguistic difference often stands in for cultural, ethnic, and racial difference, and linguistic *hybridity* is a marker of hybridity as such. Adams notes, "Often his protagonists describe themselves as hyphenated subjects who personify the mingling of French and indigenous America: a 'Canuck Fellaheen Indian' in *Maggie Cassidy* or 'Jack Iroquois' in *Book of Sketches* . . . works in which to be American is to embody racial mixture and to trace one's tangled roots across multiple borders" (153). What remains somehow redemptive in Kerouac's projections is that their weirdness (Jack Iroquois?) prevents the different sides of the equation from fusing into anything like a seamless whole, and difference as such is preserved. The strange juxtapositions of Kerouac's aliases and epithets can be read as a recuperative strategy within a "culturally homogenous modernity" threatening to relegate Kerouac's Lowell to an "unrecoverable past" (154).

While the French language is tied to home and childhood innocence, Spanish is tied to adventure, travel, and the allure of the exotic. What is most vital to Kerouac's continental "visions of America," however, are the ways in which the two overlap in a linguistic assemblage that opens onto a wide-ranging set of concerns and possibilities. As Adams says, "One invokes the other" (163). She laments the pitiful state of Kerouac's Spanish but also sees the poetic potential of lines like "Do you know what I p a l a b r a" in *Mexico City Blues*. A generous appraisal might reckon that Kerouac's pidgin is an attempt to render a Spanish equivalent of *joual* or that his willful distortions are a nod to Whitman's "camerado" and the like. Interestingly, what Adams takes exception to is not Kerouac's misprision or verbal tourism but the fact that his "willingness to identify with the Other" (166) does not go far enough and is too often "subsumed" by a compulsion to *self*-knowledge through drugs, sex, religion, and so on, leading Adams to conclude that Kerouac, and the Beats in general, "were relatively uninterested in the specific details of Mexican politics or history; its primary attraction was the cheap and permissive climate it offered for writing and recreation" (157). In Adams's account, however, a countervailing, continental situation does arise in *Desolation*

Angels, when Kerouac takes Memère with him to Mexico, narrating for her the long history of intermarriage between indigenous Americans and Spanish colonials. His mother asks, "Aw but these are good people the *Indians* you say?" Kerouac responding, "*Oui*—Indians just like the American Indians but here the Spaniards did not destroy them" (in French). "*Içi les espanols sont marié* [sic] *avec les Indiens*" (384). Here, the mestizo is a marker of the historicity of the Americas. Kerouac emphasizes singularity and contingency rather than the atemporal essentialism embedded in such a notion as his "worldwide fellaheen." Reminded perhaps of her own Unheimlichkeit as a French Canadian in Protestant New England, even Kerouac's mother, whose rabid anti-Semitism drove a wedge between her son and Allen Ginsberg, in these pages is at least open to an experience of recognition across cultures.[15]

The quest for longer histories and more capacious (though often submerged or occulted) networks of human interaction is a hallmark of Beat travel writing. It allows for Kerouac to disappear into the Mexican landscape while spinning a web of words that encompasses his native Catholicism, Maya ritual, Buddhist scripture, the American West, jazz, drugs, railroads, Spanish, French, and more. Such assemblages of influence and inspiration amount to a distinctive Beat syncretism. And in corresponding fashion, the recent studies of Kerouac by Adams and Melehy demonstrate that Beat Generation writing can be productively placed within wider trends in literary and cultural studies, that is to say, among the many critical rubrics designated by the umbrella term "transnational." With Kerouac front and center, Adams's continent stakes a claim on the middle ground between comparativism and globalism and shares with worlding a desire to think a nontotalizaling totality. What may seem like a limitation, the continent paradigm—its ostensible concern with North America alone—becomes a strength in that it can be adapted to the specific contours of other places, times, and critical projects while retaining its status as a "third term" that points to something at once more and less than the nation. And given the Beats' complex relationship with Latin America, which continue to be explored in the chapters to come, the hemispheric view has much to offer any reconsideration of Beat writing in its inter-American aspect.

Mapping the Beat Subterranean

That Kerouac continues to attract critical attention is a testament both to the persistent allure of his mystique and to the inexhaustibly protean nature of his writing. Having looked thus far at some salient features of the transnational Kerouac postulated by Adams and Melehy, I want to begin formulating a theory of worlded Beat travel that turns out to be the external, or extensive, aspect of a subterranean world that lies at the core Kerouac's oeuvre. The subterranean, like the world, is an image of creation and connectivity, where vast underground networks of influence and inspiration proliferate in the manner of the Deleuzian rhizome. There is no contradiction in positing subterranean spaces that exist *en plein air*, for the subterranean in Beat writing—and in the rich tradition of underground thought in literature, philosophy, critical theory, and cultural studies—becomes a critical term containing within itself a dialectical force subsuming depth and surface, the internal and the external, immanence and transcendence. I want to suggest that Kerouac is a paradigmatically subterranean writer and that close attention to the language of the subterranean in Beat writing can help foster a deeper and more nuanced understanding of Beat transnationalism. To revise an earlier assertion: where Kerouac is concerned at least, it is not entirely necessarily to leave the United States behind to bring the world at large into view, and this is precisely why his work is of such value to theorists of the transnational. The subterranean spaces manifested throughout his work, whether set at home or abroad, give rise to a radically expansive geographic imaginary.

Kerouac's novel *The Subterraneans* (written 1953; published 1958) is a conspicuous place to begin an investigation of the underground in Beat writing, not simply because of its title but also because it employs a set of formal and rhetorical tactics of critical importance to thinking about a worlded Beat Generation as well. Whereas an entire mythology has grown up around the composition of *On the Road*—the scroll, the three-week amphetamine blaze, no revision, years of rejection by every publisher in New York, the breakthrough of spontaneous prose, and so on—we know, thanks to a recent turn to textual studies among Beat scholars and the publication of the "original scroll edition" to mark the fiftieth anniversary of Kerouac's novel, that it was in fact heavily edited and underwent several major revisions and constant smaller ones throughout the 1950s. (This includes its translation from "Sur la route" by Jean Kerouac.)[16] What emerges from these rich textual histories is the fact that it is not *On the Road* but rather *Subterraneans* that lives up to the legend of the author's spontaneous prose. The much shorter novel was written in a mere three days, and unlike with *On the Road*, Kerouac refused to make concessions to his editor, Donald Allen, that he felt compromised his stylistic breakthroughs in *Subterraneans*.[17] Composed in a single burst of creative energy, this novel is perhaps the purest expression of what Kerouac will put down as his "Essentials of Spontaneous Prose." In fact, explaining the genesis of Kerouac's "Essentials," Ann Charters notes, "He wrote it at the request of Allen Ginsberg and William Burroughs in the fall of 1953, after he had shown them the manuscript of *Subterraneans*. His friends were so impressed that he'd written the entire book in three nights . . . that they asked him to describe how he'd done it."[18] This novel in particular reveals a kernel of truth in the Kerouac myth and for that reason alone is worth a closer look.

Moreover, not just the name but the naming of *Subterraneans* is significant and offers further insight into the collaboration between Kerouac and his earliest literary associates. It is entirely fitting that Adam Moorad, Ginsberg's avatar in *Subterraneans*, should be the one to name the group of North Beach (read Greenwich Village) bohemians on whom the novel centers. His characterization of them—"They are hip without being slick, they are intelligent without being corny, they are intellectual as hell and know all about Pound without being pretentious or talking about it, they are very quiet, they are very Christlike" (1)—remains a touchstone of Beat hipsterdom. By extension, Ginsberg names the novel itself, just as Kerouac had a few years earlier provided the title for Ginsberg's *Howl* and inspired some of the poem's most memorable lines. In his dedication of *Howl and Other Poems*, Ginsberg lionizes Kerouac for "creating a spontaneous bop prosody and original classic literature," but it is worth keeping in mind that of the eleven titles Ginsberg cites as proof of Kerouac's genius, including *On the Road* and *Subterraneans*, none were as yet published.[19] As Kerouac himself will write in the "Passing through Mexico" section of *Desolation Angels*, "Nothing could stop me from writing big books of prose and poetry for nothing, that is, with no hope of ever having them published—I was simply writing them because I was an 'Idealist' and I believed in 'Life' and was going about justifying it with my earnest scribblings—Strangely enough, these scribblings were the first of their kind in the world" (256). At the time of *Howl*'s publication, Kerouac, along with Burroughs and Neal Cassady (*Howl* was dedicated to them as well), could still be said to compose a "subterranean" literary community in the most basic sense of subterranean as underground, out of sight, unknown. Finishing one book after another while facing what would could only seem like diminishing prospects for publication after his largely failed first novel, *The Town and the City*, in 1950, who or what could Kerouac said to be writing for without some abiding sense of the subterranean as a space of radically projective, community forming potential?[20]

The Beat movement as a spatial phenomenon has long been a source of interest: over the years, books such as James Jones's *Map of Mexico City Blues*, James Campbell's *This Is the Beat Generation: New York–San Francisco–Paris*, along with Deborah Baker's *A Blue Hand* and Todd Tietchen's *Cubalogues*, have all dealt with significant locales along the Beat landscape and have documented some of the main lines of the Beats' world travels. There is much yet to be written, however, on the subject of Beat "space" per se. *Subterraneans* has a lot to say about Beat geography; Kerouac's novel maps a creative topography, and readers can follow the lines of interconnectivity from New York to San Francisco that open onto multiple spaces for writing and sex and family and spirituality—that is to say, the major obsessions of Kerouac's life and work. Through its highly compressed layers of concern, *Subterraneans*, like so much of Kerouac's work, traces an attempted line of flight (leading seemingly always back to lost youth and Lowell) but loses itself amid the dissipation and self-hatred that begin to poison Kerouac's life and relationships. The novel's very first sentence begins, "Once I was young and had so much more orientation." Its context disorients the reader as well, for although *Subterraneans* is set in the bohemia of San Francisco's North Beach, the events depicted took place on the other side of the continent in Greenwich Village. There remains a great deal of specificity of place names, but each one is marked by a shifting geography. These shifts are due in large part to the fact that the novel is very much autobiographical, and Kerouac felt compelled to protect or disguise the actors by changing their names and transplanting the entire scene.[21] But a more productive kind of transformation is also at work in *Subterraneans*. For Kerouac, the journey west always catalyzes the most intense kinds of becomings, and by rerouting the lines of a fairly banal tale of love, betrayal, and loss, it is as if he is able to redeem that loss by linking it to the creative energies and spiritual nourishment invariably associated with the West Coast in his writing.

Kerouac's decision to move the center of action from New York to San Francisco is not simply a matter of legal or editorial expediency. Seen another way, the fact that he can change the setting of the novel so convincingly and in such detail gets at the heart of the Beat subterranean as lived space. It speaks to a certain synchronicity that exists among bohemian enclaves across the country, a pulse that Kerouac finds again and again in his writing. Japhy Ryder's utopian vision in *The Dharma Bums* (1958) of a "rucksack revolution," a million young seekers taking to the road en masse, arises from similar intimations. When Bob Dylan describes his experiences in early-1960s bohemia in his memoir *Chronicles* and in Martin Scorsese's documentary *No Direction Home,* he likewise refers to an entire network of liberated zones stretching across the United States. He explains to Cameron Crowe in 1985:

> I came out of the wilderness and just naturally fell in with the Beat scene, the Bohemian, Bebop crowd, it was all pretty much connected . . . St Louis, Kansas City, you usually went from town to town and found the same setup in all these places, people comin' and goin,' nobody with any special place to live. You always ran into people you knew from the last place. . . . Where I was at, people just passed through, really, carrying horns, guitars, suitcases, whatever, just like the stories you hear, free love, wine, poetry, nobody had any money anyway. There were a lot of poets and painters, drifters, scholarly types, experts at one thing or another who had dropped out of the regular nine-to-five life.[22]

Kerouac's work, too, moves along the circuits of this ever-expanding network, or rhizome, as it extends to Mexico City, to Paris, to Tangier, and beyond. Beat notions of the worlded world are so often based on exactly the kind of hidden synchronicity and syncretism described by Dylan.

The Beat subterranean comprises both a spatial and a temporal aspect: subterranean, rhizomic space is radically contiguous and densely layered, and subterranean *time* is necessarily "out of joint."[23] Throughout *Subterraneans* the narrator maintains an intense awareness of a temporal displacement or distance between himself and the subterranean hipsters of San Francisco. This distance is expressed most poignantly early on, at the first encounter between Leo and Mardou: "She was interested in thin ascetic strange intellectuals of San Francisco and Berkeley and not in big paranoiac bums of ships and railroads and novels and all that hatefulness . . . and because ten years younger than I seeing none of my virtues which anyway had long been drowned under years of drugtaking and desiring to die, to give up, to give it all up and forget it all, to die in the dark star . . . ah time" (6). Like the rhizomic circuitry of the spatial organization of Kerouac's novels, the painful awareness of such temporal gaps serves to deflate the whole Kerouac mythos of "railroads and novels." When *On the Road* was finally published in 1957, the events depicted therein had taken place over a decade earlier in many cases. Now thirty-five years old and already beginning to shows signs of alcoholic wear and tear, the real-life Sal Paradise was not quite what readers were expecting. *Subterraneans,* published amid the tempest of Kerouac's first notoriety, painfully registers his age and "hatefulness" in relation not only to his new fans but also to a potential love interest like Mardou.

Subterraneans is hardly unique among Kerouac's novels in being organized by a circuit of motion at times productive and liberating, at times treacherous and entrapping. The nodal points of *Subterraneans* are Mardou's apartment in Heavenly Lane, the East Bay apartment of Leo's mother, and the bars and jazz clubs of North Beach. Leo maps the geography of the novel as he rushes from one node to the next in an increasingly desperate search for both escape and disciplined creativity (major themes in Kerouac's life and oeuvre). *On the Road* is structured by several cross-continent trips, *Dharma Bums* by the movement between mountaintop and city, and *Big Sur* by at least three different durations of movement. (Kerouac's desperate refrain in the novel is "One fast move or I'm gone.")[24] In *Big Sur* the first, a long-distance, or macro, movement from the East Coast to California—Kerouac's attempt to escape the crush of fame and notoriety that followed *On the Road* in hopes of solitude and recovery at Lawrence Ferlinghetti's cabin near Big Sur—is what precipitates the action of the novel as a whole. The second, a mid-level movement from San Francisco to Big Sur and back, structures much of the novel narratively and thematically. In general, the city is presented as the place of dissolution and entrapment, while the cabin and coast at Big Sur offer physical and spiritual regeneration. But Kerouac cannot hold these two worlds apart, and Ferlinghetti's cabin becomes the site of Kerouac's final (in the novel) delirium and breakdown. The third duration, the most interesting in the context of this discussion, involves a series of short or micro movements that he makes from the cabin to the coast, most often at night and to write down what would become "Sea: The Sounds of the Pacific at Big Sur," the long sound poem that forms a coda to the novel.

Once at Big Sur, Kerouac's world comprises three major elements, each with its own important and often unexpected movements and dynamics: the Raton (Bixby) Canyon bridge, the creek that flows underneath it, and the Pacific Ocean.[25] These last ocean flows from Hawaii, Asia, and beyond are fearful and violent but also vital and dynamic. They are contrasted with the circular or closed tourist flows moving up and down Highway 1 and across the canyon bridge. Together, the various movements, circuits, and flows that permeate and shape the novel converge to produce a warp zone at Big Sur, which in turn adds and is added to by Kerouac's own dissipation and paranoia. He continually emphasizes the disorienting nature of the landscape, which is registered immediately upon his arrival by taxicab: "And sure enough when he lets me off at the Raton Canyon bridge and counts the money I sense something wrong somehow, there's an awful roar of surf but it isn't coming from the right place, like you'd expect it to come from 'over there' but it's coming from 'under there.' . . . The sea roar is bad enough except it keeps bashing and barking at me like a dog in the fog down there, sometimes it booms the earth but my God where is the earth and how can the sea be underground!"[26] Kerouac's crossing under the bridge and toward the sea is most significant in its expression of the subterranean spaces and energies of Beat writing. In the novel the highway does not *even* represent commerce or the commodity, only a kind of hollow, passive spectatorship. "There they are," writes Kerouac, "thousands and thousands of tourists driving by slowly on the high curves" (43). As he attempts to move beyond the tourist flows, farther out on the coast than the coastal highway itself, Kerouac is blocked, thrown back, and rejected by the worlded flows of the ocean. Trapped here as in the city, he inevitably cracks up.

Kerouac's creative geographies often have less to do with the pure freedom of the mythic open road and more to do with Deleuzian lines of flight and escape. Here Deleuze draws heavily from D. H. Lawrence's essay "The Spirit of Place" and uses Kerouac, Burroughs, and Dylan as examples. For Deleuze, the line of flight marks the most salient, vital feature and tendency of English and American writers, whose greatest aim is "to leave, to escape," or in Lawrence's words, "to cross the horizon, to enter into another life."[27] Creating a line of flight would therefore seem to be an internal, or intensive, process, yet, according to Deleuze, "it is the opposite of the imaginary."[28] Lawrence, who figures largely in Deleuze's conception of English and American literature, describes America itself as being founded on the desire, not for "freedom" but for an "escape." He asks, "All right then, what did they [the 'Pilgrim Fathers'] come for? . . . They came largely to get *away*—that most simple of motives. To get away. Away from what? In the long run, away from themselves. Away from everything. That's why most people have come to America, and still do come. To get away from everything they are and have been." Lawrence's immensely ironic characterization of American history—setting "escape" in opposition to "freedom"—problematizes both notions. In the same way that Deleuze's lines of flight can quickly become reterritorialized and destructive, Lawrence's freedom leads more often than not to a "hopeless sort of constraint."[29] Deleuze transforms Lawrence's pessimistic, almost cynical viewpoint, however, by deemphasizing the idea that flight or escape must necessary involve physical or spatial movement. Immediately following a quotation from Lawrence, Deleuze writes, "To fly is to trace a line, lines, a whole cartography. One only discovers worlds through a long, broken flight." The British and American writers he praises "create a new Earth; but perhaps the movement of the Earth is deterritorializa-tion itself."[30] This kind of thinking seems to me to be absolutely central to the work that worlding must undertake: creating nothing less than a "new earth"—not one of territories, fixities, homogenous spaces, and immutable borders but rather a worlded world utterly deterritorialized, open, and unpredictable.

Kerouac's work is vital to Deleuze's conception of literary lines of flight, which are in turn central to understanding the subterranean in Beat writing more generally. Cultural historian David Pike has argued at some length that over the course of the past two centuries the subterra-nean itself has become inextricably linked to the city. And insofar as the Beat movement began as a primarily urban phenomenon—although the notion of the subterranean actually serves to displace the city as primary cultural locus—the Beat subterranean necessarily has a complex and in-timate connection with *the street*. To be underground is to be under the pavement. Amiri Baraka's first collection of poems, *Preface to a Twenty Volume Suicide Note*, written during his early "Beat period," opens with a quotidian image of the urban underground:

> Lately, I've become accustomed to the way
> The ground opens up and envelopes me
> Each time I go out to walk the dog.[31]

One of several valences of "beat" is, of course, the notion of being beaten down, a dead beat, and so on: a valorization of what Ginsberg has called the "bottom-up vision of society."[32] In Baraka's poem one can detect an exaggerated quality characteristic of this kind of street talk. The speaker is, in a sense, "beater than beat"—not just down on the ground but wholly underground, swallowed up by pavement. The speaker's resignation ("I've become accustomed") is also typical of the subterranean trope in Beat writing, as, for instance, in Kaufman's "West Coast Sounds—1956":

> San Fran, hipster land,
> . . . .
> Too many cats,
> Monterey scene cooler,
> San Franers, falling down.
> Canneries closing.
> Sardines splitting
> For Mexico.
> Me too.[33]

Kaufman's poem transforms the vertical movement implied by the spatial mode of the subterranean into an explicitly geographic vision of escape and exile. The resigned enclosure evoked by Baraka is carried over into Kaufman's poem through the image of the sardines, but Kaufman also manages to create a line of flight as the sardines "split" from Cannery Row, and the conditions of decay and despair generate the very means by which one may ultimately transcend those conditions.

Given the constant and easy slippage from street level to subterranean that characterizes this particular line of figuration, I do not want to be too schematic about it, but a working thesis could be put forward with the street a site of contestation and the subterranean a site of continuity. One example of this can be seen in the opening lines of Dylan's "Subterranean Homesick Blues" (1965):

Johnny's in the basement
Mixing up the medicine
I'm on the pavement
Thinking about the government.[34]

The subterranean means connectivity: the basement "medicine" provides the means Ginsberg calls the "ancient heavenly connection"; while above ground, the Whitmanian vision of the interconnectedness of all things has become a hallucinated paranoia, at once vital and destructive.[35] Dylan's own Beat period provides numerous illustrations of this dynamic, perhaps most notably in "Desolation Row" (1965) with its unmistakably Kerouacian title.

The subterranean is both a spatialized trope and troped space: the active creation of a figurative zone of encounters and energies that Beat writing employs in an attempt to conceptualize the labyrinthine processes of aesthetic and cultural production and social transformation. But the Beat subterranean is just one iteration of underground thinking to sprout up within the broad zone of literature, philosophy, critical theory, and cultural studies over the course of the twentieth century. Several times I have used the word "rhizomic" to describe Kerouac's work; my particular understanding of the subterranean in Beat writing flows from Gilles Deleuze and Félix Guattari and their theorization of the *rhizome* in *A Thousand Plateaus* and elsewhere. Developing the principles of rhizomic multiplicity and heterogeneity, they posit the immanence of the rhizome against all forms of transcendence. "A rhizome as subterranean stem," they write in *Plateaus*, "is absolutely different from roots," which is to say nonhierarchical, asymmetrical, and without a clearly defined beginning or end. They go on to say, "A rhizome ceaselessly establishes connections between semiotic chains, organizations of power, and circumstances related to the arts, sciences, and social struggles." The rhizome will always be opposed to the tree-root system, which for Deleuze signifies unity, transcendence, and a fixed nature. "There are no points or positions in a rhizome, such as those found in a structure, tree, or root," he and Guattari write. "There are only lines."[36] These lines allow the subterranean rhizomic to link up with the most diverse elements (social, political, psychic, aesthetic, etc.). And the rhizome, as opposed to the tree-root system, is centerless—a point Deleuze drives home by quoting Henry Miller's adage that grass (another image of the rhizome) always "grows between."[37]

If a rhizome has no center and no edge, then ideas of margins, marginality, and marginalization, always crucial when thinking about the Beats, begin to take on a new significance.[38] Notions of borders and transgression must also be rethought in terms of subterranean space and motion along rhizomic lines of flight. The subterranean is a figurative space where high and low, inside and outside, are but different and constantly shifting aspects of the same processes. In Sam Green and Bill Siegel's 2002 documentary on the Weather Underground—a group whose name derives, after all, from a line in Dylan's "Subterranean Homesick Blues" ("You don't need a weatherman to know which way the wind blows": the group was also known as The Weathermen)—one former member explains that the "underground" was not so much a hiding place as it was a state of mind: a new set of behaviors and patterns of activity that allowed him and his comrades to hide in plain sight. This one member marveled at the fact that he would constantly run into people he once knew "on the outside" yet would never be noticed, as if he had simply ceased to exist.

Also revealing is Weather Underground leader Bernardine Dohrn's assertion that there were "multiple undergrounds."[39] Where the subterranean is concerned, the multiple always trumps the singular, and a particular movement—literary, social, or otherwise—can be meaningful and effective only insofar as it can recognize and link up with an outside-of-itself. Iterations of a subterranean Beat genealogy often circle around the notion of an alternative or submerged tradition, as often seen in Ginsberg's relentless name dropping, in Greil Marcus's "secret history" and "invisible republic" (the latter in reference to Dylan's *Basement Tapes*), or in Anne Waldman's "outrider" tradition, which, according to Waldman, comprises "a second generation away from the New American Poetry with its branches of Beat, Black Mountain, New York School and San Francisco Renaissance [and] Umbra in the mix." She describes it variously as a "hybrid," a "curious amalgamation," and an "open system," and Waldman's *Outrider* collection even includes a long interview on the subject of a "Rhizomic Poetics."[40]

In the world of cultural studies, David Pike has been especially committed to thinking about the subterranean. In a series of books on the subject, Pike explores the rise and development of the underground as a dominant topos—like the worlded word, the subterranean is both space *and* trope—in modernity. He begins with Dante, whose *descensus ad inferos* in *The Divine Comedy* transforms older traditions of "descent" (Odysseus in Hades, Christ's Harrowing) and lays the groundwork for the next seven centuries of thinking and writing about the underworld. For Pike, the subterranean really comes into its own at the turn of the nineteenth century, when new technologies turn underground space into a new frontier:

> True enough, man-made spaces such as tunnels, sewers, catacombs, and mines were being excavated beneath the earth by convicts or slaves as far back as the twenty-sixth century BCE. The Western city has long been associated with the underworld in moral terms as the center of iniquity and dissolution. But it was only with the development of the nineteenth-century city, with its complex drainage systems, underground railways, utility tunnels, and storage vaults, that the urban landscape superseded the countryside of caverns and mines as the primary location of actual subterranean spaces.[41]

By 1800 the globe had been mapped, and the sea was waning as an engine of imagination and a sign of the radically unknown. This is precisely when the subterranean began to take over those roles, making its history intimately linked with the rise of industrial capitalism and capitalist exploitation of the earth. Pike's work maps a certain tradition of subterranean thinking, which involves on one hand a familiar privileging of the modern, the urban, in a word: the West. But, on the other hand, the subterranean also works to undermine all kinds of binaries and false dichotomies. It thus shares much in common with worlded thinking as a critical practice. Put another way, as a historical fact Pike's subterranean may be a (by)product of Western modernity, but as a critical practice subterranean thought has the potential to decenter the modern and exceed Western hegemony. The Beat Generation is usually thought of as a primarily urban phenomenon—in contrast to, say, Mother Nature's children, the hippies—but if one emphasizes instead the rhizomic, subterranean geography of the Beats' world crossings, the city (like the West) becomes just one node among many others within the transnational circuitry of Beat writing. (And the Beats' many East-West crossings are even more complex.)

For me, Pike's most suggestive and highly resonant statement about his overall project appears in a preface, where he "argue[s] that what we need now are strategies of reading that establish unforeseen connections and associations."[42] New work on the Beats should be about nothing if not establishing "unforeseen connections and associations," and I am immediately put in mind of Wai Chee Dimock and her strong emphasis on reading practices able to conjure planetary "deep time." The subterranean is a site of artistic production, and Beat writing consistently seeks to manifest its transformative, antihegemonic potential. But the subterranean also names a critical practice, and specifically one in which modes of apprehending the world around us ("strategies of looking") inform what Pike calls "strategies of reading." (The authors of *The Worlding Project*, borrowing from Michel de Certeau, prefer to speak of worlded "tactics.") Pike distinguishes between the "view from above" and the "view from below."[43] The "view from above" he characterizes as hierarchical, abstract, and homogenous, whereas the view from below—the subterranean view, Ginsberg's "bottom-up vision of society"—is marked by messiness, materiality, and heterogeneity: all the hallmarks, in other words, of the worlded world.

The rhizomic modalities of subterranean thought often blur the boundaries between artistic production and its reception and between writing and reading, art and life. Beat writing can nonetheless be located with a very distinct literary tradition that attempts, in a sense, to write the subterranean. Within this literary assemblage the underground or subterranean is a space not of dormancy and escape but of vitality and intense creative activity. This point is well illustrated by Deleuze and Guattari in their discussion of Kafka's unfinished story "The Burrow," which centers on a mole-like creature whose compulsion to build an ever more elaborate underground lair far exceeds the demands of shelter and protection. Deleuze and Guattari register this activity as a kind of man-becoming-animal, explaining, "To become animal is to participate in movement, to stake out the path of escape in all its positivity, to cross a threshold, to reach a continuum of intensities that are valuable only in themselves, to find a world of pure intensities where all forms come undone. . . . Kafka's animals . . . are distinguished only by this or that threshold, this or that vibration, by the particular underground tunnel in the rhizome or the burrow. Because these tunnels are underground intensities."[44] The subterranean figures in their reading of Kafka's story as a site of infinite possibilities, where one may be receptive to the most disparate energies and influences. The active solitude of the burrow is also a stand-in for the act of writing itself, and seen in this light Kafka's story becomes an allegory of the creative process. But what kind of process is being described here? The burrow, with its proliferation of tunnels running in every direction, is an image of the centerless rhizome. It is true that there are main tunnels and auxiliary ones, but the burrow-creature's behavior suggests a nonhierarchical conception of its underground lair. According to Deleuze and Guattari, the tunnels that lead nowhere are actually the most interesting and potentially the most instructive. Also important is the suggestion throughout the story that there are other burrows made by other creatures (to say nowhere of the innumerable "small fry" that share the protagonist's burrow). The subterranean always holds the promise of connectivity and community, and in Deleuze and Guattari's vision the burrow-rhizome is itself multiple and can potentially link up with other burrows, other multiplicities.

Looking to "The Burrow" to characterize the rhizomic assemblages of subterranean space, one could make the claim that, rather than thematizing actual space, Kafka's story *actualizes* a purely conceptual space. The burrow, like the rhizome, like the subterranean, like worlding, exists only in its active creation. This is why the burrow-maker must continually and obsessively build new passageways; he ties his own survival to the necessity to keep building at all costs. Similarly, the subterranean will always imply an active process of assemblage (a praxis, a reading practice, artistic creation, and so on). In *Notes from Underground*, Fyodor Dostoevsky's Underground Man describes a similar undertaking as that of the burrow-maker. At one point, in a fit of benevolence, he declares, "I agree— man is primarily a creative animal, condemned . . . to be continually and eternally building roads for himself, leading *somewhere, no matter where.* . . . The main thing isn't where it leads, but just that it lead."[45] This will to create through self-effacement is also reminiscent of the unnamed narrator of Ralph Ellison's *Invisible Man*, who, at the beginning of the novel, has escaped a riot by falling down a manhole and seeks lasting refuge below the streets of Harlem. The subterranean sites of Ellison's novel, like those of Dostoevsky's *Notes from Underground*, can be read as major precursors to the Beat subterranean. The Invisible Man, moreover, does not merely live underground but, as Ellison writes, "in a border area," a liminal space aligned with receptivity and productive transgression.[46]

Early champions of Ellison's work may have lauded the author for developing an American counterpart to the European existentialist tradition (the Invisible Man as isolated modern subject), but we can instead read the novel's opening scene as recognizing the potential of the subterranean as a space of affirmation and, above all, connectivity. I would argue that photographer Jeff Wall's large-format piece *After "Invisible Man" by*

Ralph Ellison, the Prologue, in which the artist stages the protagonist's underground abode, offers just such a reading. The Invisible Man sits in his undershirt off to the side with his back turned to the camera; it is evident that subterranean space itself is the subject of Wall's photograph. In this way, *Invisible Man* is written in, of, and by the underground. The most striking aspect of Wall's photograph, however, are the " 1,369 lights" that line the ceiling.[47] The viewer's gaze is drawn to the circuitry of the subterranean, and one is reminded of Ginsberg and his "bottom-up vision of society," which, in all its decrepitude, offers the best vantage on potential connections and possibilities. The obsessive wiring of these lights is analogous to the manic building of Kafka's burrow-maker or the ferocious scribblings of Dostoevsky's Underground Man.

The subterranean and the world are two aspects of the very same modes and processes, a paradoxical doubling where *going out* is *going in* and vice versa. These centripetal-centrifugal forces make it so that Kerouac's Mexico, for instance, leads both to Dean's telescopic "It's the world!" and to Kerouac's intensely introspective period of writing and dharma study there. The latter also entailed the hyperlocal Joycean wanderings through Mexico City recorded in *Tristessa*. Kerouac is a disciple of Nietzsche's Zarathustra, who exhorts his would-be followers to "*remain true to the earth*," telling them, "To blaspheme the earth is now the dreadfulest sin, and to rate the heart of the unknowable higher than the meaning of the earth!"[48] The subterranean is what grounds worlded thought and keeps its telescopic impulse to transcend firmly rooted in the "meaning of the earth." The earthbound immanence of Gary Snyder's planetary ecos/*oikos*, like Philip Lamantia's "house in the cracks of the pavement," like Kerouac's subterranean topographies, are characteristically Beat appeals to a worlded world.[49] They situate Beat writing within a definable tradition of subterranean writing through Ellison, Kafka, and Dostoevsky, as well as the looser cultural or ideological nexus described by Pike. The Beat subterranean compels a materialist reading practice that privileges the rootedness of the near-at-hand.

Kerouac's Worlded Itineraries

As an image of worlded multiplicity and Pike's "unforeseen connections," the Beat subterranean is a major key to understanding Beat transnationalism, and no one makes this more apparent than Kerouac. His "domestic" novels such as *Big Sur* and *The Subterraneans* are shaped by their subterranean spaces, and so too are the string of books including

Mexico City Blues and *Tristessa*—whose immediate geographic reference is Mexico—and *Lonesome Traveler* and *Desolation Angels*, two volumes of travel writing, in a sense, which also deal with Kerouac's experiences abroad (most notably in Mexico and Morocco). For the French and French Canadian Kerouac, the places to look are *Dr. Sax* and the late *Satori in Paris*. In these works, Kerouac consistently presents his experiences abroad in the mode of the subterranean. While living in Mexico City, for example, in the fall of 1956, Kerouac received a visit from Ginsberg, Corso, and Ginsberg's lover Peter Orlovsky. As he describes it in *Desolation Angels*, they visit the pyramids at Teotihuacán but take a greater interest in the large ant mounds scattered around the site. Kerouac sets up a clear analogy between the anthills and the pyramids, musing, "While the Teo[tihuacán] priests goofed up there these ants were just beginning to dig a real underground super market" (272). With this seemingly offhand statement, Kerouac neatly locates the subterranean as an alternative, antihegemonic space. The power dynamic between the "Teo priests" on high and the ants down below resonates with Burroughs's own fascination with the priestly caste (of the Maya, in Burroughs's case) as insidious control agents.[50] Neither Burroughs nor Kerouac presents pre-Columbian Mesoamerican society as idyllic or romanticized; they are both attuned to the power differentials—made visible by their soaring temples but also suggesting their hidden obverse: the underground pathways of the ants—that shaped those cultures and still provide insight into the workings of control and authority in the present day.

Given the intense connectivity, simultaneity, and geographic syncretism of the subterranean, Kerouac's many depictions of the "fellaheen world" are incredibly overdetermined, to be sure. In *Tristessa*—Kerouac's account of his tormented love for Esperanza Villanueva, a Mexico City morphine addict and acquaintance of Burroughs's friend Bill Garver, the legendary junky familiar to readers of Burroughs as Bill Gains—the title character is made to carry an awful lot of symbolic and ideological weight. A devout Catholic, she at times represents the Virgin Mary (and therefore conjures memories of the author's Catholic upbringing in Lowell). But during this mid-1950s period of Kerouac's intense spiritual questing, Catholicism is never far from Buddhism.[51] At one point in *Tristessa*, he writes of "the sweep of the Mexican plateau away from the Moon—living but to die, the sad song of it I hear sometimes on my roof in the Tejado district, rooftop cell, with candles, waiting for my Nirvana or my Tristessa—neither come."[52] Kerouac envisions himself a Buddhist monk in his "rooftop cell," a place of introspection but also of vast panoramas that he synesthetically *hears* in his cloistered solitude. This sensory assemblage parallels the spiritual, geographic, and linguistic assemblages that are often the fruit of Kerouac's subterranean reveries.

At other moments in *Tristessa*, Kerouac's muse is made to stand in for the whole of his now-gendered worldwide fellaheen, as when he calls her "Fellaheena" (24). These over-the-top moments are also where Kerouac maximally sets language on an expressive line of flight through characteristic wordplay that traces a worlded itinerary. A few pages after the "Fellaheena" remark, he writes, "The wild way Tristessa stands legs spread in the middle of the room to explain something, like a junkey on a corner in Harlem or anyplace, Cairo, Bang Bombayo and the whole Fella Ollah Lot from Tip of Bermudy to wings of albatross ledge befeathering the Arctic Coastline, only the poison they serve out of Eskimo Gloogloo seals and eagles of Greenland, ain't as bad as that German Civilization morphine she (an Indian) is forced to subdue and die to, in her native earth" (28). If *Mexico City Blues* had been written as prose poems, this could be a fine example. "Cairo, Bang Bombayo and the whole Fella Ollah Lot" evokes the language of Kerouac's Mexico poems, which he was actively composing during the 1955–56 *Tristessa* period. His muse has now become an image of transnational hipsterdom and placed within an even larger spatiotemporal network stretching from the tropics to the arctic with echoes of a Spenglerian world history that pits Western civilization against indigenous cultures. And Tristessa's "native earth" is echoed in *Lonesome Traveler* by Kerouac's refrain: "The earth is an Indian thing" (22–23).

Like in the poems of *Mexico City Blues*, the linguistic assemblages of Kerouac's prose in *Tristessa* give rise to other kinds of combinations. Lighting a cigarette with a votive candle in Tristessa's squalid kitchen, he says in his nonstandard *joual*, "I make a little French prayer: '*Excuse mué ma 'Dame*'—making emphasis on *Dame* because of Damema the Mother of Buddhas" (30). Kerouac's own Memère is a felt presence throughout the novella. High on morphine one night, he "see[s] the brown corners of the dream house and remember[s] my mother's dark kitchen long ago on cold streets in the other part of the same dream as this cold present kitchen with its drip-pots and horrors of Indian Mexico City" (35), and before that he thinks, "I wish my relatives from Lowell were here to see how people and animals live in Mexico" (29). In these lines there is the assumption of solidarity grounded in a shared Catholic faith and a shared positionality between the Indians of Mexico and the French Canadians of New England. After he says good-bye to Tristessa and her roommate, Cruz, following a long night of booze and drugs, he watches "the two ladies go down the sidewalk slowly, the way Mexican women aye French Canadian women go to church in the morning" (83).

The knotted relationship between faith, language, identity, and affiliation is poignantly expressed in the final chapter of *Desolation Angels*, which describes that unlikely trip Kerouac made with his mother to Mexico. Not long after crossing the border, they visit a local church and witness a penitent kneeling with arms outstretched, inspiring this exchange between Ti Jean (Kerouac) and Memère:

> "O Ti Jean, what's he done that he's so sad for? I cant believe that old man has ever done anything really bad!"
>
> "He's a *penitente*," I tell her in French. "He's a sinner and he doesnt want God to forget him."
>
> "*Pauvre bonhomme!*" and I see a woman turn and look at Ma thinking she said "*Pobrecito*" which is exactly what she said anyway." (383)

After his mother's epiphany in the church, a recognition of her fellow Catholics, the author feels confident saying, "Now she understood Mexico and why I had come there so often even tho I'd get sick of dysentery or lose weight or get pale. '*C'est du monde qu'il on du coeur*,' she whispered, 'these are people who have *heart*!'" (384). (He responds, "*Oui*.") This deep sense of shared identities and values across languages and cultures lies at the heart of Kerouac's subterranean world-visions. Granted, these identifications are often made all too easily—as when he baldly states in *Visions of Cody*, "I love the Indian, I am an Indian"—but are never made in bad faith.[53]

That is to say, what could be an essentializing move on Kerouac's part, one that elides cultural and historical differences in the name of a world brother- and sisterhood of the fellahin, has more to do with a shared position relative to a sociopolitical dominant. This is how Kerouac the French Canadian growing up in Lowell (who claimed Iroquois ancestry on his mother's side) can manage to feel a connection with the indigenous and marginalized from Mexico to Morocco. Not surprisingly, the core of this felt connection for Kerouac is always about linguistic difference. Still in Mexico with Memère, the conversation continues:

> Ma said to me: "They're afraid to talk?"
>
> "They dont know what to do. They never meet anybody. They come from the desert. They dont even speak Spanish just Indian."[54]

The variegated linguistic milieux he seems to find everywhere in his travels are precisely what bind Kerouac to the places he visits. For the very same reason, when Ginsberg and company visit him in Mexico, he expresses a particularly strong fellow feeling for Gregory Corso. Kerouac describes Corso in the act of writing: "You can actually *hear* the poem for the first and last time in the world. The scratchings sound just like Raphael [Corso]'s yellings, with the same rhythm of expostulation and the bombast booms of complaint. But in the scratchety scratch you also hear the somehow miraculous making of words into English from the head of an Italian who never spoke English in the Lower East Side till he was seven." Kerouac clearly sympathizes with Corso on account of their analogous linguistic histories as outsiders in the English language, which is perhaps why he says a few pages earlier, "Raphael Urso I liked quite well, too, in spite or perhaps because of a previous New York hassle over a subterranean girl, as I say"—referring to their completing affections for Alene Lee, or Mardou Fox, when Kerouac dramatizes the conflict in *The Subterraneans*.⁵⁵ Corso's "miraculous making of words into English" is what Deleuze and Guattari would call the "becoming-minor" of English, and the description of Corso could apply equally to Kerouac himself. Kerouac's linguistic exile proved to be immensely productive, and Melehy and Adams both name it as a major source of his strength and originality as a writer.

In *Lonesome Traveler*, a collection of travel essays published in 1960 and clearly attempting to capitalize on the fame and notoriety of *On the Road*, which was published three years earlier, Kerouac includes a brief "Author's Introduction" (presumably at his publisher's request). It fleshes out categories like "EDUCATION," "PRINCIPAL OCCUPATIONS AND/OR JOBS," and "INTERESTS," and it reads like the liner notes to an early Dylan album, ending with what could also be a précis for his entire career. In response to "PLEASE GIVE A SHORT DESCRIPTION OF THE BOOK, ITS SCOPE AND PURPOSE AS YOU SEE THEM," Kerouac writes,

Lonesome Traveler is a collection of published and unpublished pieces connected together because they have a common theme: Traveling.

The travels cover the United States from the south to the east coast to the west coast to the far northwest, cover Mexico, Morocco Africa, Paris, London, both the Atlantic and Pacific Oceans at sea in ships, and various interesting people and cities therein included.

Railroad work, sea work, mysticism, mountain work, lasciviousness, solipsism, self-indulgence, bullfights, drugs, churches, art museums, cities of streets, a mishmosh of life as lived by an independent educated penniless rake going anywhere.

Its scope and purpose is simply poetry, or, natural description. (vi)

Kerouac's "SHORT DESCRIPTION" is a thoroughly Beat assemblage. It begins with a single theme, "traveling," but the fully wrought sentences elucidating it quickly succumb to the familiar parataxis and explode into a classic Beat litany, including "Railroad work, sea work, mysticism." With the inclusion of a few more themes, namely history (personal and otherwise), literature, and *language*, one would have, complete, Kerouac's thematic canon, the central and persistent preoccupations of his oeuvre.

His canny, self-conscious introduction to *Lonesome Traveler* is a reminder that Kerouac's prose always entails an act of condensation, a process a distillation, whereas his poetry—and especially in *Mexico City Blues*, the one volume of poems to be published during the author's lifetime—is all expansive: a world-dreaming. Taken as a whole, the "242 choruses" of *Mexico City Blues* spotlight Kerouac's spatial practices and world-making tactics (with *Tristessa* and the relevant sections of *Lonesome Traveler* and *Desolation Angels* serving as a useful prose counterpoints). James Jones counts the Mexico City poems among Kerouac's most significant accomplishments as a writer. Jones's *Map of Mexico City Blues* points to the topographic nature of the poems, although his map is chiefly a figurative one, not concerned with geography per se.[56] His study is important because critics and fans alike have tended to overlook Kerouac's poetry or regard his poetic works as mere ephemera that do not quite stack up against the novels. But Kerouac wrote a great deal of poetry and prepared several manuscripts that were published posthumously. Those detailing his travels domestically and abroad include *Scattered Poems* (1971), *Pomes All Sizes* (1992), and *Book of Sketches* (2006); these and other volumes amount to a substantial body of poetic output. In fact, Kerouac's peers, notably Ginsberg and Michael McClure, have spoken of him as a poet first and foremost. (His famous "Essentials of Spontaneous Prose" is really a *poetics*.) McClure has said that he considers Kerouac's long poem "Sea: Sounds of the Pacific Ocean at Big Sur" one of the most profound and instructive pieces Kerouac ever wrote. Robert Duncan was impressed by Kerouac's "Belief and Technique in Spontaneous Prose," which he found tacked to the wall of Ginsberg's San Francisco apartment. (Duncan's "open field poetics" is a rhizomic compositional approach par excellence.) Kerouac's "manifesto" urges the poet to be "Submissive to everything, open, listening" and "In tranced fixation." Michael Davidson has even argued that Kerouac's poetics "has some affinities" with Jack Spicer's conception of poetry as "dictation." Both Spicer and Kerouac will refer to William Butler Yeats's "trance writing" as an important precedent.[57] The Jack Kerouac School of Disembodied Poetics, founded in 1974 at the Naropa Institute, is further testament to the enduring status of Kerouac's poetry among his peers.

Of the several volumes of Kerouac's poetry now in print, *Mexico City Blues* still possesses the most clarity of purpose and vision. He wrote its choruses in 1955 while living in his "rooftop cell" on calle Orizaba, and the collection was put out by Grove Press four years later, among the welter of novels published in the wake of *On the Road*. The most basic connotation of the Beat subterranean has to do with the sheer invisibility and out-of-sightness of Kerouac and his comrades during the long incubation of the Beat movement. Thinking about Ginsberg's charming dedication to his friends in *Howl*: his nod to Kerouac and the "eleven books written in half the number of years (1951–1956)... published in heaven," alas, I still wonder what could have sustained these efforts if not some deep intuition of the subterranean's obscure potentiality. The Mexico City poems were written from the depths of Kerouac's despair following his largely failed first novel and his inability to get *On the Road* published. At the time, Kerouac was writing mostly for his friends; in particular, he was preparing his elaborate notes for Ginsberg on Buddhism that would later be published as *Some of the Dharma*. Kerouac's Buddhist period (which is also to say his Catholic period), then, forms the immediate context of *Mexico City Blues*. What often gets read as Kerouac's pervasive nihilism or existentialism must be understood in terms of Kerouac's particular devotion to the Diamond Sutra, which holds that "all that has a form is illusive and unreal."

What makes *Mexico City Blues* so exemplary of worlded Beat writing is that the poems are firmly rooted in their place and time yet can expand to include the most wide-ranging influences and energies. Buddha and Christ, morphine and marijuana, "ships and railroads and novels" all exist on what Deleuze would call a single, and singular, plane of immanence.[58] Geography and thematics constantly overlap one another, making the kind of worlded mapping Kerouac undertakes in the poems far more complex as a result. Even the relatively straightforward image of Charlie Parker—the subject of a run of choruses late in the book— requires us to consider more than one location (Harlem) or one theme (narcotic self-negation) for the work to become legible. Parker, reincarnated as a Buddhist saint, is also the figure of the Beat poet: in this case, Kerouac himself. In his "NOTE" to *Mexico City Blues*, the author writes, "I want to be considered a jazz poet blowing a long blues in an afternoon jam session on Sunday. I take 242 choruses; my ideas vary and sometimes roll from chorus to chorus or from halfway through a chorus to halfway into the next."[59] The poems spin a web that takes in a vast geography, as they alternately "Commen[t] on the Great Cities / of the World" (9), describe "Mysterious Red Rivers of the North— / Obi Ubang African Montanas" of "red earth" (8), and imagine "Arabies of hot / meaning" (113). And in the stillness of their nomadic wanderings, the poems, with their multivalent language games, remain deeply informed by the author's ethnolinguistic background.

Mexico City Blues—its vast canvas coterminous with the world itself— is unthinkable in the absence of Kerouac's pocket-sized notebook; the form of the poems is therefore well worth noting. By this time, Kerouac had begun carrying around pocket-sized notebooks to fill with thoughts and observations that would inevitably become the seeds of longer compositions. But with the Mexico City poems, the notebook becomes a sort of liberating constraint in that he must confine each poem to a single small page.[60] The question, then, is *how to fit the world onto the page*. The "3rd Chorus," to take one salient example, suggests its own tactics:

> Describe fires in riverbottom
> sand, and the cooking;
> the cooking of hot dogs
> spitted in whittled sticks
> over flames of woodfire
> with grease dropping in smoke
> to brown and blacken
>   the salty hotdogs,
>   and the wine,
>   and the work on the railroad.
>
> $275,000,000,000.00 in debt
>   says the Government
> Two hundred and seventy five billion
>   dollars in debt
> Like Unending
>   Heaven
> And Unnumbered Sentient Beings
>   Who will be admitted—
>   Not-Numerable—
>   To the new Pair of Shoes
>   Of White Guru Fleece
>   O j o !
>   The Purple Paradise. (3)

The opening line, "Describe fires in riverbottom," is curious, as if Kerouac must gear himself up to write the poem. It sets out a goal for the poem, but, more pointedly, it reminds the poet to be as specific as possible, at least at the outset. The poem moves outward from the specificity of the first stanza, which describes a fairly typical Beat scene—with its transient campfire, its "wine" and "work on the railroad"—to the infinities of the second stanza, as it somewhat jarringly compares the immensity of the national debt to a Buddhist infinity of "Unnumbered Sentient Beings." The Buddhism that might seem out of place here will in fact become a major thread of the Mexico City poems, for it was in Catholic Mexico that Kerouac embarked on his most intensive and sustained study of Buddhist scripture. The "O j o !" of the penultimate line is similarly curious. The Spanish used by Kerouac throughout is hardly correct, colored as it is by English and by Kerouac's native French, but in this poem, "O j o !" is not a substantive so much as an interjection or exclamation (as in "Aha!"), and the strange typography of the word, which corresponds to its meaning in Spanish, makes it look rather like a face with two o's for eyes and a hooked j nose. Moreover, it sets up the final line in the "5th Chorus": "If you know what I / p a l a b r a" (5), and, together with its "Purple Paradise," it will be echoed in the much later "155th Chorus," when it becomes the more narcotic "Rosy / of Purple O Gate / O J O" (155). In all the ways just described, the language of the poems remains quite playful and is one of the best examples of place as transformative of language. Just as Dean was free to apprehend "the world" in Mexico, Kerouac's time in Mexico liberated his prosody to a remarkable degree. The language of the Mexico City poems is *deterritorialized* to a greater extent than in any of Kerouac's novels, and the generative potential of their linguistic *de*formations is matched only by the vastness and complexity of their thematic and geographic imaginings.

The notebook form implies a set of tactics in the sense of Michel de Certeau's "strategies–tactics" distinction. In *The Practice of Everyday Life*, Certeau opposes strategies—hierarchical, top-down, totalizing— and tactics, which involve fleeting alliances, unexpected juxtapositions, and what he calls "making do." Certeau makes a corresponding distinction between "place" *(lieu)* and "space" *(espace)*. Place (as in "everything in its proper place") is static, organized from above and fixed by the powers that be, while space, according to Certeau, "exists when one takes into consideration vectors of direction, velocities, and time variables. Thus space is composed of intersections of mobile elements. It is in a sense actuated by the ensemble of movements deployed within it. Space occurs as the effect produced by the operations that orient it, situate it, temporalize it, and make it function as a polyvalent unity of conflictual programs or contractual proximities."[61] Certeau's formulations contain clear echoes of the immanence of the Deleuzian rhizome and also point the way forward to transnationalism as worlding, where worlding is always *to world, to make a world*: to make "the world-horizon come near and become local and informed, situated, instantiated."[62] Kerouac's poetry in *Mexico City Blues* operates squarely within the realm of tactics and seeks always to "actuate" space, to create a world through its disparate juxtapositions, "vectors," "velocities," and "variables." And considering that, for Certeau, "Every story is a travel story—a spatial practice," he offers yet another way to theorize worlded Beat writing.[63]

Kerouac's language (his own "miracle of making words into English") catalyzes new linguistic, spiritual, and geographic assemblages and creates composite landscapes that bring the worlded world into view. Adams's continent is one such assemblage: Kerouac uses the term "North America" twice in the "Fellaheen Mexico" section of *Lonesome Traveler*—both times to suggest a kind of pre-Columbian unity shattered by colonialism—and twice more in *Tristessa*. The latter perhaps contains his most surprising use of the concept of North America. In a poignant moment near the end of Kerouac's novella, the narrator describes himself and two companions as "three men, from three different nations, in the yellow morning of black shawls" (84). Bull Gaines (Garver) and "el Indio" are from the United States and Mexico, respectively, which means by process of elimination that Kerouac implicitly identifies himself here not as American but as Canadian. Throughout *Tristessa*, he has already aligned himself with Catholic Mexico and its indigenous "fellaheen." Now, he seems to invoke the continent as a potentially transgressive space that exceeds or evades Western or U.S. hegemony, going so far as to disavow his U.S. origins in the name of a more heterogeneous, nomadic, and diasporic becoming-other (Canadian, Quebecois, Mexican, Indian).

The continent—like the hemisphere, the Pacific Rim, and other paradigms of the transnational—is thus a useful unit of analysis, but when it comes to Beat writing, and maybe literary production in general, once one moves beyond national borders, nothing less than the world itself will do. This is certainly the case with Kerouac, and his travels in Mexico need to be viewed alongside his travels elsewhere in the world, even if these latter were considerably less extensive. Kerouac's brief stay in Tangier with Burroughs in the spring of 1957 is generally regarded as a missed opportunity, his only real accomplishment that he began typing a clean copy of the *Naked Lunch* manuscript. (No small feat. He also played a role in naming the book; when Ginsberg misread the words "naked lust" as "naked lunch," Kerouac suggested it should be the title.)[64] Tangier will continue to be a major location in subsequent chapters; Ted Joans and Philip Lamantia, in addition to Burroughs and Brion Gysin, all spent time in Morocco. But Kerouac's apparent disinterest in Tangier, and his acute homesickness, are lamented and taken as signs of a more general lack of interest in the world at large—by which I mean the world of politics and social change, most pressingly in Morocco: decolonization and legacies of colonialism. Kerouac, who visited Tangier just following Moroccan independence, needed quite a bit of reassurance from Burroughs that it was in fact safe to travel there. He may have stayed only six weeks or so, but Kerouac's overall response to Tangier, at least as depicted in his two major statements about Morocco in *Lonesome Traveler* and *Desolation Angels*, is complex and curious and worth a closer look.

One of the first things he notices, even before disembarking from the ocean liner that brought him to Tangier, is a group of Moroccan fishermen plying Tangier Bay: "some with red fezzes but red fezzes like you never thought they'd be real fezzes with wow grease and creases and dust on them, real red fezzes of real life in real Africa."[65] Kerouac clearly relishes poetizing with the repeated word "fezzes," which evokes the buzzing activity of the port, but, above all, in my reading, those fezzes call to the narrator's attention the everyday, lived, material existence of the Moroccans. He takes what could be a hollow, stereotyped image of Morocco, the "exotic" red fez, and instead makes it real and tangible and near at hand. It thus bears a more hopeful metonymic relationship to the Moroccan people and to "real Africa." Granted, this passage does keep Morocco and Moroccans at a certain remove—safely, one might say imperially, viewed from the deck of the oceanliner—but given Kerouac's tendency to indulge in the other extreme of intimacy and identification, I find the distancing to be salutary, and the materiality of Kerouac's first vision of Tangier sets the stage for a more nuanced appreciation of Morocco than most critics have allowed.

In a letter to Malcolm Cowley, Kerouac describes his stay with Burroughs as downright idyllic: "Together we take long walks over the green hills in back of the Casbah and watch the fantastic sunsets over Moroccan fields."[66] Kerouac reads quietly while Burroughs types away at his "endless novel" (as Ginsberg memorably called it in the *Howl* dedication), the sound of clacking keys punctuated with occasional howls of laughter from Burroughs at one of his routines. It is only after an "opium overdose" sends him horrors and "snarling dreary thoughts about all Africa, all Europe, the world" that he begins to pine for "Wheaties by a pine breeze kitchen window in America, that is, I guess a vision of my childhood in America."[67] His sudden desire to leave Tangier fits into a grand narrative within Kerouac's work (in the passage just quoted he specifically links it to a literary, expatriate tradition), which he has been developing since *The Town and the City* and is given major treatment in *Dharma Bums* and *Big Sur* and *The Subterraneans*, and now in *Desolation Angels*, of constantly feeling torn between the quiet life (with his mother, his writing, his past) and the high life. Kerouac's crisis, it turns out, has less to do with disliking Tangier and more to do with an *idée fixe* that trails him like a ghost.

Even so, when Kerouac leaves Tangier it is with some regret. He remarks in *Lonesome Traveler*: "I suddenly felt sorry that I had already bought my boat ticket to Marseille and was leaving Tangier" (150). He recognizes that his time in Morocco was not without revelations—often having to do with his "worldwide fellaheen," yes, but also of a more political kind. (Morocco's politics and the larger story of decolonization in Africa and around the world will come to the fore in later chapters.) Burroughs's attitudes, for example, toward Moroccan independence were equivocal to say the least, although more legible than generally reckoned. Kerouac's writing generally disregards overtly political questions altogether, but Burroughs must have rubbed off on Kerouac in Tangier. In *Desolation Angels* he describes a volatile situation only exacerbated by the persistence of European authorities in the former International Zone:

> We saw a riot in the Zoco Grande that flared up over an argument between Spanish cops and Moroccan soldiers. Bull [Burroughs] was there with us. All of a sudden a seething yelling mass of cops and soldiers and robed oldsters and bluejeaned hoodlums came piling up the alley from wall to wall, we all turned and ran. I myself ran alone down one particular alley accompanied by two Arab boys of ten who laughed with me as we ran. . . . "Riots every day," said Bull proudly. (357)

This experience leads him to make the following observation:

> One look at the officials in the American Consulate where we went for dreary paper routines was enough to make you realize what was wrong with American "diplomacy" throughout the Fellaheen world. . . . Why didnt the American consul ever walk into the urchin hall where Mohammed Mayé sat smoking? or squat in behind empty buildings with old Arabs

who talked with their hands? or *any* thing? Instead it's all private limou-
sines, hotel restaurants, parties in the suburbs, an endless phoney rejection
in the name of "democracy" of all that's pith and moment of every land.
(357–58)

The "dreary paper *routines*" would have indicated Burroughs's presence
in these lines, even if the author hadn't named him. Kerouac perceives the
tension in Tangier as a struggle between hip and square. The diplomats in
their "neckties" would never deign to visit such "beat" spaces as "urchin
halls" or "empty buildings." Though he may couch the situation in these
coded terms, what Kerouac describes here are postcolonial legacies of
deprivation and alienation enforced by a neoimperial power structure
("the American Consulate," "the Spanish cops"). The worlded perspective on display in this last passage offers the barest glimpse of a postcolonial consciousness in Kerouac's oeuvre; it hints, finally, at the fruitfulness
of a subterranean approach to Beat Generation writing that begins to
unearth its hidden connections and concerns.

2

THE BEAT MANIFESTO: AVANT-GARDE POETICS, BLACK POWER, AND THE WORLDED CIRCUITS OF AFRICAN AMERICAN BEAT WRITING

The Beat Manifesto

The subterranean in Kerouac's writing is always connected to a potential line of flight and escape. As both Maria Damon and Aldon Nielsen have pointed out, a key reference point for the recurring images of escape in Bob Kaufman's work has to do with the Underground Railroad. Kaufman's poetry, especially those poems assembled in his best-known collection, *Solitudes Crowded with Loneliness* (1965), is able to link the U.S. counterculture and European avant-garde on one hand with civil rights and the slave narrative tradition on the other. Damon goes on to contend that for all his thematic and linguistic complexity, Kaufman has yet to enter the Beat canon, much less the U.S. or post/modernist canons. As she says, his "beatitude" remains "uncanonized"—a statement only slightly less true today than when it was made twenty years ago.[1] Why should this be the case? Kaufman first made the acquaintance of Kerouac and Burroughs in New York in the 1940s and would become a fixture of San Francisco's North Beach bohemian scene. In the late 1950s Kaufman launched a series of mimeographs under the title *Beatitude* that would serve for decades as a important outlet for West Coast writers. His 1959 *Abomunist Manifesto* is a neo-Dada masterpiece. Kaufman's relative obscurity (often self-willed) can be read productively, in the mode of the subterranean and alongside fellow African American Beat writers Amiri Baraka and Ted Joans, as having something to do with his ability to plug Beat energies into an array of extra-Beat sources, places, and times, launching from the "margins" (another term from Damon's work on Kaufman) of the Beat movement a more forceful critique of the literary and political status quo, and in the process unearth hidden linkages that are present but often obscured in the work of his Beat peers.

One thing this view from the margins has begun to clarify is the Beat movement's relationship to literary and cultural history: in particular, the history of the twentieth-century international avant-garde. Central to the avant-garde's legacy for future generations of radicals—and, really, world culture at large—is the genre of the manifesto. Exploring the ways in which Beat writers have adapted the formal and rhetorical features of the avant-garde manifesto, an initial claim is that the Beats owe as much to international traditions of futurism, Dada, and especially surrealism as they do a strictly American tradition of Whitmanian democracy and the open-road mythos. John Clellon Holmes's essay "This Is the Beat Generation," which served as a public introduction to the notion of "Beat" when it appeared in the *New York Times Magazine* on November 16, 1952, is but the first of many published attempts at self-definition and self-assertion on the part of Beat writers. While the Beats never produced a "Beat Manifesto" as such, a whole range of Beat texts contain what we might call a *manifesto function*, as key figures like Holmes, Kerouac, and Ginsberg, in addition to many "minor" Beats, felt themselves compelled to define and redefine their aesthetic and social practices and to state and restate their opposition to American conservatism after World War II. To reevaluate Beat writing in terms of its engagement with the international avant-garde is to reassess the role played by African American writers in the Beat movement as a whole. The work of Baraka, Joans, and Kaufman evinces a remarkably intense and long-standing commitment to avant-garde poetics and politics, which is central to their worlded conception of oppositional art and performative communities.

The manifesto tactics informing such disparate texts as Baraka's poem "BLACK DADA NIHILISMUS," his celebrated play *Dutchman*, and his manifesto for "The Revolutionary Theatre," in addition to Joans's *Black Manifesto* and Kaufman's *Abomunist Manifesto*, are also operative in those which, like Holmes's *Times* article, seek to define the Beat movement as such. The performativity at work in Joans's and Kaufman's manifesto-texts is a persistent feature of Kerouac's many attempts at explaining just what "Beat" means. In one of the best-known instances, his 1959 *Playboy* essay "The Origins of the Beat Generation," Kerouac's genealogy takes on cartoonish proportions as it expands to include everyone from Count Dracula to the Three Stooges.[2] Holmes's account is similarly expansive yet contains what now seems like a shocking exclusion: not a single artist, poet, or performer can be found among the myriad hipsters and hooligans who populate his *Times* article. As Ann Charters has noted, "Nowhere in this early article did Holmes refer to Beat Generation writers, because he did not think of himself or his friends Ginsberg and Kerouac in this way, although he shared with them the new sensibility he had described."[3] Such equivocation and ambivalence betray an insistent openness and a refusal of dogma that, far from sapping the strength from these texts, are a source of their lasting interest and importance to Beat studies. The conspicuous self-effacement on the part of Holmes and Kerouac reminds us that even the earliest, most canonical articulations of Beatness are anything but prescriptive or hegemonic and that the "Beat Manifesto" has been written by a diverse body of constituents, each of whom has transformed the movement in his or her own way. Even Ginsberg's "Howl," which for many does succeed in capturing the essence of the Beat Generation, registers a productive tension between the controlling vision of the poet and the absolute freedom he celebrates in his protagonists.

Holmes's *Times* article finds a precedent in Filippo Tommaso Marinetti's 1909 "Founding and Manifesto of Futurism," which marked a direct engagement with and appropriation of the forces of bourgeois journalism and the mass press when it appeared on the front page of *Le Figaro* and in papers and journals across Europe. As the manifesto became a dominant mode of self-representation among the various avant-gardes, the form became increasingly self-reflexive. Manifesto writers began to recognize the irony of announcing the radical singularity of their aesthetic project with a manifesto form that, only a few years after Marinetti's "Futurist Manifesto," was already somewhat banal. Tristan Tzara's 1918 "Dada Manifesto" begins, "To proclaim a manifesto you have to want: A.B.C., thunder against 1, 2, 3, lose your patience and sharpen your wings to conquer and spread a's, b's, c's little and big, sign, scream, swear, arrange the prose in a form of absolute and irrefutable evidence," drawing attention to what he saw as the tired predictability and general inconsequentiality of the form.[4] Parodying the rabid contrarianism typical of the manifesto, Tzara soon took to writing them on behalf of fictional characters with names like Mr. Antipyrine and Mr. AA the Antiphilosopher. But while the Dada manifestoes practically revel in their futility, the form continues to exert its strange power. André Breton's first and second *Surrealist Manifestoes* could well represent the zenith of the genre, and the richly multivalent responses to Breton's *révolution surréaliste* on the part of Baraka, Joans, and Kaufman are significant in their own right.

Ever since Marjorie Perloff's landmark *Futurist Moment*, the manifesto form has been central to our understanding of the historical avant-garde and its hallmark claims on the radically new. Two recent studies warrant particular attention. Janet Lyon has argued for a genre with rather porous boundaries, and her expanded conception is especially relevant when considering the manifesto function of Beat texts. Lyon also draws our attention to the tortuous temporality of a genre that attempts simultaneously to offer a new version of history, to create the demand for action, *now*, in the present, and to project a vision of a future in which its project will have become reality.[5] Martin Puchner has emphasized the manifesto's performative qualities, both in terms of its seeking to *create* a new movement or worldview in the very act of naming it and giving voice to its demands—there were no futurists, in other words, before Marinetti announced their birth on the front page of *Le Figaro*—and in terms of the genre's notable theatricality.[6] (The former is the performativity of J. L. Austin's *How to Do Things with Words*, where "constative utterances," statements of fact, are contrasted with "performative utterances," statements that effect some action or change in the world. The classic example of Austin's performativity is the wedding vow that, in its very utterance, *makes the marriage happen*.) But in their desire to break with tradition, to produce an event in the strongest sense of the term, manifesto writers are often confounded by a form that, as Tzara indicates, has become utterly conditioned and conventional. The performative force that both actuates and delimits the manifesto form gives rise to the characteristic impulse among avant-garde groups to continually rewrite their foundational texts, returning to the scene of the crime to recapture original energies and clarify original positions.

In *performing* a group's oppositional poetic or political practices, the manifesto is a highly transgressive genre, and the mixing and denaturing of genres has been a primary concern for manifesto writers.[7] Puchner, largely following Perloff in her discussion of Marinetti's *arte di far manifesti* (art of making manifestoes), accordingly develops a concept of "manifesto art" to read a whole series of important works of avant-garde poetry, painting, and sculpture in terms of their dual nature as manifesto and artwork. Puchner also argues most forcefully that with the *Communist Manifesto*, Marx and Engels created a model, less for the content (whether political, artistic, etc.) than for the form (the manifesto form itself), that generations of subsequent protest would take up and transform.[8] Tracing such a lineage reminds us of what is at stake when avant-garde writers and artists, the Beats included, strive to change the world with their art. For all the hits it has taken over the years, the most cogent formulation of an avant-garde politics remains that of Peter Bürger, in whose dialectical analysis the defining move of the avant-garde is "to reintegrate art into the praxis of life," to bridge the gap between art and politics, between art and the world.[9]

Perloff's discussion of collage as a signal contribution of avant-garde art highlights a certain affinity between the manifesto form and the Deleuzian assemblage with its heterogeneous, rhizomic form. She quotes Blaise Cendrars, who writes in *La prose du Transsibérien* (1913), a mixed-media text that Perloff describes as the "hub of the Futurist wheel": "I have deciphered all the confused texts of the wheels and I have assembled [*j'ai rassemblé*] the scattered elements of a most violent beauty / That I control / And which compels me."[10] Methods involving collage or pastiche are hallmarks of modernist and avant-garde art that have clearly been influenced and inflected by the Benjaminian shocks and juxtapositions of modern print media. While an obvious example of this would be the *découpage* of Picasso's synthetic cubism with its newspaper cutouts (another glimpse of *Le Figaro*) forming part of the composition, the manifesto form is also affected by similar forces of juxtaposition and the mixed-media and mixed-genre qualities of the newspaper (headlines, photography, *faits divers*, fiction, advertisements, etc.). Breton's first *Manifesto of Surrealism* is formed out of several distinct modes with completing voices, demands, and typographies. After the polemical rhetoric in first section, denouncing realism and its attendant logic and epistemology, introducing Guillaume Apollinaire's term *sur-réalisme* as a countermeasure, and praising Freud's systematized exploration of the unconscious, Breton includes a list of quotations from his surrealist colleagues before moving on to quote a seemingly random list of facsimiles of newspaper headlines. As with many manifestoes that perform a group's own practices and poetics, by incorporating these disparate elements Breton's manifesto seems to introduce the elements of chance and randomness that in many ways are at the core of the surrealist movement he is in the process of introducing.

Perloff is especially interested in the hybrid nature of Marinetti's manifestoes, and of futurist "manifesto art" more generally—its relation to the "everyday" and the heteroglossia of the public sphere. She writes, "The Futurist manifesto is also theatrical in a deeper sense, occupying as it does a 'space that lies between the arts' and conflating verbal strategies that do not conventionally cohere: the ethical and pathetic arguments of classical rhetoric, the rhythm, metaphor, and hyperbole of Romantic lyric poetry, the journalistic narrative of everyday discourse, and the dialogic mode of drama which acts to draw the reader (or viewer) into its verbal orbit."[11] Marinetti's "Founding and Manifesto of Futurism," appearing in newspapers across Europe, was a weapon in the arsenal of avant-garde tactics appropriating modern forms of popular culture and mass communication. His manifesto functions as a birth notice (the advent of the futurist movement), an obituary (for what Bürger will call "art as an institution"), and, most important, an advertisement.[12] A persistent theme of the avant-garde manifesto, testified to by Marinetti and Breton, as well as by Guy Debord and Gil Wolman in their situationist "User's Guide to Détournement" (1956) is that the (print) advertisement holds a great deal of potential for transforming artistic practices. Its potential lies in the fact that it is a more or less *empty* form, that it is a necessarily *public* form, that it can accommodate the most unexpected juxtapositions, and, for Debord in particular, that it is a *revolutionary* form in that it leads to the creation of desires that cannot be fulfilled within the reigning capitalist order.

Whereas Marinetti clearly saw the advantage of posting such a public announcement of the futurists program, later avant-gardists were more wary of mass media forms. Tzara's "Dada Manifesto," perhaps in response to Marinetti, takes several swipes at journalists, beginning with the idea that only journalists feel the need to figure out what the word "Dada" means, while the Dadaists themselves could care less: "*The magic of a word—DADA—which for journalists has opened the door to an unforeseen world, has for us not the slightest importance*," writes Tzara, whose 1918 manifesto proclaims: "DADA MEANS NOTHING" (149). Tzara compares "comprehensible" art to mere journalism, which suggests that the artist who must pander to an audience by creating easily digestible and commodifiable works of art is no better than the newspaper writer who must appeal to something like the lowest common denominator and acceptable public tastes. In its wariness of the mass press, Tzara's "Dada Manifesto" seems to prefigure Jean Baudrillard's argument in "Requiem of the Media," where, slyly adapting McLuhan's dictum that "the medium is the message," Baudrillard asserts that the very form of the mass media, whether print media or more specifically in Baudrillard's discussion, television, will always preclude its revolutionary use.[13] Citing the example of the protests that lead to the May 1968 insurrection, he argues that once televised, they ceased to be an *event*. That is to say, popular media depends on reproducibility and is therefore fundamentally incompatible with the eventness or singularity of a revolutionary event. Moreover, "broadcast" media, in print or on the air, are capable only of unidirectional communication, which is again incompatible with a truly social project. At the same time, avant-garde groups like the Dadaists have sought to co-opt notions of the popular to create performative communities based on shared beliefs and a common enemy. Werner Sollors has referred to Baraka's "populist modernism," for instance, as the bedrock of his 1960s black arts aesthetic.[14]

The manifesto is that which makes manifest. It calls forth the specter, calls on the specter to manifest itself. (Marx and Engels famously begin, "There is a specter haunting Europe.") Derrida writes, "The [*Communist Manifesto*] calls, it calls for this presentation of a living reality: we must see to it that in the future this specter . . . becomes a *reality*, and a *living* reality. This real life must show itself and manifest itself."[15] For Derrida the manifesto does not call the specter to appear now, at once. It calls, from the present moment of the manifesto, for the specter (which does not belong to any temporality or ontology) to manifest itself *in the future*, in a *future-to-come* that will not be conditioned by any manifesto. This is why the event called for in the manifesto form will always exceed the logic of the performative. The future-to-come simply cannot, or cannot simply, be made to come.

What, then, accounts for the power the manifesto still does seem to exert? Elsewhere in Derrida's work, the performative will always preclude the event (in the strong sense of the term), yet in *Specters* he opens a space for its possibility: the *Communist Manifesto* "does not consist in merely foreseeing (a gesture of the constative type) but in calling for the advent, in the future, of a manifesto of the communist party which, precisely in the performative form of the call, will transform the legend of the specter not yet into the reality of communist society but into that other form of real event (between the legendary specter and its absolute incarnation) that is the Manifesto of the Communist Party" (103). How can it be that the *Communist Manifesto* calls, not for the "advent" of the Communist Party, but for the advent, "in the future," of *a* communist manifesto? Why would the "legendary specter" be transformed, not (yet) "into the reality of communist society," but into the "real event" of a manifesto? I believe Derrida's statement—itself as circuitous as the temporal logic of the manifesto form he attempts here to navigate—*performs* the necessary and productive displacements at work in the manifesto form. If the manifesto were to have called forth the specter at once, if it had conjured the ghost only to then exorcise it, its performative call would at once exhaust the force of the unconditioned future-to-come. What Derrida instead sees operating in the manifesto is a deferral of the event—the event of a communist manifesto, the manifestation of a communist society—that in turn serves to create the conditions under which such an event might be possible. The real event of this manifesto-to-come and this revolution-to-come (always *to-come*) will, in fact, be a spectral event, unlocatable, oscillating between "the legendary specter" (*There is a specter haunting Europe* . . .) and its impossible "absolute incarnation."

The highly equivocal attempts at self-definition on the part of Holmes and Kerouac, as well as the manifestoes written by Baraka, Joans, and Kaufman, enact similar processes of deferral and displacement as those described by Derrida in his work on the *Communist Manifesto*. At the same time, the temporalities of Ginsberg's "Howl," along with its unresolved tensions between individuality and collectivity, resonate powerfully with previous discussions of the manifesto by Lyon, Puchner, and Perloff. Lyon in particular urges that we ask, whom does the manifesto address itself to, and on whose behalf? The poetics and politics of representation in the manifesto, especially in terms of representation and gender and the discourse of gender equality as it plays out in revolutionary struggle, are major questions in Lyon's book. She also writes about "negotiating universalism" in the manifesto (just as worlded thought must negotiate the global as a different kind of totality), saying that "all manifestoes pose both a challenge to and an affirmation of universalism."[16] Even as it circumscribes group identity and allegiance, the best manifesto art remains radically open and inclusive. Timothy Yu's reading of "Howl" as an inspiration and model for self-determination among a burgeoning Asian American avant-garde also speaks to the growing interest in Beat Generation writing from China to North Africa: not as something to be imported wholesale as consumable "counterculture" but as something to be *used*—to be manipulated and deterritorialized in ways that are meaningful within local contexts and histories the world over.[17]

This process of transgressive appropriation requires a worlded critical procedure equally attuned to geographic and historical specificity and to material practices that run counter to the sublime sameness of the global. To world the Beats is to emphasize not only their transatlantic linkages but also their interaction with third world and post/colonial spaces. With regard to African American Beat surrealism, a worlded perspective would, for example, consider the profound influence of Aimé Césaire, whose distinctive images of fecundity and decay are deeply rooted in Martinican soil and history and form a kind of figurative or descriptive dialect quite far removed from the language of Breton and other European surrealists. Like Césaire in his Caribbean context, Baraka, Joans, and Kaufman each argue powerfully for the African origins of surrealism as they seek to reactivate the movement's anticolonial, antiracist energies. These currents of inspiration and influence are always multidirectional. In *A Transnational Poetics*, Jahan Ramazani places Baraka within a network of criss-crossing transatlantic energies traveling from Whitman to Lawrence to Olson to Baraka to the "'black British' poets," who "complete a parallel transatlantic loop by drawing on the example of the militant, vernacular poetics of the Black Arts movement, which in turn owed debts to the Beats and Black Mountain poets . . . and to Harlem Renaissance poets such as Hughes." Ramazani, arguing for a "translocal" approach and a "particularized" understanding of literary internationalism, articulates yet another way to remap the sources and legacies of African American Beat writing.[18]

African American Surrealism and the Worlding of Beat Literature

Aldon Nielsen, who places Baraka at the center of his encyclopedic study of African American experimental writing, *Black Chant* (whose title is taken from a line in Baraka's "BLACK DADA NIHILISMUS"), will write in a later essay on Bob Kaufman:

> Kaufman's adaptations of surrealism were more historically engaged and more politically directed than were those of many among his white contemporaries. Despite the leftist and anarchist leanings of some older poets, such as Kenneth Rexroth, and younger Beats, such as Ginsberg, Ferlinghetti and McClure, few of them were ready to confront America's racial politics as forcefully as did Kaufman and Baraka. . . . More importantly, though, Kaufman's poetry joins a radical tradition of surrealism and racial politics that reaches back through García Lorca's *Poet in New York* and Aimé Césaire's *Return to My Native Land* to the radical politics of the French Surrealist Group.[19]

"More historically engaged and more politically directed"—which is also to say more worlded. Unlike Baraka, however, Kaufman figures little in *Black Chant*. The essay cited here, which discusses Kaufman's "occlusions" from histories of Beat and modernist writing, can be seen as his attempt to rectify earlier omissions in his own work. Nielsen uses very curious and evocative language to describe the fact that only a "few American critics," Maria Damon most notably, "have broken the silence surrounding what must be seen in retrospect as a veritable transubstantiation, whereby Kaufman raised the body of black arts from within the entombment of modernity, retaking at the same time the terrain of the American cultural future anterior" (136). The materiality of his description is striking. Nielsen's references to (Christ's) resurrection position

Kaufman as a martyr figure and call to mind the devastating poem "Benediction," where he writes, "America, I forgive you . . . I forgive you / Nailing black Jesus to an imported cross / Every six weeks in Dawson, Georgia."[20] They also point to Kaufman's frequent "incorporation" of modernist martyrs like Federico García Lorca into his poetry (136).

Nielsen's essay is primarily interested in Kaufman's poetry as a connective and transformative substance. Kaufman's significance lies in his ability to translate, and thereby transform, modernism through the strange logics of his pantheon. "By conjoining [Crispus] Attucks and Lorca," he writes, "Kaufman effects a yet more radical translation of Lorca and of modernism, conjuring a transmigration of African-inflected verbal innovation that transfigures modernism, placing Kaufman himself in the position of both father and son to the modern, temporally as well as racially miscegenated" (136). The temporality described here is the "future anterior" that Nielsen refers to throughout his essay, which is also the *will have been* of the Derridean future-to-come. In a more Deleuzian register, Kaufman's poetry consistently makes uses of a heterogeneous assemblage of influence—Nielsen invokes the future anterior to complicate strictly linear conceptions of literary and cultural history, which is a rhizomic gesture to be sure. With Lorca still in mind, Nielsen writes, "Kaufman rewrites and mis-remembers, dismembers, his modernist model, reauthorizing his own poetics" (139), using Lorca's words to argue even more forcefully than Lorca for the African origins of European modernism. In a move common in Kaufman's poetry, and in Baraka's and Joans's work as well, "Kaufman lays hands upon the body of Lorca's texts and makes them black American signifying structures" (139). Nielsen's insistence on the physicality of this process: "lays hands," "intimate contact," "transubstantiation," is yet another way of framing the materiality of worlded Beat writing.[21]

Critical work on Kaufman, Baraka, and Jones has tended to emphasize the disjunctions between African American Beat writing and the Beat movement as a whole. Robert Lee, for example, echoes earlier readings of Baraka's work by Nielsen, Werner Sollors, and Kimberly Benston when he tries to define a clean break between LeRoi Jones the Beat poet and Amiri Baraka the black nationalist, and a clear choice between aesthetics and politics, bohemia and the barricades. Lee writes that for the Baraka of the 1950s Beat period, "'Black' . . . signified more a call to consciousness and culture" than the basis for world revolution. He continues, "Equally, for Joans and Kaufman . . . theirs were literary black-resistance voices rather than allied to a specific politics."[22] Instead of this either/or logic, a more nuanced subterranean reading would emphasize simultaneity and overlap and mark the continued presence of early Beat and avant-garde influences throughout their later, more radical careers. Here again their marginality serves to make visible a hidden multiplicity at the center of the Beat movement. Those who study African American Beat writers (and other marginal figures associated with the Beats) are often in a better position to open up the study of the Beat Generation, not least because of the simple fact that Baraka, Joans, and Kaufman have all produced recognizably "Beat" writing that expressly acknowledges a different set of influences than those touted by Kerouac, Ginsberg, Gregory Corso, or Ferlinghetti (or give those same influences a very different inflection). Lee is exemplary in this regard when he writes,

> all three typically took up the Beat interests in Zen and Eastern-transcendental spirituality but frequently linked it to the blues—with Africa as a prime source of reference and imagery. Similarly, if their poetry could be sexually celebratory and playful, à la Ginsberg, it could also broach the racial taboos of sex, a Beat articulation (long continued in Joans and Kaufman) of the "black" senses. Given, overall, then, a heritage "up from slavery" and formed as much by jazz or spiritual or rap as by Blake and Whitman, Williams and Pound, who better to have adapted Beat to a black dispensation, . . . to have made it signify?" (162).

The almost Deleuzian turn of phrase, "a Beat articulation of the 'black' senses," immediately suggests its converse: what would a *black* articulation of *Beat* senses look like? Ultimately, "Beat senses" (and their articulation across the wider culture) are no more fixed than Lee's "black senses," and in assuming a Beat stance or inhabiting a Beat position from which to decry society's shortcomings, African American writers such as Baraka, Joans, and Kaufman also helped shape and transform the Beat movement itself.

Baraka, not surprisingly, dominates Lee's 1996 essay on the "Black Beats," but Lee's discussion of Joans's life and work is revelatory in its own way. Referring to two of Joans's best-known collections, *Afrodisia* and *Black Pow Wow*, Lee writes that Joans's best-known poetry exhibits a "largely freeform, 'spoken' poetry in which blues, jazz, sex, Black Power, Africa and surrealist motif . . . plait one into another" (167–68). The manner as well as the content of his description is worth noting. It is a typical list-form, paratactic, rhizomic description of Beat influences. These kinds of descriptions pop up everywhere in the literature on the Beats, and Kerouac himself frequently deploys them when trying to explain the meaning of "Beat." They do not signify a discursive laziness on the part of Beat scholars; rather, they are properly rhizomic descriptions of essentially rhizomic phenomena. Joans almost says as much in a 1975 interview with Henry Louis Gates Jr., where he explains somewhat cryptically, "I am connected to every living person on earth. I'm connected to the *correct* people, not the *right* people, but the correct people. There's a big difference."[23] And where Kaufman is concerned, Lee traces a poetic genealogy as rich as that of Joans or Baraka or, for that matter, Ginsberg or Kerouac. He writes that "Kaufman strikes his own Beat affinity in 'Afterwards, They Shall Dance,' a poem in which he claims a lineage with Dylan Thomas . . . Billie Holiday . . . Poe . . . and . . . Baudelaire. Only a dues-paying black Beat, one suspects, would end [the poem] in terms which resemble both Ginsberg's 'Sunflower Sutra' and a dreamy, flighted blues" (171). One might ask what exactly Lee means by a "dues-paying black Beat," but at the very least he seems to suggest that Kaufman's background and experiences allow for a more capacious vision of Beatness than that of the more canonical Beat writers.

Looking back over Baraka's long and varied career, it does become tempting to mark a clean break between his early Beat period and the developments that follow. This view is well represented by Werner Sollors, who equates Baraka's Beat-inflected writing with an ineffectual, narcissistic bohemianism in contrast to the serious, engaged commitment of his more explicitly political art.[24] I want to suggest, however, that Baraka's mid-1960s turn to black arts signals not a repudiation of the Beat and avant-garde aesthetics that characterize his early work but rather their evolution in accordance with the scope and ambition of his black nationalist and Marxist writing. Nielsen cites one interview in which Baraka explains, "I was always interested in Surrealism and Expressionism, and I think the reason was to really try to get below the surface of things . . . The Civil Rights Movement, it's the same thing essentially, trying to get below the surface of things, trying to get below the norm, the everyday, the status quo, which was finally unacceptable, just unacceptable."[25] Nielsen concludes that for Baraka surrealism has always involved "a political as well as an aesthetic logic," and the fact that Baraka produces his most self-conscious avant-garde poetry during the headiest years of the civil rights movement should not go unremarked.[26] Far from indicating a turn *away* from the world or a dismissal of political engagement, Baraka's avant-gardism reenacts the quintessential move to close the gap between aesthetics and politics, art and the world. And while the remarks cited by Nielsen deal specifically with a conflation of surrealism and civil rights, they also point the way to a sustained critique within African American Beat writing of institutional racism and imperialist domination across the globe.

Todd Tietchen's locates Baraka's initial break with both white bohemia and the mainstream civil rights movement a few years earlier in another transnational crossing: Baraka's 1960 trip to revolutionary Cuba with the Fair Play for Cuba Committee, a group of African American intellectuals that included the controversial NAACP chapter head Robert Williams. Baraka's experiences are documented in his important early essay "Cuba Libre," first published in 1960 in *Evergreen Review*. In his *Autobiography* Baraka refers to the trip as a "turning point in my life," and Tietchen argues that changes Baraka made for the revised version of his "Cuba Libre" essay (published in 1966 in *Home: Social Essays*) reflect the author's growing radicalism in their new emphasis on fellow traveler and "proto-Black Power activist" Williams. The 1966 "Cuba Libre" now sets Williams and Castro together as "transnationally aligned" revolutionaries taking part in a long tradition of armed insurrection.[27]

Baraka's radicalism, and especially his future turn to third world Marxism, clearly has roots in the time he spent in Cuba; "Cuba Libre" reveals his growing dissatisfaction with white bohemia and its hollow, essentially bourgeois revolt and with the mainstream civil rights movement. His visit to Cuba grants him a new perspective on the parochialism of racial politics in the United States. He recounts one amusing episode at the Ministry of Education, where the group of Americans has just been regaled with statistics on the vast improvement in Cuba's schools under Castro. The wife of one delegate asks the minister "if in the new schoolbooks that were being manufactured, little Negro children were portrayed as well as white . . . to show the little Negro children that they are not inferior."[28] The minister appears confused, and Baraka cannot help but laugh at the woman's well-intentioned naivety. As Baraka tells it, when the minister finally catches her meaning and hands her a newly printed book showing "five children at a blackboard, two of them black . . . the woman almost swooned" (41).

The group's visit to Cuba culminates in an overnight voyage to the Sierra Maestra by train to join the massive celebration in honor of the attacks that marked the beginning of the revolution. Thousands upon thousands of Cubans, as well as young people from all over Latin America, were making the trek, and on the train Baraka was fiercely berated by a Mexican graduate student for being a *yanqui* and—when he heedlessly admits to being a poet and therefore "not even interested in politics"—

for being a "cowardly bourgeois individualist" (57). This and similar exchanges affected him deeply, as did his brief audience with Castro. Baraka asked him, "What about communism?" and Castro replied, "I've said a hundred times that I'm not a communist. But I'm certainly not an anti-communist. . . . I said also a hundred times that I consider myself a humanist. A radical humanist" (68). Upon his return to the States, Baraka felt compelled to write of his Greenwich Village compatriots: "The rebels among us have become merely people like myself who grow beards and will not participate in politics. Drugs, juvenile delinquency, complete isolation from the vapid mores of the country, a few current ways out. But name an alternative here. Something not inextricably bound up in a lie. Something not part of liberal stupidity or the actual filth of vested interest. There is none. It's much too late" (78). By the time he returned to New York, it was clear that he had begun to rethink completely his role as a committed writer and the proper relationship between art and social change.

Baraka continued to look to the European avant-garde for guidance and precedent, however. In a series of texts from the early to mid-1960s, including "BLACK DADA NIHILISMUS" and the play *Dutchman* (both date to 1964)—William Harris calls them "transitional" in that they bridge the gap between Baraka's Beat years and his subsequent commitment to black nationalism—his continued engagement with surrealism in particular most often hinged on Breton's infamous provocation from the *Second Manifesto of Surrealism*: "The simplest Surrealist act consists of dashing down into the street, pistol in hand, and firing blindly, as fast as you can pull the trigger, into the crowd."[29] Baraka will translate Breton's dictum into specifically racialized terms, and the specter of indiscriminate murder becomes a powerful trope in Baraka's work for years to come. In an oft-cited passage from "BLACK DADA," he writes,

> Come up black dada
>
> nihilismus. Rape the white girls. Rape
> their fathers. Cut the mothers' throats.
> Black dada nihilismus, choke my friends
> . . . .
> (may a lost god damballah, rest or save us
> against the murders we intend
> against his lost white children.[30]

With "BLACK DADA" Baraka began addressing himself to, and speaking on behalf of, a "we," and the poem's deeply unsettling images of physical and sexual violence should be understood primarily in terms of their appeal to a collectivity. The scenes of racial bloodshed that appear with increasing frequency in Baraka's work of the 1960s and 1970s are never simply a matter of style or the overheated rhetoric of *épater la bourgeoisie*; they are nothing less than a call to arms and revolution. Also significant is Baraka's invocation of Damballah at the close of the poem, which registers the subversive syncretism of worlded African slave traditions that have provided a model for his own transformations of Breton's surrealist revolt.

In his celebrated play *Dutchman*, Baraka dramatizes Breton's scene of originary surrealist violence in the highly charged interactions between Clay, protagonist and self-proclaimed "Black Baudelaire," and the white Lula. While it is Clay who, finally driven into a rage by Lula's constant goading, threatens bloody murder, in a crucial reversal of events, it is Lula who takes the decisive action in which the play culminates. In his work on Baraka, Sollors does recognize Clay to be more a "Black Breton" than a "Black Baudelaire," but in Sollors's reading, Clay's death is meant to mirror Baraka's own rejection of white bohemia and its avant-garde aesthetics.[31] But if we instead read Clay as a fundamentally tragic figure, defeated by his own weakness and lack of commitment, his death then signals not Baraka's rejection of surrealism but rather his redoubled effort, absolutely following Breton in the *Second Manifesto of Surrealism*, "to make for [him]self a tenet of total revolt, complete insubordination, of sabotage according to rule" (125). Clay's death becomes a key reference point in Baraka's 1965 manifesto for "The Revolutionary Theatre."

Baraka's polemics in the "Revolutionary Theatre" manifesto follow much the same lines as those in *Dutchman* and "BLACK DADA," but what makes Baraka's manifesto especially important to the present discussion are its strongly internationalist designs and its worlded view of human oppression. When he writes, for example, "The Revolutionary Theatre is shaped by the world, and moves to reshape the world," I take him at his word as calling for a politically engaged art that indeed has the "world" as its proper object.[32] In this as well, Baraka recognizes surrealist precedents. When Ginsberg was living in Paris in the early 1960s, he discovered the censored radio recording of Antonin Artaud, the former surrealist and architect of the Theatre of Cruelty, performing his late work "To Have Done with the Judgment of God." Ginsberg obtained several copies of the recording and sent them to Baraka and Michael McClure, among others. In 1961 Jones had just started publishing the *Floating Bear* newsletter along with Diane di Prima, and they would go on to co-found the New York Poets Theatre later that year. Both *Floating Bear* and the Poets Theatre became important venues for publishing and presenting works by the Beats, the New York School, and the Black Mountain poets. Artaud's Theatre of Cruelty aesthetic would become a touchstone for the Poets Theatre, and Michael McClure even incorporated the illicit recording of Artaud's in one of his productions there. The radio performance, recorded when Artaud was in the full bloom of madness, addiction, and poverty, seems to fit rather neatly into the Beat allure of beatitude and "crazy wisdom," but there exists another, politically inflected Artaud who emerges in his writings on Mexico, offering an avant-garde critique of colonialism that Beat writers found appealing and productive in their own era of decolonization and Cold War geopolitics.

In his second manifesto for the Theatre of Cruelty, Artaud turns the tables on the imperialist West, so to speak, by describing the violent spectacle of Conquest as a *model* for the performative violence that he believed was necessary to shock the West out of its moral and spiritual complacency. For this reason, the "first spectacle" of the Theatre of Cruelty was to be called *The Conquest of Mexico*:

> The subject was chosen:
>
> 1. Because it involves the present, and because of all the references it allows to problems of vital interest both to Europe and the world.
>
> From a historical point of view, *The Conquest of Mexico* raises the question of colonisation. It revives Europe's deep-rooted self-conceit in a burning, inexorably bloody manner, allowing us to debunk its own concept of its supremacy. . . .
>
> 2. By raising the dreadfully contemporary problem of colonisation, that is, the right one continent considers it has to enslave another, it poses the question of the real supremacy some races may have over others. . . . It contrasts the tyrannical anarchy of the colonisers with the deep intellectual concord of those about to by colonised.[33]

The majority of Artaud's manifesto is, in fact, taken up by a sketch of the play in question. And to the extent that Baraka's own manifesto articulates an aesthetic for his new Revolutionary Theatre, it begins to look a lot like Artaud's program for the Theatre of Cruelty: full of wild, convulsive gestures, dissonant sounds, and violent conflict, all meant to stir the audience into action. Baraka writes, "The Revolutionary Theatre . . . should stagger through our universe correcting, insulting, preaching, spitting craziness— but a craziness taught to us in our most rational moments. People must be taught to trust true scientists (knowers, diggers, oddballs) and that the holiness of life is the constant possibility of widening the consciousness. And they must be incited to strike back against *any* agency that attempts to prevent this widening." Referring to the Theatre of Cruelty's ur-spectacle, Baraka writes, "Even as Artaud designed *The Conquest of Mexico*, so we must design *The Conquest of White Eye*, and show the missionaries and wiggly Liberals dying under blasts of concrete. For sound effects, wild screams of joy, from all the peoples of the world" (236–37).

The world, indeed. Baraka's manifesto enlists Artaud, and Artaud's Mexico, as part of a much broader, worlded conception of social upheaval and artistic practice, and Montezuma appears, as he does in "BLACK DADA NIHILISMUS," alongside a host of anticolonial and black power icons. Following Artaud's lead, Baraka proposes a first production for his Revolutionary Theatre: "The play that will split the heavens for us will be called THE DESTRUCTION OF AMERICA. The heroes will be Crazy Horse, Denmark Vesey, Patrice Lumumba, and not history, not memory, not sad sentimental groping for a warmth in our despair; these will be new men, new heroes, and their enemies most of you who are reading this" (241). Taken here to polemical heights, the transnational imaginary evident in Baraka's manifesto has, in fact, shaped Beat writing of all stripes. Baraka's worlded assemblage of avant-garde poetics, Pan-Africanist politics, and the hipster slang of "knowers, diggers, and oddballs" makes it possible to speak of an overlapping set of rhetorical tactics employed by Beat writers in their outernational contexts. His manifesto was originally going to be published in the *New York Times*, but after reading it, they decided to pass. Sollors and others have argued that Baraka abandoned his "avant-gardism" (as Sollors dismissively calls it) as well as his Beat comrades when he left Greenwich Village to found the Black Arts Repertory Theatre and School in Harlem. But it turns out that this founding document of the black arts movement, which laid the thematic and aesthetic groundwork for a new phase of black cultural nationalism, was profoundly inspired by Artaud's anticolonial critique. The next two chapters on Philip Lamantia and William Burroughs will further elaborate Artaud's legacy among Beat writers.

It would seem that by highlighting a set of texts that revel in threats of racial violence aimed, at least in part, at the author's Beat peers, and are nearly contemporaneous with Baraka's mid-1960s abjuration of Greenwich Village bohemia, I would be seeking to emphasize the *discon*tinuities between African American Beat writers and the Beat movement as a whole. The same might be said of Ted Joans's "Proposition for a Black Power Manifesto," which offers a glimpse of the poet at his most uncharacteristically polemical and makes it clear that "whiteboy, this *Ain't* your bit!!"[34] On the contrary, I believe that these texts, along with Kaufman's *Abomunist Manifesto*, do far more to reveal their profound affinities with the Beat movement at large in a shared commitment to worlded traditions of radical and avant-garde poetics and politics. While Breton's pronouncement that Joans was the "only African American surrealist" remains dubious—he clearly hadn't met Bob Kaufman—Joans's life and work are clearly marked by an avant-garde ethos indeed inspired by Breton.[35]

While Joans's debt to surrealism has been widely noted, what I want to stress is the case he makes for the transnational dimensions of even the most canonical French surrealism. In his 1975 interview with Henry Louis Gates, Joans is insistent on the point of surrealism's international character, describing the French surrealists as "internationalist" and Breton as a "man of all nationalities." In the same interview Joans is himself described by Gates as "Afro-America's Tri-Continental Poet" (4–5): a third worlding of the poet aligning him with that momentous manifestation of postcolonial consciousness and self-determination, the Tri-Continental Conference that took place in Havana in 1966. Joans's project is no less than one of remapping the world in accordance with the capaciousness of his poetic vision. In 1962 he had begun living off and on in Mali, and his work mirrors this geographic shift with an increasingly Pan-Africanist emphasis and a closer proximity to the aesthetic tenets of the black arts movement. But like Baraka, Joans never disavows his early Beat and avant-garde influences; his poetry instead becomes increasingly interested in asserting that surrealism's roots lie in African, and not European, art and culture.

Joans was born Theodore Jones on the Fourth of July 1928, in Cairo, Illinois, although not, as legend claims, on a Mississippi River steamboat. (Joans was a superb self-mythologizer.) Joans, who would often say, "Jazz is my religion and surrealism is my point of view," had been exposed in his youth to each of these central influences. His father, a musician and riverboat entertainer, taught his son to play the trumpet, and Joans was first introduced to surrealism by way of an aunt who worked as a maid for a "wealthy WASP family."[36] According to Michael Fabre in his overview of Joans's life as a surrealist, "the aunt often brought home discarded items given her by her cosmopolitan employers, who knew Nancy Cunard and haunted art exhibitions. Among those throwaways Ted found a copy of the November 1933 issue of *Vogue*, with an article about Salvador Dalí discussing surrealism; the special number of *L'Illus-*

tration on the 1931 Paris Colonial Exposition; copies of *Le Minotaure* . . . and *Révolution Surréaliste.*" A thirteen-year-old Joans, unable to read French, saved up to buy a dictionary and began translating these and other surrealist texts. "By that time," writes Fabre, "he had already begun imitating the surrealist pictures he saw, including African sculptures that seemed strangely familiar to him."[37] Inspired by Dalí above all, Joans made up his mind to become a painter, and in 1951 he received a degree in fine arts from Indiana University.

Joans set off for New York City, the capital of abstract expressionism. He met Jackson Pollock and the action painters but maintained his preference for surrealism. Joans soon established a presence in the Greenwich Village bohemian milieu, which included Beat poets Ginsberg, Corso, di Prima, and LeRoi Jones. It was Jack Kerouac who introduced Joans to the Harlem nightlife. In 1953 Joans briefly shared a one-room flat with jazz legend Charlie "Yardbird" Parker. He would later write in "Bird and the Beats," "I also gave big costume balls to raise money for rent. At one such party Bird attended, it was dedicated to surrealism, Dada, and the Mau Mau. Bird arrived late but he hastily improvised his own Mau Mau image, plus aided other hipsters. He insisted that we play no recordings of his, or Dizzy Gillespie 'his worthy constituent.'"[38] In fact, Joans's most recognizable work dates to this period, namely the message "BIRD LIVES!" that began appearing on the walls and sidewalks of Manhattan after Parker's death in 1955.

By the late 1950s Joans had begun writing poetry in earnest. Ginsberg encouraged him to read his work in downtown coffeehouses, and before long Joans had published several volumes: *Beat Poems* (1957), *Funky Jazz Poems* (1959), *The Hipsters* (1961), and *All of Ted Joans and No More: Poems and Collages* (1961). Many in the Village saw Joans as a true hipster paragon. His "employment" with the short-lived "Rent-a-Beatnik" agency, which started as an ad in the *Village Voice* reading "RENT genuine BEATNIKS Badly groomed but brilliant (male and female)," is a telling example of Joans's playful attitude toward his boho status. A 1960 *Time* magazine article documents one response that sent Joans to a "way-out coffeehouse" improvised in a living room by the wife of a business executive, where Joans explained to those gathered, "I take a bath every day, man."[39]

In 1960 Joans moved to Paris and the famed Beat Hotel. Shortly thereafter, he chanced to run across André Breton on rue Bonaparte and began meeting regularly with Breton and the surrealist group in operation at the time. Fabre mentions that "Joans was happy to learn that, during the

1931 Exposition Coloniale, the Paris surrealists had opened an anticolonialist exhibit displaying European 'tribal fetishes' like Bibles, crucifixes, and stereotyped images of blacks of the kind found on Banania cocoa boxes" (314). It is *this* surrealist movement Joans allied himself with when he called himself a "Black Surrealist." It is a reminder that the same surrealist movement behind the spontaneous insights of automatic writing, a commitment to chance and the unconscious, and all the rest, also vigorously protested French involvement in the Moroccan Rif War and remained emphatically opposed to European imperialism—a sentiment shared by mainline Bretonian surrealism and the so-called dissident surrealism of Artaud.

Early on Joans had taken to signing his poems "1714" in tribute to Breton. (Written to resemble the initials A. B., 1713 was a kind of magic number for Breton). After Breton's death in 1967, Joans wrote a moving elegy titled "The Statue of 1713." This poem, which, like so much of Joans's work, argues powerfully for surrealism's African provenance, concludes,

> trumpets roared black waves of sound
> flutes screamed and accused asthma
> the sun in all its glory spun wildly
> the statue of André Breton
> stands in the shadow of no others
> yet casting its own long distant intelligent
> shadow into hands, hearts and minds
> of men
> This immense statue created by fetishers
> festooned with gri-gri from home
> and abroad stands as a living piece
> of sculpture (a poem)
> an awesome magnetic monument
> for the beautiful women and
> brilliant men
> that felt the
> presence of André Breton![40]

Joans's surrealism is most transgressive when it resists moving into abstract notions of global or even African space. (His poetry, like much of Baraka's nationalist writing, is far less disruptive in terms of gender, as if the radicalism of their racial politics could be sustained only by an essentially conservative view of gender dynamics.) The compressed imagery and densely layered narratives in "The Statue of 1713" are properly dreamlike and hallucinatory, but they are grounded in a great deal of worlded specificity.

Written "en route Tenerife / 5 March 1967," the poem describes, according to Michel Fabre, a reverie occasioned when, "shortly after Breton's death," Joans chanced upon "Paris's small Statue of Liberty lying on its side on the Left Bank, on its way to a new location. He considered it an omen."[41] In Joans's poem, however, readers encounter the statue (now the figure of Breton himself) not in Europe but in Africa, making it explicit that surrealism is of African provenance. The revered statue of Breton has been meticulously crafted and lavishly adorned with the soil and spirit of the continent. And while elsewhere Joans is more likely to address a unified, undifferentiated Africa, in "The Statue of 1713" he describes "owl wings from Mali," "Tuareg war shots," and a pedestal of "rock that / tumbled up from Adrar des Iforhas" (220). Here, Joans's Africanist vision gives way to a worlded conception of black power, rooted in local soils but open to unforeseen crossings and connections. Far from enclosing or isolating, the worlded view, by recognizing local histories and terrains, allows them to be in even more direct and intimate contact with one another. Hence the intimacy of the "ancient poster from Montmartre" that "serves as a rug for the chief fetisher" who carves Breton's statue. On the shifting sands of the Sahara—"The desert like the metropolis is full of mirages"—the poem must constantly reorient itself, and as in all of Joans's worlded poetry, here he directs a process of geographic and linguistic mapping:

> The statue of André Breton
> leans toward the East ignoring the West
> both thumbs pointing outward
> signifying faith in the South and North. (221)

Meanwhile, other "fetish brothers" have been "entrusted to / translate the surrealist manifestos into / Tamachek thus enabling one to read them / backwards as well as forwards." The appearance of Lautréamont's Maldoror midway through the poem—"I pull my mosquito net up to allow / Maldoror a chance to enter my bed / He is a hairy tarantula tonight" (221)—points to the multiplicity of Joans's surrealist influences and acknowledges a longer lineage of avant-garde forebears. The Uruguayan-born Lautréamont allows Joans to cast a wider net spatially as well, while drawing attention to Joans's ever-present erotics of influence and inspiration. Similarly, Joans's poem "Eternal Lamp of Lam" refers to the Cuban surrealist painter Wifredo Lam, who was of mixed Asian and African ancestry. The poem basically consists of the line "AFRO CHINO CUBANO / AFRO CHINO CUBANO WIFREDO" repeated over and over again.[42] Thinking back to Joans's assertion that Breton was a "man of all nationalities," one gets the sense that, for Joans, these writers and artists are the embodiment of the worlded and worldly spirit of surrealism.

Through much of the 1960s the "tri-continental poet" called Timbuktu, Mali, home while traveling extensively throughout Africa and Europe. As the decade wore on, he gravitated toward the black nationalist movement that his former Beat colleague Amiri Baraka had been so instrumental in shaping. Joans had met Malcolm X (his "Ace of Spades") while still in New York and later befriended ex–Black Panther Stokely Carmichael. While Joans seldom adopted the violently polemical tone of Baraka's writing during this period, his work does begin to take on a more provocational edge in the volumes *Black Pow-Wow* (1969), *Afrodisia* (1970), and especially *A Black Manifesto in Jazz Poetry and Prose* (1971), where he writes in the long opening piece, "Proposition for a Black Power Manifesto":

> To free our black selves with our own Black Power
> and by any means necessary!!
>
> Our black victory can only be won by Black Power.
>
> That victory will be won the black way.
>
> Black Power is our action—now!
>
> Now ketch this shit
> I believe that the moment is at hand for the black people to rise up
> like a giant midnight ocean wave, or like a sharp fatal pain in the ass of
>   racist United States
> then with the swiftness of a cheetah's paw snatch our destinies from the
>   ofay oppressors
> Black Power can do, will do, and shall be done. (12)

And to drive the point home a few pages later: "When I say 'our,' I mean just we the blacks. I am aware that a whole lotta white motherfuckers shall buy and read this manifesto; and some will perhaps identify with it; but dig me whiteboy, This *Ain't* Your Bit!!" (15). Yet even as Joans agitated for a radically self-assertive black art, he never renounced his devotion to Breton and surrealism. Indeed, the transnational scope of

Joans's increasingly Pan-Africanist commitments can be seen as analogous to surrealism's internationalist, anti-imperialist traditions.

The black nationalism at the heart of Joans's manifesto art closely parallels Baraka's work in the late 1960s, but Joans remained somewhat more skeptical than Baraka of programmatic modes of resistance. This wariness is evident in the rather ironic earnestness of Joans's "Proposition":

> Since this a piece of prose
> Black Power prose
> a proposal for a Black Power manifesto
> and not really "the" manifesto
> I wont be mad if a black cat cops-out on what I manifest. (34)

This sentiment is remarkable in the way it seeks to avoid the limitations of resistance based in dogma by merely "proposing" a manifesto based on spontaneity and the unconditioned promise of the future-to-come. His claiming to have written not "the" manifesto but rather the proposal for a "manifesto-to-come" startlingly prefigures Derrida's argument concerning the *Communist Manifesto*, which in Derrida's reading seems to be aware of its own limitations and necessary contradictions as it enacts a series of deferrals that will never quite exhaust its utopian promise of social transformation. Joans's "Proposition" manifests the call of the unconditioned in ways very near to what Derrida sees operating in the *Communist Manifesto*. Joans declares, for instance, "Rebellion yes, rioting no! We must remain ready to act in our revolution at all times. For a moment will come when passion has infected the air, things will be tense and uptight: the black community will be so mad that it can barely breathe, and it is then that the most extraordinary events happen independently of any of the preparations that have been made." From a pragmatic point of view, the revolution must always maintain the element of surprise; when Joans's manifesto urges "that we must be cool, even though there is a 'long hot summer'" (34), it recognizes that one must move beyond predictable, and therefore containable, forms of revolt. To be successful, any mass movement must retain a core of flexibility, creativity, and freedom, and Joans has learned from surrealism the power of this disciplined commitment to chance. By formulating his call to vigilance, and ultimately to arms, in these terms, Joans places himself and his manifesto squarely within a tradition reaching back to Marx, adopted and adapted by countless radical movements and avant-garde groups around the world.

Like many avant-garde manifestoes, Joans's "Proposition" also raises important questions about genre and the manifesto form. Written in mixed verse, it nonetheless asserts itself as "as piece of prose / Black Power prose" (34) and actually forms part of a larger work titled *A Black Manifesto in Jazz Poetry and Prose*. While it could describe the whole of Joans's oeuvre, the "jazz poetry" of the title refers more specifically to the notes taken by Joans at the 1967 Newport Jazz Festival in Europe and included just after the "Proposition." Describing sets at the festival by performers including Miles Davis, Sarah Vaughn, and Thelonious Monk, who Joans calls "the surrealist of modern jazz—the Dadaist of traditional piano playing" (43), Joans judged performances on the basis of their "blackness" or "whiteness" and takes on a strong black arts quality corresponding to contemporaneous work by Baraka in that direction. Joans's notes also allow the music of "our greatest black creators" (12) to enter into his manifesto and, in a sense, answer Joans's calls for a radically self-assertive black art. The final section of the *Black Manifesto* comprises a set of poems themselves acting as manifestoes in their unyielding assertion of the primacy of African forms and modes of expression. Laying out Joans's vision of an empowered Africa, the manifesto poems are not qualitatively different from other work by Joans in the late 1960s—somewhat less playful, but with the same black nationalist and Pan-Africanist concerns. In one poem, "Ego-Sippi," Joans writes,

> i've lived at TIMBUCTOO/TANGIER/HARLEM/ & HAARLEM
> HOLLAND too double crossed the Atlantic which i shall
> rename THE AFRICAN OCEAN blue
> NOW I read my poem in 'Sippi
> and allyall know thats saying a lot. (58)

Here we have the worldliness of the speaker, the global view, the overlaying of civil rights and anticolonial struggles, and a process of worlded remapping whereby the "double crossed" Atlantic becomes the *African Ocean*. The same forces at work on the language of these poems have also pervaded Joans's "Proposition" and the *Black Manifesto* as a whole, and the manifesto-poems that relay "messages" or provide timely "warnings" recall di Prima's *Revolutionary Letters*, a highly performative piece of Beat agitprop that clearly foregrounds its manifesto functions.

Joans's manifesto-texts, and African American Beat writing more generally in its engagement with the European avant-garde, operate within the realm of *tactics*. Joans's *Black Manifesto* puts forward a vision of collective revolt and liberation based on surrealist spontaneity and what Gilles Deleuze and Félix Guattari call pragmatics rather than a programmatic party platform. Understood in terms of Michel de Certeau's strategy-tactics paradigm, the seeming contradictions that run through Joans's manifesto become vital to his larger poetico-political project. He can express the general aim: "To free our black selves with our own Black Power / and by any means necessary!!" adding, "Black Power is not an ideology of Western thought" (13); Breton, however, never entirely leaves the picture. In "Proposition" Joans also writes, "Black Power is dreams that are carried out into reality. Black Power has the real and beyond the real in which to move. Our African ancestry has enriched us with this marvelous surreality. Black Power warriors can change into invisible animals that can spring out of the electric wiring inside of whitey's house" (16). The electric presence of African surreality recalls a similar pattern of imagery from "The Statue of 1713," where "the pedestal on which it stands / made of marvelous owl wings from Mali / gives off artificial lighting / accompanied by Tuareg war shouts" and "The pedestal of Malian owl wings is weeping / causing showers of electric sparks to fall / on the sand." These sparks scare away bandits and carry "the truth of the poet" (220). Just as Baraka's "Revolutionary Theatre" manifesto does with Artaud, Joans's manifesto *makes use* of Breton, and without irony he can employ manifesto tactics to decry the entire "ideology of Western thought" within which the manifesto form developed. The circuitry in which Joans's "Black Power warriors" carry out their maneuvers becomes the image of worlded currents of resistance and revolution.

Just how densely performative these connections between black power, surrealism, jazz, and Beat poetry are for Joans is made clear in a remarkable letter he sent to Ginsberg from Paris in early May 1968:

Dear Allen G,

Received the check donated to me. I think I thank you even very much so. I hope that other white creative brothers come through. But they are perhaps very different from you when it comes to bread. . . . Anyway, I come back June to USA. . . . Surrealist group here in Paris will help also. I just need dough to cross that vast stretch of African Ocean. (I just renamed it, also the Pacific is the Asian Ocean.) Read my poems alongside the great black seer Aimé Césaire and famous white writer J-P Sartre. Jazz is being used effectively on this side for the black revolution. I introduced Stokely C[armichael] to Archie Shepp. Jazz mags now doing the job that blackshit-cow Ebony mag should be doing. Poetry is and always has been revolutionary. I didn't have to change my style like LeRoi has. Gregory C[orso] has it wrong about me. I will never forgive him since I'm not Christ and they just like killed his shadow M. L. King.[43]

Joans's train of thought gets interrupted by history in the making (i.e., May 1968), which serves to focus his attention more pointedly to the stakes of a burgeoning black power movement worldwide:

> I was just interrupted by the French students rioting in the street outside against the police and bourgeois authorities. Theirs is not, NOT a revolt! They are the sons and daughters of workers that are feeding upon the Third World's people. Guinea, Congo-Brazzaville, Tanzania, and Mali are free. But other Africa, black Africa are not. I saw a lot of things happening in Africa. Eight years of eyes and ears!! Now I must return to the land of burn, baby, burn. Poetry for the black community. Poetry for the revolutionary whites. And this time I hope to be published!!

He concludes by making clear what he believes the stakes of his own work are, and the kinship he feels with certain white Beat comrades:

> I close this thank you letter and shall keep in touch. If white America would have really *understood* what you said in your early poems, there would be more white revolutionaries of the John Brown ilk. Well Allen G, I still dig thee, for it was you that started me reading in public in the first place. May a black witch doctor raise his sun bleached rhinoceros bone toward Mecca for you, to ensure your safety in that jungle of white savagery called the Ununited States of A.
>
> Surrealistically yours, Ted

Along with his letter, Joans sent Ginsberg a flyer of the event with Sartre and Césaire that he mentions, a night of performances that also included free jazz musician Marion Brown and Black Panthers Eldrige Cleaver and Huey Newton. It must have been quite a night! *This* is the Beat Generation that my work is invested in: politically aware and involved in the world at large. This is the Beat Generation that gets lost in many readings of major figures like Kerouac, Ginsberg, and Burroughs. It also gets lost when Beat writing is considered in its U.S. context alone.

In a discursive mode similar to that of both Joans's elegy for Breton in "The Statue of 1713" and Baraka's manifesto for "The Revolutionary Theatre," avant-garde strains in Bob Kaufman's writing are borne out in a web of allusions asserting the continuity, often invisible or submerged, of the Beat movement with the various groups of the historical European avant-garde and also a longer history of radical and antinomian art. He writes poignantly of an "Ancient Rain," which becomes the presencing of that history within the immediate context of the civil rights movement, Cold War dread, and Kaufman's own struggle to come to terms with the meaning of his art. The challenge facing the poet is how to transform avant-garde texts and traditions to respond to a specific historical moment, and this remains something of an open question in Kaufman's work. In "Sullen Bakeries of Total Recall," which appears in *Solitudes Crowded with Loneliness* alongside a reprinted *Abomunist Manifesto*, he sorrowfully remarks,

> I acknowledge the demands of Surrealist realization. I challenge Apollinaire to stagger drunk from his grave and write a poem about the Rosenbergs' last days in a housing project . . . speeding to the voltage mass of St. Sing Sing, . . . And yet when I think of those ovens, I turn my head in any other direction.[44]

The "demands" of surrealism can be understood as yet another iteration of Breton's "tenet of complete insubordination"—in a late interview with Gerald Nicosia, Joans too referred to surrealist "demands"—but Kaufman's poem goes a step further, interrogating the relevance, even the possibility, of using what amounts to anachronistic avant-garde models to process the horrors of the Holocaust and the threat of nuclear war.[45] At the same time, Kaufman acknowledges the perilous debt placed on later generations of writers who would presume to speak for and with the victims and martyrs of the past. A way beyond this very real impasse, however, is already suggested by the worldly and worlded nature of Kaufman's commitment to "Surrealist realization." This recognition of the heterogeneity, multiplicity, and historical and geographic specificity of influence and inspiration, rather than distancing or isolating us from other times and places, serves to bind us ever more tightly to them and their persistent demands on us here in the present.

In a number of Kaufman's poems, one encounters the familiar *world as body* conceit, but one in which the poet's mapping procedures— Kaufman refers to them as "memory worlds" in the poem "African Dream"—are radically generative because they are always being conjured in conjunction with other moments and spaces (civil rights, the Cold War, surrealism).[46] The multiplicity of Kaufman's memory worlds is both a testament to multiple surrealisms and an uncanny artifact of the dense folds of revision and repetition that perfuse Kaufman's corpus. An untitled poem collected in *The Ancient Rain* fleshes out the dream of "African Dream" in a sequence that begins, "I dreamed I dreamed an African dream. My head was a / Bony guitar, strung with tongues." The poem continues along these lines, its oneiric, synesthetic imagery echoing that of "African Dream." Another poem, "Blues for Hal Waters," further reworks this dream content, beginning, "My head, my secret cranial guitar, strung with myths plucked from / Yesterday's straits." The easy internal rhyme of "strung with tongues" has been replaced with the somewhat headier "myths plucked with / Yesterday's straits." But the most significant substitution in "Blues for Hal Waters" is this: the entire history of Kaufman's "African Dream"—its echoes, repetitions, and surrealist transmutations—becomes the poet's *secret* song. The last version of the poem-dream contains a hidden assemblage, the secret of its own making. This and other hidden continuities will eventually become the image of the "Ancient Rain" in the long poem of that name, which "falls silently and secretly" from "a distant secret sky" and describes in the most expansive terms possible Kaufman's worlded vision of connectivity and transformation.[47]

However evocative these examples may be, nothing by Kaufman compares to his *Abomunist Manifesto* in terms of its foregrounding the multiplicity of sources and contexts for avant-garde Beat writing. Through all its wordplay and willful inanity, the *Abomunist Manifesto* remains seriously engaged with the history and rhetoric of the manifesto form, as Kaufman performs the very linguistic and semantic experimentation he calls for and forth from the world, seeming to insist more than anyone since Breton himself that an absolute poetic and artistic freedom is prerequisite for social transformation. The *Abomunist Manifesto* shares in many characteristics of the avant-garde manifesto, while also critiquing the manifesto form itself. It is in large part a parody of hipsterdom, and its very name indicates Kaufman's ironic, neo-Dada stance toward the manifesto. Part of the burden of the manifesto is to name a group, and the name Kaufman gives his "Abomunists" (which, of course, don't exist) is based on nonsense and a bizarre assemblage of terms (abominable, communist, -ists of any persuasion, read also "beatnik"). The overall form of the *Abomunist Manifesto* is also very much a pastiche composed of self-contained sections with headings such as "Lexicon Abomunon" and "Abomnewcasts," each of which cannily point to a specific aspect of the manifesto form.[48] Here, the former speaks to the need for a new language to match the aesthetic or social project of a group claiming to be radically new—while also referencing the increasingly commodified, popularized "hipster speak" of the late 1950s—and the latter to the avant-garde manifesto's appropriations of mass media forms. Fifty years after Marinetti's "Founding and Manifesto of Futurism" was printed on the front page of *Le Figaro*, Kaufman's mimeographed manifesto began circulating up and down San Francisco's Columbus Avenue announcing the demands of the Abomunists. With echoes of the revolutionary pamphlet or religious tract, Kaufman scrambles the European avant-garde into a longer history, reaching back to the "Founding Fathers," Barabbas and Christ, and Hindu scripture—complete with "music composed by Schroeder."[49] Kaufman's manifesto is at once incendiary and risible; the Abomunists dare us to take them seriously, dare us to ignore their demands.

After a brief opening salvo titled, appropriately enough, "Abomunist Manifesto," Kaufman continues with nearly a dozen addenda, postscripts, and clarifications. Out of this mélange is created a document that reenacts in one gesture the early history of the futurists or Dadaists, where an originary manifesto—Marinetti's "Founding and Manifesto of Futurism," Tzara's "Dada Manifesto"—is quickly followed by a flurry of subsequent ones defining various aspects of the movement or reasserting its founding ethos. Kaufman's manifesto playfully but cogently performs this avant-garde drama, a defining aspect of the manifesto genre and the movements it has launched. Its very form recognizes the necessary multiplicity of the avant-garde manifesto: not just multiple manifestoes from each group but also the past and future transmutations the manifesto always carries within itself. So in the *Abomunist Manifesto* we get "Notes Dis- and Re- Garding Abomunism," an immediate equivocation or negation of the platform just presented. In essence, Kaufman's is a self-negating manifesto as "dis-garding" becomes "discarding." Faint echoes of avant-*garde* can also be heard in the "dis-" and "re-" *garding* of the manifesto. Later on, there are "Further Notes (*taken from* 'Abomunismus und Religion' *by Tom Man*)," and later yet, "Still Further Notes Dis- & Re- Garding Abomunism."

The selective history put forward by the manifesto is written in terms of its projected future as it describes a past that *will have been*, and the vast, imagined history of the Abomunists is a clear concern of Kaufman's manifesto: the history of the Abomunists but also history as itself abomunist. "Abomunism," according to Kaufman, "was founded by Barabbas, inspired by his dying words: 'I wanted to be in the middle, but I went too far out.'"[50] Past Abomunists have included Krishnamurti, Edgar Cayce, John Hancock, and Benedict Arnold, these last two implicating the very founding of the United States as somehow "Abomunist" (i.e., an abomination). Kaufman's crazed name-dropping in these sections is reminiscent of the far-reaching and often unexpected Beat genealogies provided by Kerouac and Ginsberg, while early Abomunist history has been recorded in "the Live Sea Scrolls . . . one of the oldest Abomunist documents yet discovered" (82).

"$$ Abomunus Craxioms $$" skewers the axioms on which party platforms, whether hip, avant-garde, or square, are erected; Kaufman's wise-*cracks* reveal the cracks that inevitably appear in any group's doxa. The "Abomunist Election Manifesto" is one of the more parochial sections with its calls for "the abolition of Oakland" and "statehood for North Beach" (81), and as it calls to mind the long history of disenfranchisement not just in the Jim Crow South but across the United States, the "Election Manifesto" leaves us wondering about what faith Kaufman places in electoral politics. "Boms," a brief series of word sketches, evokes the martial origins of the term "avant-garde" and foregrounds their composition by "Bomkauf" (Kaufman's Abomunist nom de guerre), and they share in the poem-as-weapon thinking of Joans's "hand grenade poems" and Césaire's *armes miraculeuses*.[51] The aural and syntactic deformations at work throughout the *Abomunist Manifesto* make Kaufman's text performative in the manner of Marinetti's sound poem *Zang Tumb Tuuum*, where the creation of a new poetics (in Marinetti's case, the poetics of war) is at once demanded and fulfilled by avant-garde manifesto art.[52]

"Excerpts from the Lexicon Abomunon" and "Abomunist Rational Anthem" pile layer upon layer of verbal irony and constitute the deadly playful core of the text's lasting significance and appeal. From the early days of the Beat movement, hipster slang was easily identifiable and the beatnik argot soon appropriated by a wider public. Kaufman seems eager to disassociate himself from the Beat vernacular even as he codifies it in his "Lexicon Abomunon." He writes, "At election time, Abomunists frink more, and naturally, as hard-core Abo's, we feel the need to express ourselves somewhat more abomunably than others. We do this simply by not expressing ourselves (abomunization). We do not express ourselves in the following terms" (80). Kaufman's simultaneous avowal and disavowal of the very movement it is attempting to define—"we do not express ourselves"—is similar to the "Beat Manifestoes" of Holmes and Kerouac, who distanced themselves from what they seemed to embrace. Read as an avant-garde poetics, the "Abomunist Rational Anthem" engages even further in a productive deformation of language. "Derrat slegelations, flo goof babereo," it begins. "Sorash sho dubies, wago, wailo, wailo" (85). Its "rationality" is an appeal, not to the kind of instrumental reason decried by Breton in the first *Manifesto of Surrealism*, but rather to the distinctly surrealist "unreason" of what Césaire called "my logics."[53] In her chapter on Kaufman in *The Dark End of the Street*, Maria Damon points to the language games of the *Abomunist Manifesto* as prime examples of "unmeaning jargon" in Kaufman's work, which, Damon argues, "differs sharply from meaninglessness. His unmeaning—as in unnaming—aims to destroy actively the comfort of meaning in service of the furious, spasmodic play of jazz energy. His jargon is both the special code of initiated hipsters . . . and . . . the bubbling up and over of untamable sound." Damon underscores the political implications (and avant-garde origins) of Kaufman's "nonsense poetry" when she relates it to Césaire's surrealist project of "breaking the oppressor's language."[54]

None of this has been meant to suggest that Beat surrealism is the exclusive domain of Baraka, Joans, and Kaufman, in addition to Lamantia, who, with Joans, forms the closest *material* link between the Beats and the European vanguard. Avant-garde martyrs Mayakovsky and Lorca become important reference points in Ginsberg's life and work, and a poem like "At Apollinaire's Grave" makes it clear that Ginsberg counted the French surrealists among his poetic forebears as well. William Burroughs's postmodernist approaches to narrative and authorship build on earlier Dada and surrealist techniques and share in their commitment to the processes of chance. A case could even be made for Kerouac's "spontaneous prose" as taking part in the great surrealist tradition of automatic writing. What sets Baraka, Joans, and Kaufman apart is the much greater insistence with which an avant-garde poetics is linked to both oppositional and community-forming practices in their writing, to how they see themselves and their role as writers, and to how they understand the connection between radical art, political struggle, and social change. Even Baraka's aesthetic pragmatism, characteristic of his work in the black arts movement and often read as a disavowal of his earlier Beat experimentalism, cannot be fully appreciated without a serious consideration of its avant-garde origins. Writing from the "margins" of the Beat Generation, Baraka, no less than Joans or Kaufman, reminds us of the centrality of the international avant-garde—in particular, the tactics of the avant-garde manifesto—to Beat writing. This signal contribution to the Beat movement, with its corresponding insistence on the worlded dimensions of the European avant-garde, forms the core of their rich and enduring legacy among the Beats.

3

A MULTILAYERED INSPIRATION:
PHILIP LAMANTIA, BEAT POET

"A Voice That Rises Once in a Hundred Years"

Philip Lamantia's life and work bring together just about all the major threads, themes, and lines of inquiry under discussion thus far. His formation as a poet when a mere teenager took place among the European avant-garde in exile in New York City during World War II, and André Breton dubbed the young poet "a voice that rises once in a hundred years."[1] After the war Lamantia returned to San Francisco, where he soon found himself under the tutelage of the very worldly Kenneth Rexroth. He became active in Rexroth's Libertarian Circle, and his poetry continued to develop in new directions. The 1950s were a time of crisis and questing in which the poet published relatively little. These years mark the beginning of an itinerant period that took him to Mexico for long stretches, also back to New York and then on to Europe and Morocco in the 1960s. (By now this has become a familiar Beat itinerary.) Participation in ritual ceremonies with the Cora Indians in Mexico, followed by the trauma of a scorpion sting, brought about an ecstatic conversion back to the Roman Catholicism of his Sicilian forebears, and he all but abandoned poetry. Lamantia was one of the "Six Poets at Six Gallery" on the fateful night in the fall of 1955, when Allen Ginsberg first read "Howl" to a public audience, an event that helped launch the San Francisco Renaissance. But Lamantia chose not read his own poems that night, reading instead the work of his recently deceased friend John Hoffman. When Lamantia returned to writing poetry in earnest in the 1960s, his earlier commitment to surrealism was still very evident, but now integrated with a newfound religiosity, a Beat bohemianism, and an interest in native wisdom, mysticism, hermeticism, drugs, and ornithology. His work was now imbued with the Mexican landscape, shades of California nature poetry, and composite landscapes all his own. In the late 1970s and throughout the 1980s, his poetics were informed with a localism and a naturalism almost as intense as those of Gary Snyder. All of these factors play a role in fashioning a worlded poetic assemblage: an oeuvre as profound and complex as that of any poet writing in the latter half of the twentieth century.

Lamantia's debt to surrealism is massive and well documented.[2] While still in high school in San Francisco in the early 1940s, Lamantia sent some poems to André Breton, who was then living in New York and editing the surrealist journal *vvv*. Breton's response was so positive that the young poet left school and moved to Manhattan to join the surrealist circle that had reconstituted itself there. These exiled avant-gardists merit a fuller study than can be provided in this paltry introduction sketch—something akin to Thomas Wheatland's book, *The Frankfurt School in Exile*, which follows the Horkheimer circle to their new home at Columbia University.[3] While Wheatland emphasizes the Frankfurters' unwillingness to assimilate into American intellectual life, this was not the case with most of the avant-garde poets and painters in New York during the war. The war years were a time of intense cross-pollination, and Lamantia was an active participant in these formative events.

In a 1998 interview with fellow poet David Meltzer, two important themes emerge.[4] The first is the temporal continuity that Lamantia sees underlying French surrealism, its displaced expression in 1940s New York, the New York School of the 1950s (including abstract expressionism, which Lamantia views as an offshoot of surrealist practices), the San Francisco Renaissance, and the Beat scene on both coasts. The second theme is the spatial network of worlded influence linking Europe to New York, San Francisco, Mexico City, and indigenous traditions in the United States and Latin America. Referring to poets like himself and Gerd Stern (Jack Steen in Kerouac's *Subterraneans*), Lamantia tells Meltzer that they "were living these connections" between East and West Coast Beat and bohemian scenes. Only later came Ginsberg, Kerouac, di Prima, Ferlinghetti, and the others. In terms of Lamantia's "*origins* . . . in Surrealism," he explains that "it was during the Surrealist diaspora that Surrealism deepened what the manifestos of the 1920s initiated."[5] Publishing circles, little magazines (*Fire!!* and the Harlem Renaissance), cafés, salons, exhibitions (the Armory Show and modernism), artists living and working in close proximity—this is how movements evolve. Surrealism first took root in the United States through the introduction and history lesson provided by Breton's *vvv* and Charles Henri Ford's *View*. William

Carlos Williams was a contributor to *View*, as were Henry Miller and Paul Bowles, and Lamantia helped Ford edit the magazine through most of his stay in New York. Ford and Lamantia eventually had a falling out, and Lamantia returned to his native San Francisco. There, new energies swirled amid a postwar boom, and, along with his new mentor, Kenneth Rexroth, Lamantia was destined to play a major role in what is called the San Francisco Renaissance.

Lamantia's 1943 poem "There Are Many Pathways to the Garden," which appeared in *View* when he was only sixteen years old, points uncannily (and thus in true surrealist fashion) to the multiplicity and heterogeneity that became hallmarks of his writing for decades to come. This multiplicity is figured in the very title of the poem, while melting deserts and "colonial lizards" demonstrate a youthful exoticism that was modulated in myriad ways.[6] Those particular images echo another early poem, "The Islands of Africa," which is dedicated to Arthur Rimbaud, who famously forsook poetry before reaching the age of twenty and spent his later years as a trader (some say smuggler or gunrunner) in the Horn of Africa. Following decades of precedent, Lamantia easily conflates Rimbaud, the surrealist *avant la lettre*, with surrealism proper, and he undoubtedly identifies with the precocious *poète maudit*. Lamantia sent "The Islands of Africa" to Breton in 1944, who enthusiastically accepted it for publication in his *vvv*.

"Pathways" was reprinted in Lamantia's first full collection, *Erotic Poems*, which was published in 1946, before the poet himself turned twenty, and has the quality of an assemblage: if Ted Joans's "spiritual fathers" were Breton and Hughes, then in *Erotic Poems* Lamantia announces that his are Breton and Rexroth. By 1946 his allegiance has shifted to the latter. Back in San Francisco, Lamantia began attending Rexroth's famous Friday night salon, and Rexroth quickly took the younger poet under his wing. *Erotic Poems*, published at Rexroth's urging, marks a split between his earlier surrealist verse and his more recent "naturalistic" poems (as Lamantia called them), composed after his return to San Francisco. As he became more and more invested in Rexroth's socialist, anarchist, and libertarian politics, his writing began to replace an overtly surrealist manner and vocabulary with something more expansive and, at times, overtly political. These brief glimpses of a subterranean politics in Lamantia's poetry of the mid-1940s signal a presence that persists, just below the surface, in everything he writes and everywhere he travels throughout his long career.

In one "naturalist" piece from *Erotic Poems*, dedicated to Rexroth and fittingly titled "Two Worlds–1946," Lamantia writes of a "wingless bird, only half-a-bird," with "the power of flight / Locked in its spirit," who

"Threads through the prison seeking daylight" (44). These lines are lyrical, yet their line of flight and escape moves to actuate a latent oppositional force that resides two stanzas later in the souls of "the crucified / Who lie in absolute separateness" in "Dumb, distorted worlds" (45), or, rather, the proletariats who remain alienated from themselves and from one another, divided by the same ideologies that have just led to two world wars and already threaten another. The bird that opens the poem, lyrical image par excellence, is likely a reference to Rexroth (his collection of poems *The Phoenix and the Tortoise* had been published two years earlier), although birds continued to be potent symbols for Lamantia, profoundly shaping his turn toward an ecopoetics in the late 1970s and throughout the 1980s.

The final naturalist selection in *Erotic Poems* is also the most conspicuously political. "A Simple Answer to the Enemy" begins with a quotation from Peter Kropotkin, in which the eminent anarchist envisions a battle to the death between "the State" and "the individual and local life." Writing in 1896, the two already seem to be mutually exclusive for Kropotkin; fifty years later, Lamantia writes,

> It is an eventful year.
> We live in a nation flourishing
> On the blood of millions murdered
> And millions more being murdered
> Everywhere else in the world. (45)

He accuses the United States of base profiteering before, during, and immediately after World War II. "Peace" is a relative term, and while the war may have ended for the Americans, bringing not just normalcy but outright prosperity, the same cannot yet be said for a shattered Europe, especially Eastern Europe with the totalitarian Soviet Union now a rising hegemon. According to the poet, "The bureaucrats and idle rich / Continue their reign of permanent war / On the sweat and blood of the poor." In terms of class struggle, essentially nothing has changed. He ends the poem with this lesson:

> Whatever happens, one thing is certain:
> The end of the world it has taken
> Hundreds of years to create,
> But mere seconds to destroy. (46)

Lamantia gives voice to the first stirrings of the atomic dread brought on by Hiroshima and Nagasaki and raised to the highest stakes during the Cold War. Here is a poet grasping to find *his own* voice, borrowing shopworn phrases like "years to create, seconds to destroy" to describe the immensity of this world vision. "A Simple Answer to the Enemy" is in many ways an uncharacteristic poem, but in its most hopeful moment it also provides a clue for reading the subterranean politics of Lamantia's oeuvre. At one point he writes, "The Revolution has not won, / But it exists everywhere" (45)—forced underground, that is to say, but no less real as a result and liable to emerge in the most unexpected and unforeseen ways.

Lamantia's return to San Francisco after the war marked a turn away from surrealism and toward the "great Rexroth" and an immersion, through Rexroth, in the "sacred texts of the Western and Asian traditions."[7] While Lamantia did acknowledge his "divergence" from surrealism after his return to San Francisco, it served only to precipitate a more fundamental and productive reintegration in his life and work. He told Meltzer, "So my poetry turned naturalistic, directly in opposition to Surrealism. It seems that what I've finally gotten to now is a synthesis of these two once-divergent directions. . . . But all my books could be considered initiatory stages of a quest at once poetic and spiritual, with parallel roots in revolutionary political theory and mystical expression . . . and bracketed with an eruptive rebelliousness that marked by Beat period" (138). Lamantia did not set Rexroth and politics on one side of the equation and surrealism and mysticism on the other so much as indicate that politics and spirituality are caught up on both sides. In other words, Lamantia did not fully abandon surrealism (aligned with the unconscious and the occult) in his turn to Rexroth, nor did he need to abandon politics in his return to surrealism in the 1960s (now deepened by his experiences in Mexico and renewed interest in Catholicism).

At Rexroth's well-attended salon, that time-honored tradition of the literati, the elder statesman provided Lamantia and so many others with a political as well as a poetic education. It is still easily forgotten that Lamantia was a founding member of the "San Francisco Libertarian Circle." (At this time and in this context, "libertarian" denotes a leftist, anarchopacifist orientation.) He describes the scene to Meltzer:

> On the West Coast—Berkeley and San Francisco—there was an extraordinary convergence of poets, painters, ex–conscientious objectors, and radical anarchists—rebels of all stripes. Kenneth Rexroth was the central figure, with Robert Duncan and Bill Everson connecting the two generations. The common meeting ground was what we named the San Francisco Libertarian Circle. The regular structured meetings were announced weekly by

postcards sent to about fifty individuals. I know, since it was my specific "organizational function" to type the announcements.

Actually, the focal point of the group was every aspect of anarchist thought, researched and discussed with passion and objectivity by a small minority; within the group there were various degrees of commitment. There was special lectures more or less monthly that set the orientation for a certain period. For example, I prepared one evening a presentation of Wilhelm Reich's theories, just being published for the first time in English. Rexroth spoke on Kropotkin. A first-generation Italian introduced the most important anarchist theoretician of the early twentieth century, Enrico Malatesta, who had lived in exile in England. Some of these writings were reaching us from the British anarchist group, which also supplied us with their newspaper *Freedom*. *The Catholic Worker* arrived regularly in bundles from New York. There was even a connection with Albert Camus in Paris around his publication *Combat* and a small group around Paul Goodman in New York and the newspaper *Why?* (138–39)

Those readers familiar with the highly mannered, hermetic lyricism of Lamantia's poetry may be surprised by the language of "organizational functions" and "degrees of commitment" to anarchist and libertarian causes. I quote this passage so fully because of those revelations and the overall sense it provides of "an extraordinary convergence of . . . rebels of all stripes," spanning generations and plugged into a transnational network of radicals and freedom fighters.

But to what extent are Lamantia's anarchist leanings connected to his poetry? (We could ask the same of Rexroth.) Are the formative years with Rexroth simply a phase that ended before Lamantia reached poetic maturity, returned to the Catholicism of his youth, reembraced surrealism in San Francisco, and sought out indigenous spiritual traditions of Mexico and the American West—all of these inflected by North Beach hip culture and the factioning of the San Francisco poetry scene (vis-à-vis Duncan, Spicer, and others)? Even remaining with surrealism, one finds a formidable parallel between Lamantia's experience with anarchism under Rexroth and Breton's intellectual evolution. In *André Breton: Dossier Dada*, Tobia Bezzola writes, "Of particular significance to his later development is Breton's youthful enthusiasm for the anarchist movement, and for a style of politics that manifests itself above all in radical, extra-parliamentary activism. This clearly sets Breton apart from the *fin de siècle* decadents and their concept of *l'art pour l'art*." Bezzola's description casts Breton's "youthful enthusiasm for the anarchist movement" as leading eventually to a version of Peter Bürger's avant-garde dialectic—moving from a complete separation of "art" and "life" (i.e., *art for art's sake*) to their complete integration in the first proper avant-garde movements (Dada in particular).[8]

Rexroth wrote the introduction to *Erotic Poems* and touts Lamantia's "free association of images as an alternative to surrealism," as Richard Cándida Smith puts it.[9] Rexroth and Lamantia's sparring over surrealist *poetics*, surely overdetermined by Rexroth's opinion of surrealist *politics*, reintroduces the question of avant-garde and, by extension, Beat politics, which will continue to inform Lamantia's turn to, and beyond, surrealism; of statements by Kerouac, Ginsberg, and others about the Beat movement; of Beat poetry as revolutionary propaganda; and, finally, as in the previous chapter, of the various politically charged appropriations of the surrealist and avant-garde canon by Baraka, Joans, and Kaufman. The fundamental question here, as it was in regard to African American Beat writing, is how does Lamantia *use* surrealism, and in conjunction with what other influences . . . and to what ends? How does Lamantia set the surrealist tradition in motion in his poetry as part of a wider, more complex configuration of radical art and politics?

In Lamantia's work are combined our key concepts of *subterranean* and *world*. Insofar as the subterranean is a master trope of Beat writing, it seems as if Lamantia is putting his Beat credentials on display in the poem "Intersection," written in the mid-1950s, whose title evokes street life as well as a crossing or meeting of energies. The poem ends with this passage:

> I'm thinking some impossible drug
> flown by a hand not a hand
> > but a tongue
> not a tongue
> > but a whip
> not a whip but a cup!
> I'm thinking
> going down the street
> too long to be seen
> not wide enough to be missed

MY HOUSE IN THE CRACKS OF THE PAVEMENT! (101)

An early draft of the poem concludes with the more active and poignant "finding my home in the cracks of the pavement," suggesting that the subterranean image really is the key to the poem.[10] In either version, this last stanza would fit right in with Baraka's "Lately, I've become accustomed to the way / The ground opens up and envelops me / Each time I go out to walk the dog" and Kaufman's "San Franers, falling down"; it implies a reading that opens up an entire history of subterranean thought and writing. In Lamantia's poem the street is linked to his "impossible drug," a clear enough reference to the underground drug scene that Lamantia was no stranger to. The "cracks in the pavement" are figurative and self-referential; Lamantia's surrealism tends to the gnostic and hieratic (among writers of the San Francisco Renaissance, he often has more in common with Duncan, by way of H. D., than his fellow Beat poets in this regard), and the obscurity of the subterranean, with all its hidden meanings and connections, becomes in the poem an image of Lamantia's lyric ideal. "Intersection" originally formed part of the long-unpublished *Tau* manuscript. It was one of several strong poems from *Tau* that made their way into his next collection, *Ekstasis* (1959), which he insisted was a "very minor book."[11] When *Tau* is finally published, posthumously in 2008, editor Garrett Caples wrote in his introduction that these are likely "the very poems he *didn't* read at the Six Gallery reading," choosing instead to read the work of his friend John Hoffman, who had recently died in Mexico under mysterious circumstances.[12]

Written a few years later, at the apogee of the North Beach Beat scene, Lamantia's poem "High" was published in *Destroyed Works* (1962) and later anthologized in Ann Charters's *Beat Reader*. The poem is paradigmatic in the way it assembles the poet's disparate voices:

O beato solitudo! where have I flown to?
stars overturn the wall of my music
as flight of birds, they go by, the spirits
opened below the lark of plenty
ovens of neant overflow the docks at Veracruz
This much is time
summer coils the soft suck of night
lone unseen eagles crash thru mud
I am worn like an old sack by the celestial bum
I'm dropping by eyes where all the trees turn on fire!
I'm mad to go to you, Solitude—who will carry me there?
I'm wedged in this collision of planets/Tough!
I'm ONGED!
I'm the trumpet of King David
the sinister elevator tore itself limb by limb

You can not close
you can not open
you break yr head
you make bloody bread! (200)

In Lamantia's frequent appeals to a Beat mystique throughout the poem, the phrasings and diction of his Beat peers are plainly registered (which may explain the poem's place in anthologies like Charters's). "Celestial bum" and "sinister elevator" would not look out of place in "Howl," while "ovens of neant" and "soft suck of night"—even the more obscure "I'm ONGED!"—are reminiscent of Kerouac's phrasing in *Mexico City Blues*. The opening line: "O beato solitudo! where have I flown to?" may sound like it could have been written by Gregory Corso, but it is a distinctly Lamantian flourish. In tongue-in-cheek fashion, the poet wishes to take "Beatitude" back to its roots not in the New Testament but in the Roman Church. Lamantia's Beatitude is "canonized" in both senses of the term, although the authority of the Church is significantly undercut in the poem —by the vapid internal rhyme in the opening line itself, by salvation manifested in the parodic image of the "celestial bum," and by the bit of doggerel that ends the poem with an image of a profane Eucharist.[13]

With its religious, and specifically Catholic, references, "High" calls to mind another of Lamantia's poems of this period. "All Hail Pope John the Twenty Third!," which also dates to the late 1950s, ratchets up the irreverence. The speaker implores the new pope, architect of the Second Vatican Council, "Oh Pope John save us from the Light haters" and "bring back the East to us / Rejoin us to the International Christ."[14] Lamantia repeats his point about the internationalism of the Church when he counsels, "Commission the Watusi to compose Masses for all Africa, for the whole world!" (On the other side of the Catholic-surrealist divide, this line will find its complement in Ted Joans's "Statue of 1713," when "fetish brothers . . . translate the surrealist manifestos into Tamachek.") Lamantia then figures the pope as a kind of beatnik savior, asking, "Why O Pope of Divine Madness and Holy Sanity / Why has the world gone evil, mammon crazy, middle class and more stupid than ever?" He calls him a "Mystic Funny Man" and ends his pontificating with the biting flippancy of "Amici, I'm hip to the Catholic Scene!" (132).

Perhaps Lamantia's facetiousness and iconoclasm in "All Hail Pope John" can be traced back to another source; namely, Breton's mentor, Guillaume Apollinaire, who, near the beginning of his major poem "Zone" (published in 1913), writes,

You alone in all Europe are not antique O Christian faith
The most modern European is you Pope Pius X
And you whom the windows look down at shame prevents you
From entering a church and confessing this morning.[15]

In "Flaming Teeth," a poem from the 1970 collection *The Blood of the Air*, which marks the poet's return to surrealism, Lamantia once again connects surrealism and Catholicism through an image of unholy consecration: "Here come the flagons of Isidore Ducasse / The speed which is happening / And the grave compassion / The riot was mainly in my mind" (276). Here proto-surrealist Ducasse (Comte de Lautréamont) and his chalice of sacred wine are set against the more earthbound "speed" of amphetamine vision, while the "riot" of the mind runs parallel to Breton's *révolte de l'esprit*.

It turns out that Lamantia likely *did* have Apollinaire in mind when he wrote his paean to Pope John. Fully forty years later, he will return to similar subject matter, this time with explicit reference to the French poet. One of the last works Lamantia would publish during his lifetime, "Ultimate Zone" (2000), not only takes its name from Apollinaire's poem, it also takes the "most modern European is you Pope Pius X" line for its epigraph and opens with a quote from Apollinaire's 1917 manifesto "The New Spirit and the Poets." Lamantia contrasts this "new spirit" with the contemporary zeitgeist, which is embodied by the current pontiff:

It can not be said that you Pope John Paul II are the epitome of post-modernism
since for two decades you have been one of its most responsible critics
Now after so many changes so many revolutions so many end worlds
poetry itself pronounced dead in these disunited states. (419)

Gone is the cheekiness of "All Hail Pope John." This later poem is a somber reckoning with the state of the Church and the plight of artistic culture "in these disunited states." According to the editors of the *Collected Poems*, "Ultimate Zone" was composed during a "flurry of poetic activity . . . precipitated by a mystical vision Lamantia had at the National Shrine of St. Francis in North Beach, San Francisco."[16] (He will refer to this as his "August breakthrough.")[17] After nearly a half century of devoting himself to the muse of poetry, Lamantia is still capable of new breakthroughs, new conversions. His last poems, including "Ultimate Zone," invite new readings of older works as they reshuffle the materials of the assemblage.

Apart from bookending his persistent yet ever-conflicted fascination with the Church, both as spiritual nourishment and as poetic fodder, Lamantia's pair of pope poems is instructive in a more general way: one that is central to the theme of this book. Particularly in their invocation of Apollinaire and his poem "Zone," they suggest how one might arrive at a more historically rooted, materially grounded understanding of Beat Generation writing. Apollinaire, who coined the term *sur-réalisme* in 1917, is, along with Breton and Antonin Artaud, a figure within the surrealist tradition whom Beat writers have been particularly drawn to. In Kaufman's "Sullen Bakeries of Total Recall," the poet feels compelled to interrogate Apollinaire's (and by extension surrealism's) relevance in a post-Auschwitz world, a desire that speaks more to Kaufman's own "anxiety of influence" and misgivings as a writer. Ginsberg, on the other hand, and in typical fashion, has no problems declaring Apollinaire and the surrealists poetic forebears. Ginsberg's 1958 poem "At Apollinaire's Grave," written around the same time as Lamantia's "All Hail Pope John," in fact, is an earnest and tender tribute. He too singles out "Zone with its long crazy line of bullshit about death"—Ginsberg's play on "line" alluding to his preoccupation since "Howl" with the extended "breath line."[18] ("Zone" does feature longer lines than most of Apollinaire's poems.)

What, exactly, is the Beats' inheritance from the French poet? Judging from Ginsberg's elegy, it is primarily a poetico-spiritual legacy that Apollinaire leaves for future generations of avant-gardists. It exists within the realm of *spirit*, from his *esprit nouveau* to the *inspiration* of Ginsberg's breath line. From this point of view, the Zone that Apollinaire writes about and that both Ginsberg and Lamantia find so compelling would seem to be equally abstract: a dislocated region of pure potentiality and surrealist becoming (and not unlike the Inter-*zone* of William Burroughs's *Naked Lunch*, which, for all its parallels with and references to the International Zone of twentieth-century Tangier, still gets read by Barry Miles and others as first and foremost a "landscape of ideas.")[19] This would be all the more proof, in other words, that the Beats—like the surrealists before them—are interested above all in a revolution of the mind (*de l'esprit*). Such a perspective, however, ignores that fact that Apollinaire is invoking a very real place in "Zone," namely, the *zone non aedificandi* extending from the 1844 wall constructed in Paris during the July Monarchy.

Built to secure the capital against foreign invasion (and possibly to protect Versailles by containing the ever-rebellious Parisians), the unpopular enclosure soon became obsolete and was eventually demolished during the 1920s, but not before various encampments of squatters had sprouted up all along the wall. Many of these *zonards* had been displaced by the rapid modernization of Paris under Napoleon III and his Prefect of the Seine, Baron Haussmann. Today the Boulevard Périphérique, which separates Paris from its *banlieue,* follows the former path of the 1844 wall and reinforces the site's long history, marked by division and conflict along class (and now racial, ethnic, and religious) lines.[20] Apollinaire's poem is embedded in this same history, as contemporary readers would have certainly understood, especially those in the poet's immediate circle. Its urban topography makes "Zone" resemble a typical flânerie poem in the tradition of Baudelaire. The flaneur, or "stroller," is the one who feels at home, and yet set apart in the crowd, and thus better able to observe and critique (and also praise) the conditions of modern life. The flaneur leaves him- or herself (whether it is always necessarily a gendered category has been a much-debated question) to the mysterious working of chance and the shock of unexpected juxtapositions that modernity makes inevitable—hence the allure of flânerie for the surrealists, the basis for traveling tales like Breton's *Nadja* and Louis Aragon's *Paris Peasant.* This is a tradition that eventually led to the radicalized situationist dérive in the 1950s and to today's school of critical geographers.

The comic variation in Apollinaire's poem is that the flaneur is none other than Pope Pius X, that "most modern European," who "walk[s] through Paris all alone in the crowd" (121). After Pius has taken in the sights—Notre Dame, Montmartre, and so on—the poem's geography begins to spin farther outward. From Paris to the Mediterranean and then on to Amsterdam and Prague, the poem's centrifugal force is analogous to the one that led Sal and Dean from Mexico to "the world!" at the end of *On the Road,* and impelled Baraka, Joans, and so many others to move from civil rights in its narrow U.S. context to an internationalist concern for "all the peoples of the world." And as is so often the case, the most fully worlded moment in Apollinaire's "Zone" occurs when the poem is also the most grounded in its own time and place. Still addressing Pope Pius in the poem's final stanzas, he writes,

> You walk toward Auteuil you want to walk home on foot
> To sleep among your fetishes from Oceania and Guinea
> They are all Christ in another form and of another faith
> They are inferior Christs obscure hopes
>
> Adieu adieu
>
> The sun a severed neck. (127)

Auteuil, a former commune on the Bois de Boulogne at the edge of Paris, was literally cut in two (it had its neck severed) by the 1844 wall. The Auteuil quarter had long been associated with wealth and ease and thus makes a fitting new "home" for Pius, especially after his return from the far reaches of the empire ("Oceania and Guinea"). Lamantia would likely agree with the pope's sentiment that these fetishes from distant lands "are all Christ in another form," although he may not share Pius's arrogance about their inferiority and obscurity. The colonial consciousness that suddenly arises in these final lines, and especially the violence of the very last line, conflates the wall's slashing through the city—which brings the mansions of Auteuil into stark contrast with the squalor of the Zone—with the colonial violence that is always the corollary of the metropole's splendor and security. Aimé Césaire will put the thematic richness of the poem's finale to new uses in his 1947 collection *Soleil cou coupé*. How familiar Lamantia, Ginsberg, and others were, if at all, with the material context of Apollinaire's poem is not the point. The subterranean histories inscribed within the older poet's work "flash up," as Walter Benjamin puts it, "in a moment of danger," and the past struggles wait to be redeemed by present ones.[21]

In the Lamantia mythos, the period of spiritual disquiet that characterized the 1950s for the poet culminates around 1960 with an act that the *Collected Works* editors describe as "one of the signal events of Lamantia's artistic life: the burning of most of the poetry he'd written but not published since *Erotic Poems*." They go on to say, "The exact circumstances and sequence of events around this act aren't fully known, but it was a deliberate, premeditated renunciation of his life as a poet, a continuation and amplification of the spiritual crisis begun on his conversion and compelling him to suppress his own work at the Six Gallery reading." The archival work of the *Collected Poems* editors, however, reveals that these years of silence and disavowal were quite productive indeed. It turns out that, in addition to the *Tau* manuscript, whose publication he also suppressed in 1955 and which appeared only posthumously half a century later, a significant number of works survived the conflagration. Most notable among these is an unpublished typescript fittingly titled "Destroyed Works," which Lamantia put together before burning his poems. Then, in 1962, he decided to publish a collection of poems under the title *Destroyed Works*, although this new volume, likely composed between 1958 and 1960, contained nothing from the original typescript. The editors conclude that now "the title refers to the event itself . . . rather than the actual poems in the book. Lamantia seemingly used the 'Destroyed Works' typescript as a model . . . but filling [it] with more recent content."[22]

Garrett Caples concludes that "Lamantia thought nothing of condemning a whole body of his own work on the basis of its perceived philosophical, moral, or spiritual failings."[23] Creative destruction has long been a watchword of the avant-garde, from Marinetti's *distruggere i musei* to Valerie Solanas's one-woman Society for Cutting Up Men. In his own way, Lamantia manages to take what appears to be an absolute dead end: the "renunciation of his life as a poet," and turn it into yet another kind of inspiration. For readers of Lamantia's work, the 1950s are a vexing period, fraught with contradictions and disavowals yet necessary to come to terms with to grasp the now worlded multiplicity and complexity of the poet's oeuvre. The aesthetic and political radicalism of Breton and Rexroth remains, but it is now enriched by Lamantia's interest in and experience with indigenous cultural practices in North America—filtered in part through the dissident, "anthropological" surrealism of Antonin Artaud—his ever-deepening immersion in a variety of hermetic and occult traditions, and by the fertile ground of the Beat movement and San Francisco Renaissance. Following Rob Wilson's understanding of conversion as necessarily multiple and ongoing, I want to suggest that this entire period, which encompasses *Tau*, *Ekstasis*, and *Destroyed Works*, is for Lamantia one of continual and intensely productive conversion, an always proliferating line of flight.[24]

The brief poem "Scorpion Bite" that appears in *Ekstasis* is only a thinly veiled account of his initial conversion experience in Mexico:

> mozart the light of day light beams are fingers
> are antique clouds
> are loadstones
> light beams entangled, heaven and the god enter my breast
> Christ is the marvellous! (92)

Lamantia later described his ordeal with the scorpion in similarly epiphanic terms.[25] The final line of the poem, which identifies Christ with "the marvellous" (i.e., the surreal), stages surrealism's supersession by the Church in Lamantia's life and writing. The reference to Mozart that opens the poem might feel incongruous, but it actually points back to the Cora *yahnah* ceremony that also played a role in the poet's spiritual crisis. In his interview with Meltzer, he recalled, "Once inside the open temple, about forty men seated themselves, a third of them wearing stylized priestly garb of glimmering cloths. On one side of the circle I remember about five of them playing curious-looking bow-and-string instruments; others played flutes. . . . Musically, I heard complements to Bach, Mozart,

Balinese classical music, and Indian ragas! An amazing experience, communal and transcendent." This worlded musical assemblage is evoked at the very beginning of "Scorpion Bite" and hints at a multiplicity of causes for the poet's conversion. The painful sting of the scorpion may have precipitated his reaching out to the Virgin of Guadalupe, but the stage had already been set by the Cora ceremony. "It was there," he told Meltzer, "that I began to return to the Church, to my own roots, inspired by their vision and ritual" (143).

But elsewhere, Lamantia equivocated. In his interview with John Suiter he said, "I had converted, or thought I had," to explain his decision not to read his own work at the Six Gallery.[26] A key sequence from the posthumously published "Destroyed Works" typescript reenacts Lamantia's drama in Mexico. In section 27 he writes ecstatically, "I see *you* ghost of the scorpion that God bless it bit me / Scorpion that drove me in a poisonous 24 hr circuit / to LA MUERTE / death (o yes! yes! yes!)." But in the very next section he is profoundly ambivalent, even self-mocking:

What's all this howling about
Do you really want to break out
If you did where would you go
Do you want poetry

It's above you
Do you seek nirvana grace joy
It is under you. (166)

Here Lamantia slyly alludes to the Beat world of "howling" poets (e.g., Ginsberg) who must "seek nirvana" where else but down below, on the pavement, underground. These lines are playful enough, reminiscent of "High" ("O beato solitudo! where have I flown to?"), but they also betray a deep-seated conflict about Lamantia's future and purpose as a writer. They expose a psyche struggling to assimilate what the poet calls a "multilayered inspiration."[27] Section 36 of "Destroyed Works," which he titles "Cora"—it is one of the longer sections and one of only a few given a title—Lamantia concludes with these lines:

Saw the high priest and chief
a shriveled up old man in the morning
sweeping out his thatch hut like an old woman
He grinned, too,
            when I told him of the Washo Circle,
      peyote rite of the half moon

"No! no!—here little white boy we've got the FULL MOON
not just this half moon you've been raving about
but, sonny, you're not going to see it!
                NOT FOR A HUNDRED YEARS!" (172–73)

Although Lamantia does not spell out the immediate cause of this sudden resentment from both parties, but clearly the speaker is seen by the
"high priest and chief" as an interloper, one who could never really hope
to gain access to the tribe's secret magic. The "Washo Circle" refers to a
peyote rite that Lamantia had participated in at Lake Tahoe, California,
in 1954. By then, he was something of a peyote connoisseur; many credit
him with introducing the hallucinogen to the Bay Area bohemian scene.
Lamantia had hoped to follow in Artaud's footsteps by participating in
a peyote ceremony with the Cora, but he arrived in the Sierra Madre at
the wrong time of year. The final line of "Cora," however, expresses an
even greater, epistemic asynchronicity between their ceremonial calendar
and the solitary questing of this "little white boy." The speaker perhaps
consoles himself by calling attention to André Breton's praise of the poet
as "a voice that rises once in a hundred years," but given that the conversion dramatized in "Destroyed Works" is at first a conversion *away* from
surrealism, his past achievements offer little consolation.

Lamantia sounds like Paul Bowles describing the Tangier of yore when
he discusses Mexico City with Meltzer. "Mexico City was wonderfully
habitable in the 1950s" (143), he explains, also echoing Burroughs's
assessment in letters to Kerouac from the early 1950s, urging Kerouac
to leave the States and join him there. In fact, some unpublished prose
pieces that Lamantia wrote in Mexico sound an awful lot like Burroughs
(channeling Dashiell Hammett); for example, "I was moving into Mexico for the bribe. A hundred dollars to Sanchez, the border official in
Juarez. With the five thousand under my belt, I could flood with Aztec,
Zapotec, and Mayan. Perez would be waiting for me in Mexico City
with the contacts in the villages throughout the south, where in each of
them local Indian dealers would have the objects or go collect them."[28]
A little further along, he sounds even more like Burroughs: "Sitting in a
torpor, late afternoon, after guzzling two bloody Marys—still too early
to write—suddenly remember Dr. Rivera who provided me few times
with prescriptions for morphine," and he writes of an acquaintance in
Mexico, "Her addiction is classic." For Lamantia no less than for Burroughs and Kerouac, Mexico clearly represents a space of transgression,
one involving, yes, drugs and dissipation, and apparently in Lamantia's

case the black market of Indian artifacts, but, more important, the kind of performative, textual transgression that opens up his work to a panoply of worlded influences.

Lamantia continues to conjure images of Mexico with Meltzer, describing Mexico City as "a great city, enormous, on a giant plateau stretching for miles in all directions. I walked a good part of it by day and by night. Rich with sights and smells, very unlike the United States in those days, and certainly not at all like Europe, though there were many baroque churches, many of them with subtle Indian interlacings" (143). His image of Mexico City on its "plateau"—another favorite of Deleuze—corresponds topographically to the rhizomic textual networks that structure such works as *Tau* and *Mexico City Blues*. Both geographically and figuratively, Lamantia's "plateau" extends across Mexico to form a heterodox assemblage that transgresses borders of religion, race, and nation. Lamantia figures this entire process as a "crisis of conversion" leading to the rupture described earlier.[29] Unlike Burroughs, Lamantia openly acknowledged Artaud as a trailblazer; for Artaud as well as Lamantia, their experiences in Mexico ultimately led back to the cross (though much to Artaud's chagrin, anyway).[30] But Lamantia's was not a simple return to the Catholic faith of his youth. Within the assemblage of influence, there will always be a trace or remainder of other forms and histories; much like the "subtle Indian interlacings" on Mexico's churches, Lamantia's poetry was henceforth woven from the diverse strands of Catholic and Native American wisdom and tradition, Eastern religion, European surrealism, "revolutionary political theory and mystical expression."[31]

Lamantia's interest in Latin American baroque art and architecture is to be expected. It calls to mind Alejo Carpentier, who defined the baroque not as a style but a spirit that transcends (transgresses) the fixed periods of art and literary history. According to Carpentier, the baroque "arises where there is transformation, mutation or innovation" and allows him to speak of the Zapotec temple at Mitla in the same breath as Beethoven and Schoenberg.[32] Carpentier's description of "proliferating cells" (97) that abound in baroque art and literature resonates in turn with Deleuze's book on the baroque, *The Fold*, where *fold* comes to stand in for the assemblage, or rhizome, as the Deleuze's primary figure of multiplicity, immanence, and heterogeneity. Carpentier's genealogy of the baroque reads like Breton's surrealist genealogy in the first *Surrealist Manifesto* and includes Rabelais and Cervantes alongside Baudelaire, Ducasse ("the Montevidean"), and Rimbaud. Carpentier considers surrealism itself to be "totally baroque" (98). The indigenous carvings admired by Lamantia, like the Cora altar constructed "at the far end of the church, away from the Catholic altar," provide a model for the kind of indigenous transmutation that will lead eventually to baroque transformations of European modernism in Latin America and the Caribbean through Martí, Césaire, Etienne Léro, and others.[33] Like the diasporic surrealism that, in Lamantia's view, fulfilled the originary promise of Breton's earlier manifestoes, all kinds of creative activity arise from the tension between rootedness, dynamism, and movement and must be oriented toward the future. This is as true of Lamantia's surrealism as of the ecopoetics of his later work.

"A Close Phalanx, Radical, Ardent, Progressive"

The San Francisco Renaissance far exceeds the involvement of its Beat participants, yet even Michael Davidson, who sets out to tell a different story of the Renaissance, begins his account with the Six Gallery reading —if only to call it an "enabling fiction" that helped establish the San Francisco Renaissance and continues to condition its critical reception in the decades since.[34] To open up a new history, Davidson highlights the distinctions between individual poets and between rival camps. Describing the evening billed as "Six Poets at the Six Gallery," an event that, ironically for Davidson, "has come to epitomize the spirit of the age," he notes the following:

> Despite Kerouac's ecstatic picture of it [in *The Dharma Bums*], the San Francisco Renaissance was by no means unified, nor did it necessarily revolve around the figures who read at the Six Gallery. Two of them—Gary Snyder and Philip Whalen—were absent from the scene during many of the crucial years. Rexroth was, for the most part, a reluctant participant— and ultimately an antagonist. Two major poets of the period—Robert Duncan and Jack Spicer, both of whom were intimately associated with the formation of the Six Gallery—were not part of the reading, nor did they identify the Beat movement as "their" renaissance. Sectarian rivalries among persons, manifestoes, and subgroups within the city fragmented the scene, and when journalists attempted to define some kind of common ground, they had to fall back on vague references to exotic religions and anti-establishment attitudes.[35]

Are the writers and artists of the San Francisco Renaissance really any different from the Dadaists or the surrealists or the situationists, each group with its infighting and its expulsions and its "enabling fictions"? The San Francisco Renaissance, like the various movements of the historical avant-garde, is thoroughly and necessarily heterogeneous. As F. O. Matthiessen's pioneering work was keen to show, the American Renaissance of the 1850s had its tensions, but, like Davidson, he was also able to demonstrate that such tensions were more productive than destructive, "enabling" writers, in a dialectical manner, to develop and transform and become self-aware and self-critical.[36] The Beat movement in and around San Francisco in the 1950s and 1960s may not be synonymous with the San Francisco Renaissance either, but that one evening at the Six Gallery—its context and aftermath—has largely determined the reception of Lamantia's poetry. A brief look at those involved that night (and those who were conspicuously absent) will illuminate the contours of a very different literary assemblage. Finally, much of the thinking that emerges from the Renaissance—however one chooses to define it—does so in the mode of the subterranean rhizome: from Davidson's emphasis on (oppositional) *community*, to Jack Spicer's *poetry as dictation*, to Robert Duncan's *open field poetics*, to Gary Snyder's worlded *ecos*.

The poets who participated in the reading were Michael McClure, Philip Lamantia, Allen Ginsberg, Gary Snyder, and Philip Whalen. The sixth poet was master of ceremonies Kenneth Rexroth, the grandfather and impresario of the San Francisco Renaissance. Jack Kerouac famously took donations for wine, got drunk, and shouted *Go!* during Ginsberg's reading of his then unfinished "Howl." The reading was an assemblage in the sense that the six poets came from very different places with very distinct poetics and aesthetics and very different views about the role of the poet and of poetry. Even as these six visions merged to form the central "enabling fiction" of the San Francisco Renaissance, their differences remained incommensurable. The rhizomic or subterranean text-network, like the Beat movement, is heterogeneous and multiple, and this heterogeneity manifested itself even at the "inaugural" event of the Six Gallery reading. Some divergences are clear: Snyder's nature poetry, for example, is a world apart from Ginsberg's apocalyptic urbanism in "Howl," while the different approaches to Buddhism represented by Japhy Ryder (Snyder) and Ray Smith (Kerouac) in Kerouac's *Dharma Bums*—which famously opens with Kerouac's account of the Six Gallery reading— become the source of that novel's productive tensions. Michael McClure later points out such differences in an interview with Jonah Raskin, who reported, "From McClure's point of view, Allen manifested his 'socialism' at the Six Gallery reading night. Snyder manifested his 'Buddhist anarchism,' while Phil Whalen manifested his 'gentleness of consciousness and conscience,'" and so on.[37]

The following day, Lawrence Ferlinghetti, owner of City Lights books, sent Ginsberg a telegram reading, "I greet you at the beginning of a great career. When do I get the manuscript?"[38] Echoing Emerson's famous praise for Whitman upon first reading *Leaves of Grass*, Ferlinghetti establishes a direct line between what was transpiring in San Francisco back to the so-called American Renaissance a century earlier. Born in New York City, Ferlinghetti had moved to California after receiving his PhD from the Sorbonne, where he studied with the assistance of the G.I. Bill. Drawn to the city in large part by Rexroth's long presence there, he taught briefly at the Jesuit-run University of San Francisco before becoming involved with and eventually purchasing City Lights. The bookstore became a meeting place in the great tradition of Sylvia Beach's Shakespeare and Company in Paris. City Lights press was an important front in the paperback revolution, and its eclectic back catalog is an assemblage unto itself that includes not just the well-known "Pocket Poets" series but also the *Artaud Anthology*, Deleuze's *Spinoza*, and works by Genet and Lorca. The manner in which Ferlinghetti describes his first impressions of San Francisco as a displaced *European* city in the early collection *Pictures of the Gone World* (1955) can be compared to the layered geographies of Latin America and Morocco in Burroughs's *Naked Lunch* or to Kerouac's topographic syncretism in *Mexico City Blues*. (Paul Bowles drew Burroughs from South America to Morocco just as Rexroth drew Ferlinghetti from Paris to San Francisco.)

Longtime Beat scholar Bill Morgan's recent travel guide *Beat Atlas: A State by State Guide to the Beat Generation in America* makes little to no distinction between the Beats and non-Beat iterations of the same rebellious spirit among midcentury U.S. writers. On the East Coast the Beats share the page with New York School and Black Mountain poets, and on the West Coast the San Francisco Renaissance is treated very much as a unified movement. If in his work on the Renaissance, Davidson laments the fact that in standard literary histories of the period Beat hegemony has forced out or to the margins figures like Spicer, Robin Blaser, and to a lesser extent Duncan, Morgan's move toward inclusivity means that readers can glimpse the Renaissance in all its messiness. He writes quite a bit about Spicer, for example, who was openly hostile to Beats yet integral to the story both Morgan and Davidson wish to tell. Rexroth emceed the Six Gallery reading, but he wouldn't exactly be called pro-Beat. Spicer, a founding member of the Six Gallery, was absent that night. Spicer helped shape the Berkeley poetry scene with Duncan and Blaser, then through his very presence in North Beach and his "Poetry as Magic" workshop at San Francisco State University, where Lamantia would briefly teach in the early 1970s. The circle that included Spicer, Duncan, Blaser, also Joanne Kyger, was an important foil to the Beats, whom Spicer felt were mere tourists and interlopers, more interested in poetry as a lifestyle choice than as pure devotion to the Muse.

Duncan remained on better terms with Ginsberg, and the two had a definite impact on each other's poetry. Duncan's unprecedented 1944 essay "The Homosexual in Society" set the stage for the frank sexuality of "Howl." Duncan was impressed by Kerouac's "Belief and Technique in Spontaneous Prose," which he found tacked to the wall of Ginsberg's San Francisco hotel room, and Duncan's "open field poetics," with its emphasis on the "breath line," captivated Ginsberg in turn. In the notion of a rhizomic assemblage of influence, "influence" does not simply (or even primarily) refer to one writer's influence on another writer but rather to everything that enters into and shapes a text: this rhizomic approach to composition that applies to Duncan's *Opening of the Field* as much as to *Mexico City Blues*. Perhaps it is not surprising, then, that Davidson places Kerouac's spontaneous prose in the same category as Spicer's "dictation" theory of poetry, arguing that Kerouac's method, particularly in *Mexico City Blues*, "represents an analogous attempt to capture the very contingent and occasional nature of reality without representing it" (21). Along with Duncan's "open field" poetics, Spicer's dictation is yet another iteration of the aesthetics of assemblage that Beat poets share with nonaffiliated Renaissance poets, a fundamentally nonpersonal view of artistic creation—in the first of his three major "Vancouver lectures," given just months before his death in 1965 at age forty, Spicer describes poetry as a "thing from Outside"—and an understanding of literary influence that has much in common with the Deleuzian rhizome.

The heterogeneity of any assemblage is what allows books like Davidson's (and Matthiessen's) to be written. "The point to make here," according to Davidson, "is that, even in its self-described inaugural moment, the San Francisco Renaissance was diverse, relying for its unanimity on a spirit of camaraderie and fellow-feeling more than on shared aesthetic beliefs" (4). But is a movement more properly based on "shared aesthetic beliefs" than on a Whitmanian "camaraderie and fellow-feeling," as Davidson seems to imply? Perhaps the Beats are a model for a movement based on the former. This is certainly the spirit of Morgan's *Beat Atlas*, which translates the Beat phenomenon into wholly spatial terms: "Being so diverse in origin, their writings were not dictated by a single, regional characteristic, so the Beat movement became a national thrust, a joining of like-minded, kindred spirits."[39] It turns out that such disjunctures—geographic, aesthetic, political—are precisely what allow a space for community to develop within the cracks and interstices. Davidson goes on to say, "Although there is little continuity among the San Francisco poets, there are points of general agreement that derive from the activist position," meaning that *politics* united the various factions of the San Francisco Renaissance much more than aesthetics ever did.[40]

The central theme of community runs like a thread through the many accounts of the San Francisco Renaissance, including the queer cultures of Michael Davidson's account.[41] According to Davidson, the writers of the San Francisco Renaissance manifested "their collective role as a kind of oppositional sign" (27), and the Beats in particular are significant for having developed "alternative forms of community." One could use the term "oppositional community" here in ways that point both inward and outward. Davidson admits, "Literary infighting and warfare, rather than undermining the sense of community, are important components in strengthening resolve and developing a strong platform." The new communities of the San Francisco counterculture "were based on shared literary interests, to be sure, but they also reflected sexual and social preferences as well, some years before the sexual and gay liberations. And because sexual preferences often led to (or derived from) alternative theories of family and group, they prefigured the communalist 'lifestyle' movements of the late 1960s" (28). Like Snyder, Davidson sees the link between the Beats and the hippies as a shared commitment to communalism and "totally integrated world culture."[42] He writes, "The attraction of such community has to do with its ability to synthesize matters or art, politics, and social theory into lifestyle, which can then be inherited and extended to the larger culture" (29). One might say, with Peter Bürger, that as a proper avant-garde group the Beats sought to dissolve the boundaries between art and politics and the "praxis of life." Finally, in terms of the San Francisco Renaissance as an assemblage, Davidson's analysis is instructive when it urges that "we should see their work as a collage of sources, both romantic and modernist, that attempts to revive some sense of community destroyed by war" (32).

To tell the story of the San Francisco Renaissance is to tell the story of the eventual shift from the Beat Generation to the Hip Generation, from the beatniks to the hippies. Richard Brautigan would be an interesting figure to consider in this regard, as would Ken Kesey and the Merry Pranksters (Neal Cassady from Beat muse to prankster hero). Within the Six Gallery network, it is Gary Snyder, somewhat surprisingly, who turns out to have been one of the most eloquent and sympathetic chroniclers of this transitional moment, and in ways that resonate with our worlded vision of the Beats. (In 1969 William Everson would call Snyder "the best earth man now writing.")[43] What Snyder chose to read at the Six Gallery—the poem "A Berry Feast"—reflected his training in anthropology and interest in the native cultures of the Pacific Northwest, an interest both aesthetic and ethical and having to do with learning to live in and with one's *ecos*, or home. In his most significant prose work during the pivotal years of the mid- to late 1960s, Snyder recast the San Francisco Renaissance in terms of his worlded view of social formations and social change. The texts collected in *Earth House Hold* include journal entries from his time in Japan and India, reflections on the U.S. counterculture, and notes on "Buddhism and the Coming Revolution." Its title, which puns on the root of "ecology" (*ecos* is Greek for "house") and breaks the conventional bonds between "house" and "hold," implies an act, as in *worlding*, of creating a world in the act of gathering it to oneself, gathering oneself and others into a community. *Carpe mundum.* Gathering oneself *into* the local environment and seeing it in the nearness of its totality.

Of particular interest is Snyder's pair of sympathetic essays on the hippies. One, drawing its themes in part from Whitman's poem, is evocatively titled "Passage to More Than India." At a basic level, this is Snyder's way of saying the revolution will be a revolution of the mind. One does not necessarily have to follow in his footsteps and go study Zen in Japan for two years, taking a break to travel through India studying erotic carvings in temples. In fact, Snyder writes, "Those who do not have the money or time to go to India or Japan, but who think a great deal about the wisdom traditions, have remarkable results when they take LSD. The *Bhagavad-Gita*, the Hindu mythologies, *The Serpent Power*, the *Lankavatara-sūtra*, the *Upanishads*, the *Hevajra-tantra*, the *Majanirvana-tantra*—to name a few texts—become, they say, finally clear to them. They often feel they must radically reorganize their lives to harmonize with such insights" (108–09).

A transformation in consciousness can happen anywhere, but for Snyder enlightenment is still a matter of knowing one's place. Just a couple pages earlier, he has written, "Peyote and acid have a curious way of tuning some people in to the local soil. The strains and stresses deep beneath one in the rock, the flow and fabric of wildlife around, the human history of Indians on this continent. Older powers become evident" (107–8). Expanding one's consciousness is neither a *going-out* there nor a *going-in* here (i.e., one's mind/ego). It is, rather, a *going-down* into the soil, into one's own rootedness in space and time—what Nietzsche's Zarathustra calls "the meaning of the earth."[44] And connecting all this to the great wisdom traditions becomes yet another way of bringing near the "world-horizon" and recognizing that the over there is the right here right now.

The occasion for these reflections is the Great Human Be-In (January 1967), the "Gathering of the Tribes" that laid the groundwork and set the stage for the so-called Summer of Love. This is where Timothy Leary told those gathered to "turn on, tune in, drop out." Snyder begins his essay with a consideration of the two famous posters announcing the event. He describes them, the event, and those who participated:

> The two posters: one based on a photograph of a Shaivite sadhu with his long matted hair, ashes and beard; the other based on an old etching of a Plains Indian approaching a powwow on his horse—the carbine that had been cradled in his left arm replaced by a guitar. The Indians, and the Indian. The tribes were Berkeley, North Beach, Big Sur, Marin County, Los Angeles, and the host, Haight-Ashbury. Outriders were present from New York, London and Amsterdam. Out on the polo field that day the splendidly clad ab/originals often fell into clusters, with children, a few even under banners. These were the clans. (103)

Snyder then launches into a kind of hippie ethnography, describing their communes, their living arrangements, their kinship dynamics, their beliefs, and other details. Most important for Snyder, the hippies are creating alternative forms of family and plugged into a communal awakening. In "Passage to More Than India" and its companion essay, "A Gathering of the Tribes," Snyder is being tongue in cheek, but not entirely; he sincerely (at least in 1967) wants to give these "new," or "ab/original," modes of living their proper due and legitimacy. His play on words: "ab/original" —as in *not* original—brings us to the heart of Snyder's argument. The hippies are reenacting older forms and making them live again, creating a true assemblage by whatever means are at hand: drugs, Eastern religion, Marxism, rock and roll, and so on. And along with the local groups, or "tribes," Snyder acknowledges the presence of "outriders" (which becomes an important term for Anne Waldman) and fellow travelers who form a network stretching across the nation and, indeed, across the globe.

Snyder appeals the figure of the Indian, or rather "The Indians, and the Indian," but when he writes about a new sensitivity to "the human history of Indians on this continent" in a piece that also invokes Whitman's "Passage to India," Snyder's juxtaposition creates a curious (for Snyder) relativism and even validation of Columbus's originary malapropism. Snyder knows better, so what's the point? When he refers to the two posters for the Be-in, that too evokes the familiar Beat syncretism of

Kerouac's "worldwide fellaheen," but something more productive and worthwhile is happening as well. Just like the book's title, *Earth House Hold*, the connection exists only in the act of noting it or, rather, *creating* it. "The Indians" are not equivalent to "the Indian," but just as the hippies are seeking to create (gather together) a new community by returning to older social forms with a difference (because assembled), the connection is always going to be anachronistic, idiosyncratic; revolutionary time will always be out of joint. Something similar occurs in Snyder's "Buddhism and the Coming Revolution," where he points to the historicity of all religions (even Eastern ones): "Historically, Buddhist philosophers have failed to analyze out the degree to which ignorance and suffering are caused or encouraged by social factors. . . . Consequently the major concern of Buddhist philosophy is epistemology and 'psychology' with little attention paid to historical or sociological problems" (90). Snyder then fashions what I am calling a dialectic of Buddhism that points to a third way between capitalism and communism, one also informed by "recent findings in anthropology and psychology" (91), by anarchist politics and the Industrial Workers of the World, by the then burgeoning ecological movement, and so on. For Snyder, the revolution is imminent and *immanent*; he quotes the IWW slogan, "Forming the new society within the shell of the old" (92), and voices the almost Burroughsian desire to see that this new society will be, in short, a "totally integrated world culture" (93).

With *Earth House Hold* Snyder also wants to move beyond, or find a middle path or third way between nationalism and individualism. This is why the "tribe" appeals to him so much. He does call the hippies a "specifically 'American' incarnation" of a much-longer antinomian tradition (104), but the fact of their Americanness is contingent rather than essentialist and matters only insofar as the U.S. counterculture is rooted in more local soils. The history that Snyder lays out in "Passage to More Than India" is a familiar one; it links the hippies to mystical traditions in Europe and in the East, to Christian heretics, to Sufis, to Hindu tantrics. Each group is plugged into a unique time and place and so retains a subversive power, perhaps stronger than Kerouac's (through Spengler) worldwide fellaheen. And yet they form "outcroppings" in the worlded, earthly topology of what Snyder calls the "Great Subculture which runs underground all through history." What links these various "outcroppings" is the continuity of the subterranean, and what separates them from the established order at any given time is their "transmission" of a "community style of life" (115–16).

Both natives of San Francisco, Lamantia and Snyder are seldom men-

tioned in the same breath, even in Beat studies, except maybe when talking about the lineup at the Six Gallery. Snyder's rugged naturalism seems
worlds away from Lamantia's mannered verse. But, starting in the late
1970s, Lamantia began to immerse himself in the world of nature. He took
up bird watching and spent lots of time traveling up and down the West
Coast, camping, observing the flora and fauna, and studying the indigenous cultures of California. His writing during this period morphs into
something akin to what would now be called ecopoetry, but of course
with a distinctively Lamantian flair—always bringing surrealism, mysticism, and various hermetic traditions into and out of the picture: forming new assemblages and revealing new multiplicities that were there all
along. The poet's interest in nature and ornithology should not be seen
as a quaint diversion or a wrong turn; these new concerns are integral
to the poetics of his late career. Birding in particular becomes a means
for Lamantia to organize and even reconceive the dharma, or practice,
of his life's work; as he says in the title of a late poem, "Passionate Ornithology Is Another Kind of Yoga." The poet who reemerges in the 1981
collection *Becoming Visible*—which inaugurates the period of nature
poetry that culminates in *Meadowlark West* (1986)—strives to obtain
an anthrotopographical perspective, that is to say, a deep understanding
of the ways in which human cultures, particularly the indigenous cultures of the American West, have attuned themselves to their geographic
surroundings. He is interested how a group's rites and rituals, folk tales
and characters, dance and music, are manifestations of the surrounding
landscape, and what those links suggest about our lived experience of the
world around us. And only from the profound rootedness of all culture
arises the planetarity of a shared *oikos* or "earth house hold" (as Snyder
figures it).

Lamantia's curiosity in this direction did not simply appear ex nihilo
in the late 1970s. Or it might be more correct to say his later ecopoetics
now informs his understanding of prior experiences and travels, including his travels in Mexico. Talking with John Suiter about his two months
in the Sierra Madre with the Cora Indians, Lamantia makes the case that,
to fathom Cora society, one must take in the immensity of the landscape
as well: a remote, dramatic totality of valley and plateau, stone and sky.
"It's the rise of Nayar," he says. "Everything there is. They're the Nayarit
[or Cora], and that's their river, and their territory—and they are *unde-
feated* to this minute." With his exultant description Lamantia stresses
the correspondence between language, landscape, and identity: Nayar/
Nayarit. Such symmetry, he seems to suggest, between name, place, and

being is what makes poetry possible—the logocentric dream of an originary poetry of *naming*. Such themes of culture's rootedness and human
landscape analogies are not at all departures from Lamantia's surrealism,
either. A major preoccupation of the surrealists, especially the so-called
dissident surrealists around Georges Bataille and the journal *Documents*,
has to do with what James Clifford calls "surrealist anthropology." Artaud
displays a similar mindset in his influential writings on the Tarahumara,
where he describes a kind of living archaeology present all around them.

In "Redwood Highway," the long (by Lamantia's standards) poem in
six bulleted sections that opens the collection, readers are immediately
presented with the near-far dialectic that organizes so much worlded
Beat writing. The poem signals Lamantia's new immersion in the natural
world—which on the surface, at least, *does* seem like a radical break
from the kinds of hieratic and hermetic poems he had been writing since
a teenager in the 1940s, and its title provides readers with a very real
and specific setting: the redwood forests of northern California. Yet, after
setting up clear expectations of localism, the poem begins with references
to Giordano Bruno and Ibn Arabi, a seventeenth-century Italian panthe-
ist and astrologer and a Sufi master. As its name suggests, "Redwood
Highway" is a traveling poem, and Bruno and Arabi and the wisdom
traditions they suggest are soon connected to more local cartographies:

> The powers from out there on the western horizon of Walpi
> The San Francisco Peaks blowing their tops
> Runners from the Chumash sprayed
> Teleported
> Over sierras hot lands deserts
> . . . .
> Shamans at Mount Diablo touched by antlers of light. (295)

The poem's several pages move mostly across California's variegated terrain, and the most insistent pattern of reference has to do with local features,
in terms of both geography and culture (with characteristic wordplay):

> Climbing your *rig-ridge*
> > *rigorous nose*
> . . . .
> To keep memory of you Yurok of the north
> Albino deer dancers dream over Mount Shasta
> On these Ohlone shores of the central dream
> Moon dancing the sun. (297)

The long form of the poem allows the poet to weave in a multiplicity of allusions. Painter Giorgio di Chirico makes an appearance, and the speaker takes us "Through waves of lemonade seas ah Charles Fourier" (298). A number of curious references to Mount Shasta and Lemuria appear in "Redwood Highway" and other poems of the period. Lamantia is tapping into a whole mythology surrounding the Cascades peak, which has it that the inhabitants of an Atlantean lost continent, Lemuria, have reemerged on Shasta. It must have been quite alluring for Lamantia to consider this locus of theosophic and occult thought right here in his backyard. The fairly extensive notes to the poem (atypical for the poet) suggest that Lamantia is becoming much more concerned with the immediate spatiotemporal contexts of his work, a tacit assertion that an awareness of these contexts and their referents is now necessary to fully appreciate the poem's meaning.

"Redwood Highway," like *Becoming Visible* as a whole, marks a transition from the gnomic verse of the 1960s and 1970s to the full-on ecological consciousness of the 1980s. And as is often the case, this new-found eco-consciousness goes hand in hand with a raised *political* consciousness. In a sense, Lamantia has come full circle in the poems leading up to and included in *Meadowlark West*, the last full volume of new poems published during his lifetime. They are a logical extension of his turn toward naturalism and radical politics with Rexroth four decades earlier. His interest in ornithology and birding is reflected in the fact that birds are now the central image of his *Meadowlark West*–era poems. Birds have always been a potent element of Lamantia's symbology. But up until now, they have been primarily that—symbols. (One can think back to the "wingless bird . . . half-a-bird," threading through its prison, that opened his poem to Rexroth, in *Erotic Poems*, to take one particularly apt example.) Starting in the early 1980s, birds will take on a much greater presence in Lamantia's writing; they are real entities with a material existence independent of their lyric value. They are also a barometer, it turns out, of all kinds of world-historical forces. The poetic assemblage grows denser still. In the poem "Meadowlark West," published separately in 1982, birds are still connected to legend and myth and native wisdom: "Coyote Hummingbird Owl are rivers of thought / . . . pits of correspondence over the land / Birds the dream tongues warble Iroquois Mojave Ohlone" (334). The brief poem "Birder's Lament," published a few years later, is poignantly domestic and deceptively simple:

Robin, rare Robin at my window
below the introduced tree, pecking black seeds

> Blessed be, this
> otherwise difficult day
> gracious vision, Robin, of your mandibles
> to counterbalance the Killdeer birds crushed
> on their nests by giant tractors at Crissy Field. (335)

Behind every beautiful thing lies a horror—the ethical image par excellence. Crissy Field is the former U.S. Army airfield on San Francisco's northern bayshore, whose construction laid waste to an important estuary and migration site. (With the airfield decommissioned, the area has since been allowed to revert back to marshland.) An ironic twist occurs in the second line, with the "introduced tree" a quiet corollary to Crissy Field's violent invasiveness. Much of San Francisco itself was built on sand dunes and landfill: we are all "invasive" here, the poet seems to say.

The more substantial "Poetics by Pluto," published alongside "Birder's Lament," fleshes out a similar connection between militarism (e.g., Crissy Field) and ecological degradation. It also begins at home before ballooning outward: "The dendrophobe across the way just demolished nests / of finches sparrows other possible birds." But in the following lines there is also the possible for renewal and rebirth through the turnings of far greater world-cycles: "Wild in the city with green teeth up through the pavements Phoenix is that bird / From ashes of the kali-yuga / another root in the great tradition." "Green teeth" might have been just one more vaguely surrealist image of the sort that abound in the poet's corpus, but the preceding several poems have by now prepared readers for this now beatific reference to a plant sprouting up from a crack in the city sidewalk. It quite literally makes its "house in the cracks of the pavement!" In "Poetics by Pluto," birds may augur a coming utopia: "Better falconry / than the definitive end Better the poetry of the birds / Up from salty deeps, Dianas, to rule us and reweave a scallop shell sacred to Venus / There's a cleavage possible" (335). A turn occurs about halfway through the poem with the full force of an ecological apocalypse:

> Mockingbirds are returning to Frisco
> to lift the ancient taboo
> hummingbirds by the milliards at the feeder stations
> Meanwhile empires are vomiting
> not some nineteenth-century phano-sphere of coming blight (trotting
>   castles) but
> sudden death for a whole continent of forest here & everywhere
>   sparrows strangled midair with the last condors

> situate Acid Rain and the Green House Effect [cf. Snyder's *Earth House Hold*]
> plague-lined trees oil-slick birds. (336)

Sparrows and finches, mockingbirds and hummingbirds: these are not exotic images. They are the urban everyday, where inspiration or terror is never far off. A few lines later, he points to a likely culprit in the event of global annihilation: "How do I feel? rotten, misnamed 'hysterical' who calls freely for the Annulment of / Nuclear Physics / as if technē were the issue and / not a cosmic catastrophe" (336), a point he drives home in "Elegy on the Migrating Nightingales Massacred by Nuclear Physics at Chernobyl." The immediate cause of this poem is clear enough, and so is Lamantia's manner of engaging with the subject matter by looking specifically at the nightingales' sad end. That most lyrical of all birds, whose name "has never ceased to signal the harmony of the world" (340), has been sacrificed on the altar of a technological arms race.

Asked by Meltzer about the differences between the East and West Coast scenes of the 1950s, Lamantia replies that "San Francisco was more political, utopian, and environmentally aware" (146), and when asked about the 1970s Bay Area punk scene, he confesses, "I find all that perfectly in line with most of my life, starting in the revolutionary heart of Surrealism and later in the Beat rebellion." The punkers who once convened at North Beach's Mabuhey Gardens and the On Broadway likewise sought to obtain Ginsberg's "bottom-up vision of society." At the same time, Lamantia derides the post–San Francisco Renaissance language poets as "floating over San Francisco" (148)—that is to say, about as far as one can get from one's *house in the cracks of the pavement*. In *Earth House Hold*, Gary Snyder used the Human Be-In as an occasion to reflect on the legacy of the Beats, to show how the Beats of the 1950s have passed the torch to the next generation, the hippies of the 1960s. He suggests in true Blakean fashion that both the Beats and the hippies are manifestations of an ancient tradition of antinomian thought. In their alternative living arrangements in particular, the hippies were actually returning to a very traditional mode of living: communal, egalitarian, and ecologically tuned in.

Snyder was far from the only one during this period making such connections, especially between the Beat Generation and the Hip Generation. In 1968 a San Francisco–wide art festival declared that a "Rolling Renaissance" was taking place, one that linked the Beats of the mid-1950s back to earlier bohemian formations, to Rexroth and his circle, to innovations in postwar visual art (primarily through abstract expressionism and action painting), dance, music (jazz, etc.), poetry (the Berkeley, then San Francisco, Renaissance of Duncan, Spicer, and others), and ahead to the hippie era. As the renaissance rolled from North Beach to Haight-Ashbury, it also tapped into the *longue durée* of bohemianism and avant-garde movements in the United States and Europe, as it drew clear inspiration from that earlier American Renaissance of Emerson, Whitman, and Thoreau. All these points are made rather explicit in the program and essays marking the 1968 event.[45] The writers and artists whose work was celebrated under the Rolling Renaissance banner and who contributed their reflections on the recent history of the San Francisco scene for the program make up a wonderful cross-section of the arts. Recognizing that poetry (especially through ties to Beat poets like Ginsberg and Ferling-hetti) had come to dominate the public's impressions of the San Francisco Renaissance, they consistently stress the multiplicity of arts thriving in postwar San Francisco.

The Rolling Renaissance ephemera offer a ground-level glimpse of a movement taking stock of itself and forging connections to something larger. The fact that its contributors are working and writing from *within* the hippie moment means that a lot of claims are made about what separates them (or not) from the prior Beat Generation. The Beats are presented as alienated individual(ist)s catching the tail of the existentialist comet, whereas the hippies are communalists in art as in life. Here is a sampling of what they had to say.

Poet David Meltzer: The idea of the Beatnik, living in his strange cave with his strange brood of illegitimate kids, common-law wife, bongos and narcotics, became much more important to the public than the literature that created it. Nevertheless, a barrage of literary magazines and presses began printing, hexographing, mimeographing new work—sometimes all a publication would be would be carbon copies of a work limited to the endurance of the carbonpaper and the typist.[46]

Art critic Thomas Albright: Ten years later, the action shifts from Grant Avenue to Haight Street, and history seemingly repeats itself, but more so. . . . [This retrospective] is attempting to define some of the links in a continuing chain of creativity which has made San Francisco a major world center of underground activity since the second World War. . . . The distinctions exist, but there is a larger reality to the popular notion that lumps them all together in a growing revolutionary army, the underground spirit of the 1960s.[47]

Author and psychiatrist Francis Rigney: Here in San Francisco, there has been

an almost continuous bohemian tradition since the 1860's, when Bret
Harte's contributions to a local journal, the *Golden Era*, were signed "The
Bohemian." . . . The very first bohemian colony [in the United States] had
fraternal poverty, used opium, and suffered with malnutrition and T.B. It
also included Walt Whitman.[48]

That "very first bohemian colony" was known as the Pfaffians: a group
of artists and eccentrics who met at Pfaff's Tavern in Manhattan and
did indeed include Whitman—one more way in which Whitman's example prepares the ground for the Beats, who are now figured as "the last
of the Bohemians."[49] Taking things a step further, from bohemia to the
avant-garde and all that the distinction implies, consider the following
passage from Whitman, published in 1851, when he was still writing
for the *Brooklyn Daily Eagle*. It concerns a recent art exhibition, but as
Matthiessen notes, "most of his space was given over to arguing that a
vigorous augmentation of power would come to the work of our isolated
painters if they were joined together in a close group."[50] In a review titled
"Something about Art and Brooklyn Artists," Whitman writes,

> What a glorious result it would give, to form of these thousands [of Amer-
> ican artists] a close phalanx, ardent, radical and progressive. Now they
> are like the bundle of sticks in the fable, and, as one by one, they have no
> strength. Then, would not the advancing years foster the growth of a grand
> and true art here, fresh and youthful, worthy this republic, and this greatest
> of the ages? Would we not, at last, smile in return at the pitying smile with
> which the old art of Europe has hitherto, and not unjustly, regarded ours?[51]

This really is astonishing; barely halfway through the nineteenth century, Whitman already seems to be calling for the development of a true
avant-garde movement among America's most "ardent, radical, and progressive" artists. He even uses the same kind of martial diction ("a close
phalanx") that would later serve as the basis for the very term "avant-garde."
One may balk at Whitman's rhetorical chauvinism in the "Brooklyn Artists" review, but what Whitman means by "America" always exceeds the
nation and nationalism, and in politics to an even greater degree than in
art. Inspired by the revolutions of 1848, he declared, "I am the sworn poet
of every dauntless rebel the world over."[52] It is *this* Whitman—worlded
and radicalized—whose legacy the Beats inherit a century later.

The last couple of chapters have tried to demonstrate the usefulness,
indeed the necessity, of looking at Beat Generation writing in relation to
the historical avant-garde. At the very least, such connections help clar-

ify the Beats' place in cultural history and literary tradition, even if that tradition is what Apollinaire calls the "anti-tradition" of the avant-garde. These chapters have also begun to suggest what a Beat politics might look like, both in the abstract terms of Bürger art-life dialectic and in regard to the very real political struggles that have occupied the attention of any number of Beat writers over the years. The internationalism of the avant-garde is no less consequential for future generations of experimental, transgressive writers and artists: the worlded contours of the Beat movement are an extension of this same transnationalist impulse among earlier groups like the Dadaists and surrealists. Baraka, Joans, Kaufman, and Lamantia each created new assemblages by placing surrealism in particular in conjunction with still other influences and energies. The dense, rhizomic tangle from which Lamantia fashioned his poetry has been the subject of the present chapter. With different purposes in mind, Baraka and Joans amplify surrealism's antihegemonic potential by linking it to the black power movement in the United States and to anticolonial struggles around the world. Their work sets the stage for a broader discussion of what I venture to call a postcolonial consciousness within Beat writing.

4

CUT-UPS AND COMPOSITE CITIES: THE LATIN
AMERICAN ORIGINS OF *NAKED LUNCH*

Like Déjà Vu: "The Secret" and the Spatial Turn

Paralleling wider trends in literary and cultural studies, the past several
years have seen a spatial turn in critical approaches to the work of "Beat
Godfather" William S. Burroughs.[1] Whereas previous scholars have
tended to view Burroughs's landscapes primarily as hallucinated, night-
marish abstractions, recent critics are beginning to understand prominent settings like the Interzone of *Naked Lunch* as firmly grounded in
lived space and time. Exploring the relationship of geography, history,
and biography, Brian Edwards and others have shown how Tangier in
particular—Burroughs lived there for several pivotal years in the 1950s
and 1960s—played an active role in shaping some of Burroughs's most
important literary production and, conversely, how his work formulates
a sophisticated response to the social and political realities of Morocco
during the years just before and after independence from colonial rule.

In his chapter on Burroughs in *Morocco Bound*, Edwards argues that
"critics have in one way or another avoided a serious inquiry into the
relationship between Burroughs's major text [i.e., *Naked Lunch*] and his
response to Tangier, pushing the role of the city into the passive background" (159). He goes on to say that critics have "discounted the importance of Tangier as more than imaginative construct, even while sensing
the importance of thinking about the materiality of Tangier," which "has
led to confusion about Burroughs's political position and the Moroccan
and geopolitical context of his work" (160). The "confusion" Edwards
refers to is a response to the uncomfortable (from our enlightened, post-
orientalist vantage point) ambivalence Burroughs seems to display in
Naked Lunch and elsewhere toward decolonization in North Africa and

around the world on one hand and toward the United States' neoimperialist economic and military policy during the early years of the Cold War on the other. Ironically, in his efforts to resituate *Naked Lunch* within its specific historical and geographic contexts, Edwards all but ignores the novel's deep roots in other soils, specifically Latin America. I fully agree with him when he writes, "Rereading *Naked Lunch* in its Tangier context demonstrates the ways in which Burroughs's piercing indictment of a culture of control and a society of hypocrisy emerges from an especially rich global imagination that helps provide the energy and terms of his disruption" (161), but to truly grasp the richness of Burroughs's "global imagination" means locating Tangier and *Naked Lunch* in a much broader zone of reference and worlded critique.

This wider view brings the story back to a part of the world Burroughs called home in the early 1950s and had hoped to settle permanently before deciding to relocate to North Africa. Burroughs wrote three of his most important books in Latin America—*Junky, Queer,* and *The Yage Letters* —and, in a very real sense, he never left. Or better yet: Latin America never leaves Burroughs (textually speaking, at least). Long-unpublished material such as his 1953 "Latin American Notebook" and the assorted manuscripts of the "Interzone" period of 1953–58 reveal the extent to which the locales and landscapes of Mexico, Panama, and the Upper Amazon continue to dominate Burroughs's imagination during that crucial transitional period leading to the publication of *Naked Lunch* in 1959. And key scenes, images, and characters from Burroughs's Latin American works reappear not just in *Naked Lunch* but for decades to come: notably in the *Nova,* or "cut-up," trilogy of the 1960s and the *Red Night* trilogy of the 1980s. Chief among these textual recurrences is Burroughs's utopian vision of a great "Composite City," where "all human potentials are spread out in a vast silent market."[2] Recording a dream vision that Burroughs experienced during his trek through Peru and Colombia in search of the hallucinogenic plant known as yagé, or *ayahuasca,* the Composite City scene becomes the centerpiece of *Yage.* It undergoes many permutations in later works, but it appears almost verbatim in *Naked Lunch.* The Composite City, like *Yage* as a whole, is therefore vital for understanding the author's attitude toward Tangier and Morocco. A worlded reading of Burroughs's breakthroughs in *Naked Lunch* reveals that the novel's origins lie not only in Tangier's Zoco Chico or Paris's Beat Hotel but also in the jungles of South America.

Reading Burroughs can often provoke a feeling of déjà vu. Repeated words and phrases, often entire scenes, come and go, presenting themselves as so many variations on a theme, and a familiar cast of characters, including Dr. Benway, Clem Snide, Lola the junk pusher, Hauser and O'Brien, and of course Burroughs's doppelganger, William Lee (aka Inspector Lee, Agent Lee, and Willie the Rat), all make their way on and off the stage, leaping from one book to the next over the course of decades. To some extent all writers return to familiar themes and images and even verbal formulations across different works—giving rise to what is generally referred to as an author's "style"—and this is no less true of Beat Generation writers. But in Burroughs's case these repetitions and returns appear so frequently and so intensely that anyone hoping to better understand Burroughs's corpus must try, following Oliver Harris's lead, to unlock the secret of repetition as such in his work.[3]

I use the word "secret" very pointedly, for Burroughs repeatedly warns readers that the allure of the secret may turn out to be a siren song or—given the Raymond Chandleresque tone of early works like the long-unpublished *And the Hippos Were Boiled in Their Tanks* (cowritten with Jack Kerouac in 1945) and his first published novel, *Junky* (1953)—a red herring. In *Junky* he in fact writes, "There is no key, no secret someone else has that he can give you," referring to the life of a junky and to the world of junk.[4] Very little of what Burroughs says, however, especially about his own writing, can be taken at face value. From a certain point of view, his disclaimer would seem to be at odds with the entire motivation behind writing the book, which was to provide an unvarnished, unsentimental account of the drug underground, one that would run counter to the lurid sensationalism proffered by the mainstream press, and to attempt to correct the misinformation that had led to misguided U.S. drug policies. In the end, Burroughs both promises and withholds the truth, or the secret, of junk, offering readers a glimpse while at the same time denying access to that world.

Upon publication by Ace Books in 1953 (under the pseudonym William Lee), *Junky* was consigned to the dime-store paperback rack, ironically making Lee's hard-boiled voice and persona quite a good fit among the pulp titles of the day. This voice would become characteristic of Burroughs's writing for years to come, developing in highly innovative and imaginative ways to shape works from *Queer* and *Yage* to *Naked Lunch* to the *Nova* trilogy and beyond. Along with the constant repetitions noted earlier, Burroughs's distinctive voice—recognizable through all the later permutations—is a major source of the continuity that exists in his body of work as a whole. It is not surprising, then, that the "secret" alluded to in *Junky* (though defined negatively) is elsewhere closely allied with the author's voice, in particular with the experience of finding his voice: a complicated, intimate personal history that also illuminates the most outward-looked, indeed worlded, aspects of Burroughs's work.

Burroughs's voice is itself a performance. He is a master ventriloquist, and the performative dimensions of his writing are inseparable from its power as political and cultural critique. But after *Queer*, his follow-up to *Junky*, failed to find a publisher and after he found himself in a more or less permanent exile (sentenced in absentia for the shooting death of Joan Vollmer in Mexico City), Burroughs experienced a period of uncertainty and renewed addiction. The years from 1953 to 1958 were also a time of great productivity. After leaving South America, where he had been traveling for several months in search of the mythical hallucinogen yagé, for Tangier, Morocco, in 1954, Burroughs produced mountains of prose. Under the working title "Interzone" and sometimes referred to as the "word hoard," this material would provide the basis for Burroughs's best-known book, *Naked Lunch*, and furnish material for his "cut-up novels" in the 1960s. In a short piece titled "The Conspiracy," cut from the "Hauser and O'Brien" scene that would appear in *Naked Lunch*, Lee writes poignantly, "Since early youth I had been searching for some secret, some key by which I could gain access to basic knowledge and answer some of the fundamental questions." Then, in language taken straight from *Junky*, he describes some of the "clues" he has followed related to pleasure and addiction before going on to say,

> The final key always eluded me, and I decided that my search was as sterile and misdirected as the alchemists' search for the philosopher's stone. I decided it was an error to think in terms of some secret or key or formula: the secret is that there is no secret.
>
> But I was wrong. There *is* a secret, now in the hands of ignorant and evil men, a secret beside which the atom bomb is a noisy toy. And like it or not, I was involved. I had already ante'd my life. I had no choice but to sit the hand out.[5]

Tracing the contours of an overarching plot that unites "Interzone" and *Naked Lunch* with everything that follows would reveal an unceasing struggle to wrest the secret away from these "ignorant and evil men." This struggle is fought in the past, present, and future simultaneously, in lands known and unknown, with weapons familiar and undreamed of. Burroughs's novel *Cities of the Red Night* (1981), with its protagonists the loosely federated band of pirates and partisans living under the "The Articles" and battling, as ever, the agents of Control—the enemy figured, significantly, in the novel as a colonial power—concludes by imagining an all-out arms race reminiscent of the passage from "The Conspiracy" (cons-*piracy*) just quoted: "I have blown a hole in time with a firecracker. Let others step through. Into what bigger and bigger firecrackers? Better weapons lead to better and better weapons, until the earth is a grenade with the fuse burning."[6]

Cataclysm isn't always a bad thing in Burroughs, and the final lines of *Cities* can be read as downright utopian. The future is unknown, but the freedom fighters of the novel, like the Wild Boys, like Agent Lee fighting the Nova Mob, are attempting to *create* the future through (sometimes violent, sometimes tender) acts of transgressive performativity and utopian world making. Gilles Deleuze has referred to the act of writing as "creating a weapon," and it is hardly a coincidence that Deleuze found Burroughs's writing to be a source of such fascination and generative potential.[7] For Burroughs, finding one's voice in writing, which amounts to finding the secret, transforms not just the self but potentially the world. Or to put it a slightly different way, the repeated trope of the secret—as an example of the dense layers of connection and continuity in his work and as the very image of that continuity—overlays an intimate, interpersonal set of concerns and another, equally important set of concerns grounded in political and historical forces on the largest scale.

In another piece from the "Interzone" period, Burroughs discusses the unique status of Tangier, his new home, in the run-up to Moroccan independence from colonial rule. He writes, "It is frequently said that the Great Powers will never give up the Interzone [i.e., Tangier] because of its value as a listening post. It is in fact the listening post of the world, the slowing pulse of a decayed civilization, that only war can quicken. Here East meets West in a final debacle of misunderstanding, each seeking the Answer, the Secret, from the other and not finding it, because neither has the Answer to give."[8] Similarly, in *Queer* he writes, "The Westerner thinks there is some secret he can discover [from the East]."[9] Once again taking language more or less straight from *Junky*, Burroughs is now using the trope of "the Answer, the Secret" to interrogate and confound orientalist discourses of the relationship between East and West, self and other, that have long served to naturalize Western imperialism and colonial domination. More immediately in this passage the secret has to do with Cold War geopolitics at the moment of decolonization in Africa and elsewhere. As "the listening post of the world" (65), Tangier fits into his worlded view of political maneuvering and political unrest; for Burroughs's Interzone to be grasped in its full complexity and critical force, it must be understood as one locus in a much wider spatial network.

In a 1955 letter to Allen Ginsberg, Burroughs explains the ongoing "Interzone" project, writing, "This novel is a scenario for future action in the real world. *Junk, Queer, Yagé*, reconstructed my past. The present novel is an attempt to create my future. In a sense it is a guidebook, a map."[10] Here, too, I hesitate to take him entirely at his word. Given the massive overlap and continuity evident in *all* of Burroughs's work, a strict delineation cannot be made between past and future. The formal and thematic breakthroughs of what would become *Naked Lunch* have their origins precisely in those earlier texts that Burroughs mentions to Ginsberg and in a sense tries to disown by relegating them to his past. Critics have tended to follow his lead, however, in downplaying the role and even the visible traces in *Naked Lunch* of the early trilogy.[11] Burroughs's entire body of work can be read as "a guidebook, a map." And for Burroughs, as for Kerouac, Joans, Lamantia, and other Beat writers, writing is a mapping procedure that performatively creates the time and space it endeavors to describe.[12] Insofar as he seeks to describe what amounts to entire worlds: the junk world, the yagé world, and so on, writing for Burroughs becomes nothing less than a process of active world making.

The repetition in Burroughs's work has a thematic basis, as the author returns obsessively to the scene of the crime, revisiting the same images, the same turns of phrase, the same narrative situations in book after book. The repetition in Burroughs's work is also an artifact of its textual history, which has slowly been uncovered in recent years as assiduous editors, critics, and archivists like Oliver Harris, James Grauerholz, Bill Morgan, and Barry Miles have pieced together letters, journals, and unpublished manuscripts to reveal a much fuller picture of Burroughs's method as a writer and of the complicated backstories of his best-known works. The editorial sleuthing and profound insights of Harris in particular have been indispensable to my own understanding of Burroughs's corpus as a vast, rhizomic network of intertextual reference and worlded concern. He has highlighted both the continuity and the "sheer contingency" of much of Burroughs's published work in terms of what has gotten published when and where and as what.[13] Portions of the *Queer* manuscript, for example, were removed and added to the Mexico City section at the end of *Junky*. Burroughs meant *Queer* to be an immediate sequel to *Junky*, but it would not be published for another twenty-five years. When *Queer* was finally published, an epilogue was added to make up for the pages cannibalized by *Junky*. This epilogue, titled "Mexico City Return," was not originally written for *Queer* but for Burroughs's next project, began in 1953 and published ten years later as *The Yage Letters*.

There is evidence to suggest that Burroughs imagined all these pieces as facets of a single work in progress, "a series of seemingly cryptic notes" from his 1953 "Latin American Notebook," where, as Harris writes, "he plots out an entirely different future for his material."[14] Burroughs's notes are as follows: "When Lee quit junk—unexpurgated version—First trip to S.A. with Allerton. Return to Mexico. Left out—Allerton goes and returns—Back to S.A. No word from Allerton, S.A. trip and back to Mexico. Everything lost."[15] By the time *Yage* was published in 1963 in its (mostly) final form, readers had already encountered some key scenes, in only slightly amended form, in *Naked Lunch* (1959), which was assembled mostly from the mass of writing Burroughs had produced during the Interzone period of 1953–58. Nonetheless, the notebook solidifies the importance of Latin America to Burroughs's development as a writer, not just in the early work but in everything that comes after. Covering the second half of 1953, that is, the period immediately following his initial composition of the *Yage* manuscript, the notebook bridges the gap between the more straightforward, naturalistic early writing and the outrageous experiments of *Naked Lunch*, underscoring the crucial role of the Latin American context in catalyzing those experiments.

Burroughs's work offers a different take on a possible theory of Beat travel and Beat space. Harris writes that "Jack Kerouac's journeys on the American road made travel central to beat writing, but of the three major figures the real travel writers were Burroughs and Ginsberg. They journeyed further and for longer, nomads geographically and imaginatively, because each knew they were internal exiles—aliens in their own land, even in their own bodies."[16] Deleuze's definition of writing—drawing in large part from the example of Beat writers—as a creative line of flight certainly fits Harris's assessment of Burroughs and Ginsberg, but Burroughs's "exile" in South America was also very real indeed: he had fled Mexico City after the tragic shooting death of his wife, Joan Vollmer. The immediate cause of the yagé travels, however, is mostly occluded from *Yage*. The only reference comes when Burroughs writes to Ginsberg from Lima, "which is enough like Mexico City to make me homesick," telling him, "Mexico is home to me and I can't go there. Got a letter from my lawyer—I am sentenced in absentia. I feel like a Roman exiled from Rome" (34). Vollmer's absence from both *Yage* and *Queer* is troubling and conspicuous; it also helps structure the whole of Burroughs's early work. Her death, as Harris points out, is the "Left out" written into the textual itinerary Burroughs maps in his "Latin American Notebook."

So perhaps "the secret" can be formulated otherwise; it is necessary to return to the beginning—and isn't this fitting—and look *again* at the déjà vu brought on by reading Burroughs. As Freud has said, déjà vu is an experience of the uncanny. It is the uncanny return of the repressed and the compulsion to return again and again to the scene of the crime. The scene of originary trauma in Burroughs's life as a writer is undoubtedly Vollmer's death, and this may account for the compulsive repetitions seen everywhere in his writing and—his skepticism about Freud and psychoanalysis notwithstanding—go some way in explaining the entire manifestation of Latin America in work after work.[17] At the very least, and in truly Freudian fashion, one can say that he sublimates his guilt over his wife's death by writing. He says as much in his introduction to *Queer* when the novel was finally published in 1987, where he notoriously writes, "I am forced to the appalling conclusion that I would never have become a writer but for Joan's death, and to a realization of the extent to which this event has motivated and formulated my writing. I live with the constant threat of possession, and a constant need to escape from possession, from Control. So the death of Joan brought me in contact with the invader, the Ugly Spirit, and maneuvered me into a lifelong struggle, in which I have had no choice except to write my way out."[18] This is a stunning admission, to be sure. And difficult to reconcile with the fact that Joan is almost completely absent from the writing her death has apparently motivated. He can now safely point to this tragic event as the catalyst for all the writing to come, and he confesses that it was Brion Gysin who forced him to recognize the truth and full weight of Vollmer's death, which had been repressed both psychically and textually for a long time.[19] It would not be too much of a stretch to say that the death of Joan Vollmer speaks to a much larger dynamic concerning women and Beat Generation writing. They drive the plot but must themselves remain silent. But the specter always returns, and Vollmer's spectral presence in Burroughs's writing (like the spectral presence of *Yage* and Latin America running all throughout *Naked Lunch*) is profoundly felt.[20]

Text and Drugs: Generic Transgression in Burroughs

Adding yet another layer of complexity (and contingency), Burroughs at this time was increasingly relying on letters, especially to his friend, agent, editor, and former lover Allen Ginsberg, to generate material. He even tells Ginsberg, referring to what would become *Naked Lunch*, that "maybe the real novel is letters to you."[21] This statement, and his use of letters in general in the creative process, speaks to the intensely interpersonal nature of his writing. As Burroughs also says in relation to *Queer* (another text with a strong epistolary basis), he writes to "contact" another.[22] Such statements, then, make *The Yage Letters* a very strange case. Originally conceived of as the third installment of a trilogy that also included *Junky* and *Queer*—an excerpt was published in 1958 as "Naked Lunch, Part III: In Search of Yage"—*Yage* would seem to take Burroughs's penchant for filling his letters to Ginsberg with material that would find its way into a later manuscript to its logical extreme, with Burroughs now simply publishing the letters themselves. But once again, nothing can be taken at face value, for the epistolary trappings of *Yage* mask a supreme fiction, and the strategic manipulation of genre in *Yage* raises questions of paramount importance for unlocking "the secret" of Burroughs's work taken as a whole.

Transnational studies must incorporate a theory of transgression, a means of understanding how the physical act of crossing borders (as of a nation-state) bears a complex and intimate relation to other kinds of transgression (racial, ethnic, political, sexual, and so on). The borderlands critique of Gloria Anzaldúa and José David Saldívar, like Gayatri Spivak's postcolonial critique, interrogates power dynamics that are always involved in crossing borders of one kind or another. As (mostly) white, male, and American, Beat writers possessed a certain privilege to cross freely, and as Harris, Edwards, and others have pointed out, this fact was not lost on Burroughs. Much of the complexity and ambiguity of his "travel writing," whether he is in Morocco or Mexico, stems from Burroughs's ambivalence toward the relations of power that have resulted in such privilege. At times, Burroughs (often in the guise of doppelganger William Lee) clearly relishes playing the role of "Ugly American," but the crucial point is that he sees it precisely as a *role*. Burroughs is performing the ugly American routine, exaggerating it to grotesque proportions to expose its ideological underpinnings. To miss this point is to remain forever dissatisfied with Burroughs's politics.

Worlded space—with its fluid, polyvalent interplay between the local and the global, with its lack of respect for borders whether national or otherwise—is at its core transgressive space. As if to disavow or somehow make up for the privilege bestowed on them as Americans traveling abroad (often in the "third world"), Beat writers *performed* transgression: to be sure, through sex and drugs, and in Burroughs's case guns, but also through their writing. Beginning with the Composite City comprising "all human potentialities," Burroughs begins to imagine radically transgressive—particularly queer—identities, and after *Naked Lunch* (namely in the *Nova* and *Red*

Night trilogies) his work becomes increasingly invested in queering revolution by revolutionizing queerness.

Moreover, the formal innovations of Beat writing, whether it be the jazz-chorus notebook-sketch form in the poems of Kerouac's *Mexico City Blues*, the "routine form" that Burroughs began experimenting with in Mexico and would perfect in Tangier, or the "cut-up method" that Burroughs and Brion Gysin developed together in Paris (Gysin had lived in Tangier for a number of years), are unthinkable without the Beats' worlded and worldly travels. Burroughs's work is perhaps most interested in genre and generic transgression. Critics still refer to *Naked Lunch* as a novel only for lack of a better term; he professed to have little need for quaint notions like narrative stability or authorial integrity. Burroughs's two most important innovations where form is concerned are the routines, which Jennie Skerl has described as "satirical fantasies"—brief, self-contained literary grotesques—and the cut-ups, whose lineage extends at least as far back as Dada experiments with chance and found writing.[23] (A contemporary analogue can be found in the lettrist/situationist practice of *détournement*, which recontextualizes language with humorous and often subversive results.) But his breakthroughs don't end there, and *Yage* comprises a set of texts with an especially high degree of formal and generic experimentation.

Yage's epistolary form masks a fiction: the fiction being that although it has all the trappings of real correspondence, and although much of the text did originate in actual letters written to Ginsberg from South America, the *Letters* as finally published in 1963 are a literary construction. As Harris puts it in his excellent introduction to the 2006 *Redux* edition of *Yage*, "Burroughs fabricated its epistolary appearance by adding such as the letter's formal tops and tails, by changing the tense to create an improvised effect of reporting live, and by cutting out tell-tale lines."[24] The question then becomes, what did the epistolary form allow Burroughs to do that could not have been done otherwise? Throughout the *Letters* are intimations that Burroughs could find meaning in his "exile"—as he refers to it in the May 5, 1953, letter from Lima—only in interpersonal or relational terms, with Burroughs playing the part of sage and Ginsberg that of willing pupil. The two shared an intense but short-lived love affair upon Burroughs's return to New York from South America, lending a certain emotional urgency and need to *get across* in the letters. Such a fraught narrative context nonetheless creates an immediate and intimate connection between author and audience; at the same time, the intimacy of the epistolary form assures readers that they are getting the unvarnished, uncensored truth about ayahuasca, about South America, and about the author's ordeal in the Amazon. The illusion of the letters also provides an imagined connection to home, or at least to an "elsewhere." They emphasize Burroughs's distance from the United States, from the "beat scene" that was beginning to form in his absence. Finally, plot becomes much less of a priority in the epistolary form; Burroughs is free to experiment with narrative and other literary conventions. If a plot does emerge, it can be more fragmentary and selective.

Insofar as *Yage* promises an unvarnished account of his travels and of the ayahuasca experience, it shares that motivation with the earlier *Junky*. Both are written as a kind of exposé: *Junky* gives readers the truth about the heroin underground; *Yage* reveals the secrets of a more exotic drug. And both texts share the same clear-eyed, hard-boiled, dime-store tone. Ginsberg's surmising, then, however spurious, that Burroughs first heard about ayahuasca in "some crime magazine" or "goofy tabloid" is revealing.[25] One of the voices that Burroughs assumes in *Yage*—one that he had already employed in *Junky* and would continue to refine in *Naked Lunch* and later works—is that of the pulp novel or dime-store rag. One could imagine (as Ginsberg himself does) the lurid tales of yagé madness penned in a style much like Burroughs's. But like Burroughs the ugly American, this voice is at the same time a put-on, a ventriloquism. In his "January 15, 1953" letter, the first of the series published in *Yage*, Burroughs deflates the genre while admitting its strange allure: "I had a magazine article with me describing a joint outside Panama City called the Blue Goose. 'This is an anything goes joint. Dope peddlers lurk in the men's room with a hypo loaded and ready to go. Sometimes they dart out of a toilet and stick it in your arm without waiting for consent. Homosexuals run riot'" (4). While in Panama, Burroughs cannot resist seeing the Blue Goose for himself, even as he points out the obvious absurdity of the magazine article.

If he first learned about ayahuasca from a similar article, what can that possibly say about the likelihood of success in his impending yagé quest? In truth, relatively few lines are devoted to describing the actual yagé experience. Burroughs's several accounts are contradictory and inconclusive—a great deals depends on preparation, dosage, and the presence of a second, catalyzing compound (just as Ginsberg catalyzed Burroughs's writing of the *Yage Letters*)—and, with one notable exception, are written with the same economy and matter-of-factness as those letters describing the most mundane aspects of his travels. I suspect that one who reads the *Letters* solely for vicarious "yagé kicks" will be disappointed, but any withholding of knowledge or failure of insight on Burroughs's part should be read as a failure only in terms of our earlier notion of a *productive* failure that allows for a much greater insight to arise. The following section shows that the letter beginning, "On my way back to Bogota with nothing accomplished" (16), leads almost immediately to one of the most cogent and piercing critiques of the prevailing world order to be found anywhere in Beat writing; what seem at first like dead ends in *Yage* will sometimes open onto considerably more expansive vistas than at first imagined.

Apart from, but in fact not wholly unrelated to, the dime-store style, another kind of writing that Burroughs lampoons while still utilizing to great effect is the ethnographic report. Burroughs studied anthropology as a graduate student at Harvard in the late 1930s and later took classes in Mesoamerican archaeology at Mexico City College. While in South America he even accompanied renowned Harvard ethnobotanist Richard Schultes on one of his Amazon expeditions. It was with Schultes that Burroughs records his first experience taking yagé, and an early, non-epistolary draft of the *Yage* manuscript looks very much like ethnography. Through this lens, *Junky* begins to resemble a ethnographic report—from a native informant, no less—on the heroin subcultures of New York and New Orleans, and readers will recognize something of the anthropological in Burroughs's later depictions of Interzone in *Naked Lunch* or the civilization described in "The Mayan Caper" episode from *The Soft Machine* or the six "Cities of the Red Night" in the novel by that name.

Burroughs's "scientific" account of yagé and the native rites surrounding it may be as much a fiction as the letters themselves. The opening lines of "In Search of Yage" (the name of the original batch of 1953 missives from Burroughs to Ginsberg) suggest as much. He begins, "I stopped off here [Panama] to have my piles out. Wouldn't do to go back among the Indians with piles I figured" (3). Harris suggests that with this frank admission Burroughs immediately relinquishes any claim to objectivity in what follows.[26] But at a deeper level what this too-personal tale calls into question is the entire notion of scientific objectivity and transparent ethnographic knowledge. Burroughs thus anticipates the breakthroughs of poststructuralist anthropology by some years, whose practitioners (Clifford Geertz, James Clifford, among others) would seek to account for the power differential inherent in the relationship between observer and subject, questioning the ideological assumptions that shape all knowledge of the Other.

The first edition of *Yage*, published by City Lights in 1963 (ten years after Burroughs's journey through the Amazon) is a textual assemblage that brings together not only the original set of "letters" but also a second section, "Seven Years Later," which includes Ginsberg's long letter from 1960 detailing his own ayahuasca experiences, as well as Burroughs's cryptic reply; and a 1963 "epilogue" containing "I Am Dying, Meester?" a cut-up largely assembled from fragments of the 1953 letters. By 1963 portions of the text had appeared independently in such places as *Black Mountain Review*, *Big Table*, and *Kulchur*. In 1961 LeRoi Jones and Diane di Prima, coeditors of *The Floating Bear*, were arrested on obscenity charges for publishing a particularly daring bit of text called "Roosevelt after Inauguration," (In an earlier issue of *Floating Bear* Jones and di Prima had published Burroughs's 1960 reply to Ginsberg, which provides instructions for the cut-up method that he was then developing with Brion Gysin.)

Although "Roosevelt" was not finally published with the rest of *Yage* until the 1988 City Lights edition, readers of earlier editions would have found the piece referred to in Burroughs's "May 23, 1953" letter, where he writes, "Enclose[d] a routine I dreamed up. The idea did come to me in a dream from which I woke up laughing," and a footnote most likely written by Ginsberg himself reads, "This is Burroughs's first *routine*, 'Roosevelt After Inauguration.'" The form then took on a life of its own, like the talking asshole in *Naked Lunch*; subsequent letters to Ginsberg developed much of the material of that volume."[27] "Roosevelt" may have been the first *published* routine, but by the time of its composition in 1953 Burroughs had been working out the routine form since at least the previous year when he was writing *Queer*. The routine happens to be the defining innovation of Burroughs's long-published second novel: a verbal high-wire act that protagonist Lee employs in a series of increasingly desperate attempts to "contact" Allerton, the reluctant object of Lee's desire. But it is not until *Yage* that the routine appears *as such*. In the actual May 23 letter that Burroughs sent to Ginsberg containing the text of "Roosevelt," he calls it a "skit" ("Enclose a skit I dreamed up").[28] Together, these additions and inventions—"Roosevelt after Inauguration," the 1960 reply to Ginsberg, "I Am Dying, Meester?—all point to the fact that *Yage*, as a hybrid and highly performative work, is able to contain the entire sweep of Burroughs's experiments from the routines to the cut-ups.

Given both the tortuous textual histories of individual texts in the Burroughs corpus—their extreme instability or contingency—and the exceptional continuity across texts, it can be dangerous to ascribe primary importance to any one or another of them. Some have pointed to *Junky*, with its major themes of addiction and control, as the key to unlock all the others; some, like Harris, have argued for *Queer*'s elevated status, especially in terms of a more politically and historically grounded understanding of Burroughs.[29] Some consider the *Nova Trilogy* to be the fullest expression of the author's postmodern transgression; and Ken Kesey has even declared *Cities of the Red Night* to be Burroughs's "best work."[30] In some sense, though, these are all attempts to wrest the spotlight away from *Naked Lunch*: a recognition that his widely declared masterpiece was not created ex nihilo or, as Burroughs once claimed, in an extended state of delirium of which he has no recollection.[31]

Rather than ascribe a special status to any particular work, existing as they do in a rhizomic network of dense intertextuality, I prefer to highlight particular *moments* in Burroughs's writing that make possible the densest connections, the most active linkages across an entire text-network. This network extends well beyond the limits of Burroughs's oeuvre; it extends beyond the literary altogether. The moment I am most interested in is his depiction of the Composite City. Its world-conjuring potential and deep resonance with themes that will occupy Burroughs for decades to come make the Composite City a singularly compelling creation. It has the capacity to reshape and maybe even resolve some central questions and debates involving not just Burroughs but Beat writing as a whole.

From the Composite City to the Cut-Ups:
Development of a Method

After Burroughs's first, inconclusive experiment with ayahuasca—he accuses the medicine man of "misappropriating half the vine"—he recounts a curious dream that clues us in not only to the fiction of the "letters" but also to what, for Burroughs, becomes the real significance of the yagé experience. He writes, "That night I had a vivid dream in color of the green jungle and a red sunset I had seen during the afternoon. Also a composite city familiar to me but I could not quite place it. Part New York, part Mexico City and part Lima which I had not seen at this time. . . . I cannot say whether these dreams had any connection with Yage. Incidentally you are supposed to see a city when you take Yage."[32] Harris points out that, in the world of the letters at least, Burroughs will not see Lima for another two months.[33] The temporal slip in the dream report, however, also makes for a clever bit of foreshadowing that could not have been achieved otherwise. The "Composite City" he refers to will become the setting for the extended yagé sequence in Burroughs's final letter from

South America. I would argue that the Composite City provides a model for the Interzone in *Naked Lunch* and later works, providing key images, characters, and even phrases that appear again and again in Burroughs. He is being disingenuous when he suggests that "these dreams" (now plural) may or may not have "any connection with Yage"; his vision of the Composite City—meaningful in terms of its spatiality and its hybridity—is utterly inseparable from his conception of the drug. But this is not to say its status as a dream should be discounted.

Throughout *Yage* Burroughs consistently presents dreams and dream states as radically generative. His initial Composite City vision could still be said to arise from the dream rather than the drug. "Roosevelt after Inauguration," which anticipates the stylistic of *Naked Lunch* by several years, likewise came to him in a dream. The last yagé sequence begins, "Last night I took last of Yage mixture. . . . This morning, still high. This is what occurred to me: Yage is space time travel" (50). Whether Burroughs's further insights into the nature of the Composite City were also dreamed is again inconclusive, but something is nonetheless happening in these visions that aligns pharmacological experimentation and oneiric revelation with spatial mapping and literary invention. Yagé is best understood, then, as a trope. Like travel itself, it is that which creates a maximum of connections, casts the widest net, or whatever allows one to *make contact*.

The author's fullest description of the Composite City appears in a (real) letter he wrote to Ginsberg from Lima on July 10, 1953. After five months in South America and mostly frustrated attempts to discover the secrets of yagé, Burroughs was finally getting somewhere. He had learned about the crucial addition of a second plant to catalyze its psychotropic properties and had now consumed the yagé mixture several times. In his July 10 letter he prefaces the passage in question by telling Ginsberg that it was "like I was taking dictation."[34] (He uses the same "dictation" metaphor in *Queer* to describe his routines and in reference to composing parts of the "Interzone" manuscript.) The Composite City passage was the first portion of what would become *Yage* to be published, in the spring 1958 issue of *Black Mountain Review*, which was coedited by Allen Ginsberg and featured the work of several Beats.[35] Burroughs's piece ran under the heading "From Naked Lunch, Book III: In Search of Yage." The passage as finally published by City Lights begins,

> Yage is space time travel. The room seems to shake and vibrate with motion. The blood and substance of many races, Negro, Polynesian, Mountain

Mongol, Desert Nomad, Polyglot Near East, Indian—new races as yet unconceived and unborn, combinations not yet realized passes through your
body. Migrations, incredible journeys through deserts and jungles and mountains (stasis and death in closed mountain valleys where plants sprout out of
your cock and vast crustaceans hatch inside and break the shell of the body),
across the Pacific in an outrigger canoe to Easter Island. The Composite City
where all human potentials are spread out in a vast silent market. (50)

I imagine, however, that most readers encounter the Composite City in
Naked Lunch, where Burroughs's yagé vision is reproduced in full in
the chapter titled "The Market." There, Burroughs draws a direct link
between the Composite City and Interzone, writing, "Panorama of the
City of Interzone. Opening bars of East St. Louis Toodleoo . . . at times
loud and clear then faint and intermittent like music down a windy street.
. . . The Composite City where . . . " So when he goes on the describe a
landscape of "minarets, palms, mountains, jungle," it would in part seem
to evoke Tangier (although he did not set foot on Moroccan soil for another six months after composing the original passage). After a couple
paragraphs the back story is alluded to in the form of a heading: "Notes
from Yage State." Burroughs then restarts the entire passage, beginning
with "The room seems to shake and vibrate with motion."[36] To further
synchronize the Composite City passage with its new setting in *Naked
Lunch*, the author interpolates this line about halfway through: "In the
City Market is the Meet Café" (98). In its Tanjawi context, "City Market" would refer to the Zoco Chico with its bustling cafés, but the market
is already a central image in Burroughs's original vision of the Composite
City. When the Meet Café is described in greater detail a little later on
in *Naked Lunch*, many of those details are again derived from *Yage*. It
is clear that Burroughs's perceptions of Tangier as recorded in *Naked
Lunch* are heavily filtered through his experiences in Latin America.

Apart from individual images and motifs—many of which reappear
in later works with predictable regularity—the Composite City connects
to Burroughs's project as a writer on another, much deeper level. Harris's
greatest insight into *Yage* has to do with the fundamental *textuality* of
the yagé experience. Referring to the "July 10" letter, Harris writes that

yagé is dramatically defined as "space time travel." This in turn became
Burroughs' definition of *writing*, and the rest of his oeuvre is governed by
this understanding. It is therefore essential to recognise the particular textuality of this extraordinary drug-inspired vision. In this phantasmagoric
scene, meeting point of "the unknown past and the emergent future," the

experience of traveling in space and time is not only described but actually *produced* for the reader, who encounters a collage of phrases and images taken from the preceding letters. Creating uncanny flashbacks, this literally composite text is a special kind of "travel writing," and an augury and precedent for [later] experimental practices.[37]

Those "experimental practices" include the cut-ups, which precede the publication of *Yage* by half a decade. As Harris has written elsewhere, the "collage aesthetic" of the Composite City letter "renders the *yagé* experience of visionary possession by being based on the wholesale recycling and transformation of phrases already read in the earlier letters, so generating cumulatively an uncanny sense of déjà-vu." Déjà vu indeed—Burroughs will take these operations a step further with the 1963 text "I am Dying, Meester?" which is a more extensive cut-up of the original yagé material, and Harris argues that the inclusion of both the "July 10" letter and the cut-up text "invites the reader to see Burroughs' cut-up technique as a systematic development of the earlier, *yagé*-inspired, bricolage text, and so recognize cut-up as the textuality of *yagé* experience."[38]

Understanding the yagé experience as primarily a textual experience offers a useful framework for reading Burroughs's work as a whole. Thinking about his first novel, one could say that *junk* is also a textual experience. It is certainly a linguistic experience: as an ethnography of the criminal underworld, the novel is especially interested in capturing the junky argot. It ends with a glossary of terms, after all, and Lee the narrator delights in explaining things like "When I first hit New Orleans, the main pusher—or 'the Man,' as they say there—was a character called Yellow." The scene in a ward at the Lexington Narcotic Farm is a pastiche of junky lingo that approaches a distinctly cut-up aesthetic.[39] The emergence of the routine form in Burroughs's next novel, *Queer*, is a similarly textual affair. (In the opening pages of *Naked Lunch* he will ask, "Ever notice how many expressions carry over from queers to con men?")[40] Even though Lee's elaborate linguistic performances are born out of "a desperate need to maintain some special contact with Allerton," his love interest, the routines begin to take on a life of their own—even in the absence of Allerton or any listener at all (besides, of course, the reader). Burroughs foregrounds this complicated narrative situation:

> Lee paused. The routine was coming to him like dictation. He did not know what he was going to say next, but he suspected the monologue was about to get dirty. He looked at Mary. She was exchanging significant glances with Allerton. "Some sort of lover code," Lee decided. "She is telling him

they have to go now." Allerton got up, saying he had to have a haircut before going to work. Mary and Allerton left. Lee was alone in the bar.

The monologue continued.[41]

Language in Burroughs's novel is "queered" in the sense that it is no longer a simple, straightforward matter of communication between sender and receiver. Lee's failure to contact Allerton is sublimated and redeemed through the birth of Burroughs the author, and the dictation metaphor consistently signals key breakthroughs in his development as a writer: the routine form, the Composite City vision, the Interzone manuscript. And at every turn a primary concern with textuality reestablishes itself. With *Naked Lunch* the routines steal the show, functioning like variations on a theme that never cease calling attention to themselves as textual constructions. The cut-up novels of the 1960s, then, become a logical extension of this desire to foreground of the materiality of language.

And yet Burroughs's obsession with language *as such* does not amount to mere abstraction. As Harris puts it, "Nothing Burroughsian is abstract: the force of his ideas will not be separated from the effects of his words. That is why his work can be so potent and so extraordinary, stamped as it is with a strictly literal, overpoweringly *visceral* force."[42] His work seeks to activate the transgressive power of language, not neutralize it. When Burroughs says in his 1974 *Rolling Stone* interview with Bowie, "Writing is seeing how close you can come to make it happen," and that "the artists should take over this planet because they're the only ones who can make anything happen," he points to exactly this performative dimension of artistic and literary creation.[43] When leftover material from the "word hoard" of the Interzone years would eventually appear in the *Nova* trilogy, it is now also shaped by the cut-up techniques Burroughs had been developing in Paris with Gysin at the Beat Hotel.[44] Now that the raw material has been radically decontextualized and transformed by their cut-up techniques, text has become theme and form has become content. Burroughs continues to write against "Control" in all its forms, but now with the cut-ups, the word itself—its material presence—is being deformed and deployed as a weapon in that struggle. His war against the "word virus," central to *Nova*, requires a defetishization not only of the author-function but also of the text as autonomous and self-sufficient. The word virus is itself an attempt on Burroughs's part to materialize language, and the cut-up method is one tactic among others that have existed in "larval form"—as Burroughs himself might have put it—from his earliest days as a writer.

Within this swirling matrix of themes and concerns from throughout Burroughs's corpus—textuality and performativity, genre and voice, identity, transgression of all kinds, travel and temporality—the Composite City exists as a key nodal point. It draws attention to the importance of *Yage* as a whole; in turn, and in truly worlded fashion, that "epistolary" account of his four-month trek through Peru and Colombia sheds light on the vexing matter of Burroughs's Tangier politics. Burroughs's quasi-ethnographic travelogue is full of barely concealed political content. Burroughs arrived in Bogotá in the midst of Colombia's long-simmering civil war (known as *La Violencia*), and in *Yage*, he takes every opportunity to criticize U.S. military and economic policy in Latin America. The predation described throughout *Yage* is characteristically set in sexual terms but represents world-historical forces, which appear as the not-so-hidden underbelly of Wallerstein's world-system, or a sinister variation on Dimock's deep time. After his first, failed trek into Colombia's Putumayo region, Burroughs recounts,

> On my way back to Bogota with nothing accomplished. I have been conned by medicine men (the most inveterate drunk, liar and loafer in the village is invariably the medicine man), incarcerated by the law, rolled by a local hustler (I thought I was getting that innocent backwoods ass, but the kid had been to bed with six American oil men, a Swedish Botanist, a Dutch Ethnographer, a Capuchin father known locally as The Mother Superior, a Bolivian Trotskyite on the lam, and jointly fucked by the Cocoa Commission and Point Four). Finally I was prostrated by malaria. (16)

Not only have the power relations between predator and prey been inverted in Burroughs's getting ripped off by the "local hustler," but in one long parenthetical aside he lays bare the entire colonial and postcolonial history of oppression and exploitation in the Americas: economic, political, religious, and otherwise. And by including the "Swedish Botanist" and "Dutch Ethnographer" in his litany, he even foregrounds the notion of scientific knowledge as epistemological violence of a kind his own narrative is attempting to circumvent. It should come as no surprise that he recasts this history in terms of (queer) sexual violation. Throughout *Yage*, sexuality in general carries with it the potential for a deeper and more human understanding of one's environment and encounters—what Burroughs calls "making contact." Again and again, upon meeting someone new, he asks himself, *is so-and-so queer?* and *would I go to bed with him?* It is therefore quite telling that whenever discussing Colombia's civil conflict, Burroughs makes sure to point out that the Liberals are much more attractive than the Conservatives, and that the "Policia National [*sic*] . . . is the most unanimously hideous body of young men I ever laid eyes on, my dear," adding, "I only saw one I would consider eligible and he looked ill at ease in his office. If there is anything to say for the Conservatives I didn't hear it. They are an unpopular minority of ugly looking shits" (10–11).

Both as an individual—"I thought I was getting that sweet backwoods ass"—and as an American citizen, Burroughs, through the persona (Lee) that emerges in his narration of *Yage*, writes himself into this long history of domination and abuse. Harris writes, "The Lee who unites with the anti-colonial aspirations of Latin American peoples . . . is also the Lee who plays the imperialist Ugly American abroad," concluding, "Such contradictions give his writing its unsettling power."[45] A further contradiction is that the force of Burroughs's critique derives in equal measure from his complicity and from the critical distance provided by his status as an "exile." If utopian literature is always a comment on extant social institutions and norms, then travel writing is always directed homeward; as critical as Burroughs often can be of the people and places he encounters in *Yage*, he reserves his sharpest commentary for the United States, using South America as a foil or contrast to critique *yanqui* culture and especially U.S.–Latin America political and economic dynamics. He does not seem to mind the privilege his gringo status affords him. But more often than not, Burroughs is *playing* the ugly American, and for very strategic rhetorical purposes. In a telling series of episodes, Burroughs is mistaken for "a representative of the Texas Oil Company travelling incognito" and "treated like visiting royalty," explaining that the "Texas Oil Company surveyed the area a few years ago, found no oil and pulled out. But everyone in the Putumayo believes the Texas Company will return. Like the second coming of Christ" (24). Burroughs fails to correct anyone and instead uses these instances of misprision to expose the profound psychic consequences of economic imperialism. He sees U.S. interests in Latin America as overdetermining all sorts of interpersonal relationships as well. When a customs agent "who had fought in Korea" tells him, innocently enough, "I like you guys," Burroughs reflects, "I never feel flattered by this promiscuous liking for Americans. It is insulting to individual dignity, and no good ever comes from these America lovers." It is worth noting that when Burroughs criticizes the locals, he rarely does so in an absolute sense; he is more critical of the effect, corrupting or otherwise, that their region's relationship with the United States seems to produce in them. When Burroughs writes of "the predatory toothless smile that greets the American all through South America (11), he merely describes the sad inverse of a very real history of neo/imperialist predation in Latin America and around the world.

Viewed as a whole, *Yage* gives the lie to the common complaint that Burroughs was either uninterested or simply unaware of the contemporary sociopolitical situation of the places in which he traveled and lived. This point of view is well represented by Barry Miles's contention —only half correct—that Burroughs and his compatriots at the Beat Hotel "could have been living anywhere."[46] It is true that in his writing Burroughs almost instinctively transforms his immediate surroundings into something approaching a surrealist dreamscape, but this process of geographic transmutation is what gives Burroughs's travel writing (in the broadest sense) much of its critical force. As critics like Harris, Edwards, and Hibbard have been increasingly at pains to show, the author's "landscape[s] of ideas" are deeply informed by the specificity of local histories and contemporary political struggles. In the Tangier context, disappointed readers may feel that Burroughs's apparent ambivalence toward Moroccan nationalism is no more than an apology for colonial rule, but in *Yage* Burroughs's politics are unambiguous. His treatment of the causes and outcomes of Colombia's armed conflict are especially significant when considering the extent to which *Yage* set the stage for *Naked Lunch* and the all writing to come. Throughout *Yage* Burroughs gives constant reminders of the precarious political situation in Colombia while repeatedly expressing his solidarity with the Liberals and, by extension, the Colombian people. "The majority of Colombians are Liberals," he notes (13). This is to suggest that conservatism is something, like Christianity, imported from Europe, while the natural disposition of South America is liberal.

At one point in the narrative, prevented from leaving the town of Puerto Asís while his tourist card is set in order, Burroughs muses, "If I was an active Liberal what could I do . . . aside from taking the place over at gun point? (22–23), implying that he *is* one in spirit or sympathy and that it would not take much to force him over the line. This sentiment is echoed in a (real) letter written to Ginsberg at the time; Burroughs tells him, "Wouldn't surprise me if I ended up with the Liberal guerillas," a statement that anticipates his "Jihad Jitters" routine. Musing to Ginsberg in a 1956 letter about the possibility of rioting and revolution in the streets of Tangier, Burroughs writes, "If they stage a *jihad* I'm gonna wrap myself in a dirty sheet and rush out to do some jihading of my own.[47] Keeping *Yage* in mind here could impart some nuance to what appears to be a mocking and reckless response to the Moroccan situation. Later on in *Yage* Burroughs writes, "What *we* need is a new Bolivar who will really get the job done."[48] The author's disdain for the Conservative Party stems largely from its association with the Catholic Church, agent of deathliness and repression and a most "sombre" bearer of "the dead weight of Spain" (10). He recounts watching a Conservative propaganda film featuring a Catholic priest who "sat there in his black uniform nakedly revealed as the advocate of death . . . exuding a musty odor of spiritual decay." Burroughs's description hints at the deeper meaning of his own superficiality (i.e., the Liberals are better looking than the Conservatives) as having more to do with appearance versus reality. The ugliness of the Conservative Party and its allies is hypocrisy shining through the facade, revealing "cancerous activity sterile and blighting" in the place of so-called social progress or good works (13).

Worst of all, the Conservatives have managed to suffuse the entire country with an atmosphere of paranoia and dread. Describing the capital of Putumayo, Burroughs writes,

> Mocoa has about 2000 inhabitants and sixty nacional cops. One of them rides around all day through the four streets of the town on a motor bicycle. You can hear him from any place in town. . . . The police have a brass band they bang around three or four times a day starting in the early morning. I never saw any signs of disorder in this town which is well out of the war zone. But there is an air of unresolved and insoluble tension about Mocoa, the agencies of control out in force to put down an uprising which does not occur. Mocoa is The End Of The Road. A final stalemate with the cop riding around and around on his motor bicycle for all eternity. (17)

The Policía Nacional, which Burroughs described earlier as "the Palace Guard of the Conservative Party" (10), have created the kind of surveillance state that will become an obsession in Burroughs's writing. Phrases like "final stalemate" and "for all eternity" also seem to suggest that the malaise he sees all around him runs much deeper than the immediate political straits.

This much longer, multilayered history becomes visible in the palimpsest of Beat travel writing, and a markedly expansive view of South American culture and human history pervades *Yage*. Burroughs is traveling in southwestern Colombia and stopped over in the Andean town of Pasto when he writes, "I went into a cantina and drank aguardiente and played the mountain music on the juke box. There is something archaic in this music strangely familiar, very old and very sad. Decidedly not Spanish in origin, nor is it oriental. Shepherd music played on a bamboo instrument like a panpipe, pre-classic, Etruscan perhaps. I have heard similar music in the mountains of Albania where pre-Greek, Illyrian racial strains linger. A phylogenetic nostalgia conveyed by this music—Altantean?" (14).[49] Like Kerouac's "Fellahin Indians," the "Illyrian racial strains" Burroughs hears in this "mountain music" is straight out of Oswald Spengler, and the notion of an aboriginal race that remains outside of history and so survives the rise and fall of Western civilization undoubtedly informs Burroughs's characterization of Latin America. The status of music in this passage—its ability to convey a "phylogenetic nostalgia"—is also worth remarking, as is the reference to a "panpipe," which resurfaces in the following chapter in reference to both Gysin and Paul Bowles. The same charges of orientalism that apply to Kerouac's essentialist depiction of the indigenous Mexicans he encounters in On the Road could certainly apply here, but the following passage works to temper such a viewpoint:

> Nothing human is foreign or shocking to a South American. I am speaking of the South American at best, a special race part Indian, part white, part God knows what. He is not, as one is apt to think at first fundamentally an Oriental nor does he belong to the West. He is something special unlike anything else. He has been blocked from expression by the Spanish and the Catholic Church. What we need is a new Bolivar who will really get the job done. This is I think what the Colombian Civil War is basically about—the fundamental split between the South American Potential and the Repressive Spanish life-fearing character armadillos. I never felt myself so definitely on one side and unable to see any redeeming features in the other. South America is a mixture of strains all necessary to realize the potential form. They need white blood as they know—Myth of White God—and what did they get but the fucking Spaniards. Still they had the advantage of weakness. Never would have gotten the English out of here. They would have created that atrocity known as a White Man's Country. (38)

Burroughs's South Americans are now portrayed as actors in their own history (i.e., "the Colombian Civil War"). With this shift, he has introduced a good deal of history contingency, not just in terms of Colombia's immediate conflict but also in terms of the entire colonial history of Latin America. The "Myth of White God" refers of course to Cortés as the embodiment of the Mesoamerican deity Quetzalcoatl. When Burroughs suggests that indigenous Americans "need white blood as they know," he again acts to restore to them a certain agency, for however spurious the interpretation may be, in Burroughs's mind it's the Aztecs' myth, not the Europeans'. When he adds, "and what did they get but the fucking Spaniards," he reminds us that things could have gone another way. Most important in this passage, however, is Burroughs's insistence on South American hybridity, his claim that "South America is a mixture of strains all necessary to realize the potential form." This notion of a genetic assemblage, of humanity as "composite," form the basis of key passages describing not only the yagé experience but also the Interzone of *Naked Lunch*. Just as Burroughs asserts the historicity and historical contingency of those he encounters in his yagé quest, he also conceives of their future: one in which we all have a stake in realizing the potential human form.

The future envisioned in Burroughs's Composite City is worlded and worldly, composed of "the blood and substance of many races, Negro, Polynesian, Mountain Mongol, Desert Nomad, Polyglot Near East, Indian —new races as yet unconceived and unborn, combinations not yet realized" (50). Such potentialities are expressed in transgressive combinations of mongrel hybridity, and the "market" in *Yage* and *Naked Lunch* is the locus and mechanism of that expression.[50] The transactions that take place there are not calculated or calculable in economic terms; they are negotiations in the Deleuzian sense of engendering mutual transformation and leading to unpredictable outcomes. And, like everything Burroughsian, these take on a (geo)political edge. According to Brian Edwards, in *Naked Lunch* Burroughs "stages" an anal economy that, in particular, queers the "American supremacist logic" of the Cold War period.[51] Site of bizarre fetishes and "obsolete unthinkable trades," the Composite City's market, which becomes Interzone's City Market, perverts the flow of capital and commodities between core and periphery, North and Global South, and mocks the acquisitiveness of a Cocoa Commission or a Texas Oil.

The yagé vision comprises a vast geography, and Burroughs uses the force of that vision to direct a (by now familiar) process of psychic and linguistic remapping. Its terrain is reminiscent of Kerouac's worlded landscapes in *Mexico City Blues* and in the passages from *On the Road* explored in chapter 1. But while Kerouac is concerned with "the essential strain of the basic primitive, wailing humanity that stretches likes a belt across the equatorial belly of the world," Burroughs's city, with its "vast silent market" of "human potentials," is dynamic and mutable and open to the unknown possibilities of a future-to-come.[52] Far from imaginary, Burroughs's vision arises and is formed from the very real geography, history, and politics of South America. The "mountain music" he heard earlier on the cantina jukebox gave him a similar kind of "phylogenetic nostalgia" (14) as his yagé visions, and what he later calls "the South American at [his] best, a special race part Indian, part white, part God knows what" (38) is a manifestation *in time* of the generative, even utopian, hybridity of the Composite City.

For Burroughs, yagé (like writing, like traveling) is about making connections, making contact. When he met Doc Schindler—the figure of ethnobotanist Richard Evans Schultes, who traveled extensively in the Amazon researching indigenous use of hallucinogenic plant species—the first thing Burroughs asked regarding ayahuasca is "about the telepathy angle" (9), which he had already made reference to in both *Junky* and *Queer*. The potential for a deeper kind of interpersonal communication to develop through its use is in large part what compelled Burroughs to seek out the drug. The fictive audience for his yagé letters, Ginsberg, as friend, lover, protégé, enables Burroughs's epistles to become a kind of telepathy as well. In *William Burroughs and the Secret of Fascination* and elsewhere, Harris highlights the negative potential of the "telepathy angle." Indeed, the first mention of yagé in the final pages of *Junky* connects the drug to "Russian experiments on slave labor," writing, "They want to induce states of automatic obedience and literal thought control. The basic con. No build-up, no routine, just move in on someone's psyche and give orders."[53] His "no routine" reference is fitting: as Harris notes, "Lee's fantasy of controlling and objectifying Allerton through *yagé*" in *Queer* also motivates his increasingly elaborate verbal routines in the novel.[54] Yet Burroughs ultimately views telepathy as a disruptive force, one that short-circuits the usual relations of power. Of the Soviets he writes, "The deal is certain to backfire because telepathy is not of its nature a one-way set-up, or a set-up of sender and receiver at all."[55] This last statement, while it seems to foreclose what Lee says he's after in *Queer* and *Yage*, also points to the positive, liberatory potential of telepathy—along with everything that Burroughs might substitute for telepathy in a metonymic chain that includes, finally, writing itself. In *Wising Up the Marks*, Timothy Murphy places the emphasis on telepathy's connective and even community-forming potential, although he notes its provisional status in Burroughs's oeuvre: "The 'telepathic community' will become a limitation for Burroughs later, but for now [in *Queer*] it suffices."[56]

Understanding yagé is a matter of recognizing and uncovering hidden linkages and relationships. Describing the *brujo* who initiates his first successful (if rather overwhelming) ayahuasca experience, Burroughs writes, "The medicine man was around 70 with a baby smooth face. There was a sly gentleness about him like an old-time junkie" (25). The medicine man is a Beat character, no doubt. But what Burroughs continues to stress is the insistently geographic (and worlded) character of the yagé experience. There with the *brujo*, feeling the first effects of the ayahuasca, "The hut took on an archaic far-Pacific look with Easter Island heads carved in the support posts" (26). The journey to Easter Island, this time "in an out-rigger canoe" (50), will be retraced in the final Composite City episode: another example of the subtle interplay of space and time in *Yage* and one that points to a dense network of worlded energies suffusing the very landscape of South America.

The Composite City is a "collage of phrases and images taken from the preceding letters," but one that cuts across not just *Yage* but Burroughs's entire body of work.[57] In an addition to the original scene in his "Notes from Yage State" in *Naked Lunch*, he mentions a further yagé-becoming: "I feel myself turning into a Negress, the black color silently invading my flesh" (99). In *Yage* Burroughs had declared, "The only element in Panama I contact are the hip spades" (5). The strange condition called "Latah," which is first described to Burroughs by Doc Schindler in these terms: "Latah is a condition occurring in South East Asia. Otherwise normal, the Latah cannot help doing whatever anyone tells him to do once his attention has been attracted by touching him or calling his name" (30) that appears throughout *Naked Lunch* is one facet of that novel's exploration and interrogation of "Control."[58] Without downplaying the importance of Morocco and International Tangier in the years just prior to independence to the creation of *Naked Lunch*, in a Burroughs-ian world-imaginary where textuality and geography, text and world, are co-constitutive, one must recognize the Interzone as a vastly more complex spatial configuration. It is Tangier, but it is also Latin America, and given Burroughs's rather unambiguous politics in *Yage*, readers must also reconsider any easy conclusions about his politics in *Naked Lunch*.

Interzone Intertext: Burroughs and Artaud

The *Yage* text-network extends beyond Burroughs's writing alone. In his Latin American notebook, for example, he writes, "St-Perse. *This is Yage poetry*," referring to French diplomat and Nobel Prize winning poet Saint-John Perse.[59] But there is a more significant, though mostly unremarked, precursor to Burroughs and the yagé quest, and that is Antonin Artaud, who is turning out to be a major reference point in worlded Beat writing: influencing Baraka and his Revolutionary Theatre, inspiring

Michael McClure's plays and Allen Ginsberg's poetry, and informing the hieratic syncretism of Philip Lamantia's lifelong vision quest. I would like to suggest that *Yage* is a rewriting of Artaud's *Voyage au pays des Tarahumaras* (published in English as *The Peyote Dance*), which documents his 1936 travels through Mexico's Sierra Madre in search of the nearly lost peyote rites of the Tarahumaras. The striking parallels between these two texts involve far more than a shared interest in hallucinogens, and just as reading *Naked Lunch* through *Yage* has opened up new readings of both, reading *Yage* through *Peyote Dance* clarifies even further the stakes of their worlded imaginaries.[60]

If *Yage* is structured by a performative and parodic ethnographic knowledge, Artaud plays the role of junky archaeologist. After being waylaid in Mexico City for some weeks, he is finally on his way to meet the Tarahumaras, traveling on horseback and wracked by the pain of opiate withdrawal. He records visions of oddly shaped stones peering out at him from the forest, writing, "The land of the Tarahumara is full of signs, forms, and natural effigies which in no way seem the result of chance. . . . Of course, there are places on the earth where Nature, moved by a kind of intelligent whim, has sculpted human forms. But here the case is different, for it is over the whole *geographic expanse of a race* that Nature *has chosen to speak.*" Artaud goes on to say, "If the greater part of the Tarahumara race is indigenous, and if, as they claim, they fell out of the sky into the Sierra, one may say that they fell into a *Nature that was already prepared.*"[61] Artaud refers to these "natural effigies" of tormented and crucified human forms throughout his writings from the Sierra Madre. For Artaud the archaeologist, the earth reveals *itself*, and his intensely paranoid anthropomorphism wants to suggest the closest correspondence between the Tarahumara and the land they inhabit. Perhaps too close for comfort, from our vantage point, wary of the "orientalist trap"—as when Artaud claims that the Tarahumara live somehow outside of history, one with the earth—but Artaud's essentialism becomes much more interesting when we see what it is pitted *against*.

The habitually destitute Artaud financed his trip to Mexico by traveling as a cultural envoy of the French government. It was the French Ministry of Education that organized a series of well-attended lectures delivered by Artaud at the National University in Mexico City. The best known of these is titled "Surrealism and Revolution." In it, he described his break with André Breton and the surrealists a decade earlier, precipitated by Breton's growing allegiance to the Communist Party. Artaud declared that Breton's surrealism had itself "become a party."[62] He described Marxism as a kind of spiritual imperialism, another nefarious product of Artaud's dirty word: "civilization." He likewise took the opportunity to speak directly to the "youth of Mexico" (as he repeatedly, almost affectionately, called them), urging them to abandon Marx and instead embrace the native traditions of their land. This is a theme Artaud will return to again and again in his writings from Mexico: the need to refound the revolution on indigenous principles that, for him, will lead to a much more profound revitalization of the human spirit and become a model for the rest of the world.

For Artaud, the need for a third term, or a way out, is especially acute because the "progressive" forces of nationalist Mexico have proven as hostile to indigenous, and potentially subversive, cultural practices as the Spanish missionaries before them. One local government official he befriends told him, "The trouble is that when they have taken Peyote, they no longer obey us."[63] Artaud reports that a peyote crop had recently been destroyed by federal soldiers under orders to prevent its cultivation, and in an open letter to the governors of Mexico, published in *El Nacional*, he extols the virtues of their native cultures and pleads with them to help preserve these cultures. In this, Artaud's project is remarkably similar to that of Paul Bowles when he travels around Morocco in the late 1950s, recording indigenous music for the U.S. Library of Congress, native cultural traditions he felt were under threat of extinction amid the modernizing fervor of many Moroccan nationalists.

This all may sound rather presumptuous: Western Man come to restore the native to his or her proper, essential way of life. Artaud asked in despair, "And all this, for what? For a dance, for a rite of lost Indians who no longer even know who they are or where they come from and who, when you question them, answer with tales whose connection and secret they have lost" (46). Yet Artaud's dual mission in Mexico—his participatory psycho-ethnography among the Tarahumara and his polemical instigations among the students and intelligentsia in Mexico City—remains significant in that reconciling or aligning modern political history with more ancient struggles and ways of being is central to his entire project as a writer and artist. His gaze cast back over the millennia is also forward-looking, and in this way the Tarahumara and their mysteries constitute a middle path, or a third term, for Artaud: between colonialism and nationalism, capitalism and Marxism, culture and civilization.

When he named a chapter of his Tarahumara book "Supplément au voyage au pays des Tarahumaras," Artaud placed himself in a tradition of travel writing as social critique that stretches back to the Enlightenment.

The reference is to Denis Diderot's *Supplément au voyage de Bougainville* (1772), a satirical "addition" to Louis-Antoine de Bougainville's famous travelogue. Along with Bernardin de Saint-Pierre's *Paul et Virginie* (1788) and similar works, Diderot's *Supplément* makes it clear that, just as utopia is at some level a critique of the world *as it is*, every travel narrative is also about one's place of departure. What is so remarkable about Artaud's "Supplément" is that he turns his critical gaze back on himself and acknowledges the epistemological limitations of his peyote quest. Like *Peyote Dance*, Burroughs's quasi-ethnographic travelogue is full of barely concealed political content, taking every opportunity to criticize U.S. foreign policy in Latin America. But he makes that critique all the more trenchant by recognizing and then refusing to disavow his own complicity.

A worlded critique is one that looks beyond the nation-state and toward a totality not yet captured by the deracinating transcendence of the global and globalization. From Mexico in 1936 Artaud offers us a prescient warning about the consequences of our ever-flattening world. In another piece written for *El Nacional*, he writes, "The present civilization of Europe is in a state of bankruptcy. Dualistic Europe no longer has anything to offer the world but an incredible pulverization of cultures. To extract a new unity from this infinity of separate cultures is a necessity. . . . Although there may be a hundred cultures in Europe, there is only one civilization—a civilization which has its own laws. Anyone who is not provided with machines, guns, airplanes, bombs, and poisonous gases inevitably becomes the victim of his better-armed neighbor."[64] Artaud specifically refers to the recent invasion of Ethiopia by fascist Italy. He suggests, however, that in the face of Western hegemony, Mexico possesses the "secret of its eternal culture" that will render it invulnerable. Artaud, in other words, uses the very rootedness and singularity of the Tarahumara to suggest how we might achieve the furthest reaching social transformation. In his second Theatre of Cruelty manifesto, composed three years before his trip to Mexico, Artaud had already demonstrated his conviction that indigenous beliefs and ways of being were the only possible antidote to the culturally bankrupt West. Burroughs echoes Artaud's cataclysmic sense of the future when he writes of Tangier as "the slowing pulse of a decayed civilization, that only war can quicken."[65]

Recent critics interested in how *Naked Lunch* has been informed by its author's Tangier milieu have registered a deep ambivalence on Burroughs's part when it comes to Morocco's struggle for independence. This ambivalence often hinges on a distinction between his sympathy with the oppressed Moroccan people and his contempt for what he felt were the self-serving interests of nationalist party leaders—a conflict that in *Naked Lunch* plays out between the Party Leader and the "Ordinary Men and Women" in the routine by that name. As Allen Hibbard puts it, "On the one hand, in contrast to some of his fellow expatriates who seemed to lament the loss of the colonial period, Burroughs remained open to possibilities for change; on the other, he registers a degree of skepticism toward the nationalists' motives."[66] Critics have also noted that Burroughs's ambiguous attitude toward Moroccan independence stems from a more fundamental critique of the nation-state itself: "His disapproval of the nation form," argues Edwards, "extends to the Maghrebi nationalists' projected imposition of a new nation and culture of control to substitute for French colonialism."[67] For Burroughs, a victory for nationalist Morocco would be no victory at all, and this sentiment aligns him with Artaud and Bowles and their sense that the nation form is ultimately incompatible with what Marx once called our "species-being."

Especially vexing is Burroughs's response to the civil unrest in the turbulent years prior to and following Moroccan independence: the riots that swept across Morocco and threatened to erupt in Tangier as well. In a letter to Ginsberg meant to allay Kerouac's fears about traveling there, he writes, "TANGER IS AS SAFE AS ANY TOWN I EVER LIVE IN. . . . ARABS ARE NOT VIOLENT. . . . Riots are the accumulated, just resentment of a people subjected to outrageous brutalities by the French cops used to strew blood and teeth over a city block in the Southern Zone." In an earlier letter to Ginsberg, he writes, "The possibility of an all-out riot is like a tonic, like ozone in the air. . . . I have no nostalgia for the old days in Morocco, which I never saw. Right now is for me."[68] At moments like these Burroughs is clearly sympathetic to the Moroccans' anticolonial aspirations, but he can also be cynical and mocking; in *Naked Lunch* he portrays imagined riots as grotesque orgies of violence. Writing about such scenes, Kurt Hemmer is sharply critical of Burroughs's distortions. He argues that "the violence associated with Arabs in *Naked Lunch* severs their connection to imperialism's despotism by becoming so shocking as to eclipse any semblance to the immediate politics behind the images." Hemmer goes on to assert that "the riots in Tangier were stimulating not only intellectually but, more important, aesthetically," and as a result "an immediate engagement with the Moroccan revolution is lost in the excessiveness of both form and content."[69] Nothing in Burroughs, however, is ever *merely* aesthetic, and here too the example of Artaud can be useful. The shock of aestheticized violence in Artaud's Theatre of Cruelty—inseparable from the West's original sin of colonialism—becomes a tool and a necessary first step in the revolution to come. Amiri Baraka recognized this and premised his own Revolutionary Theatre on the salutary function of performative violence. In a similar vein Burroughs's kaleidoscope of obscene violence in *Naked Lunch* is used to launch an avant-garde critique of colonialism that reverberates far beyond that one work and its immediate Moroccan context.

Allen Hibbard and Kurt Hemmer have both sought to reconsider the role played by Tangier in Burroughs's best-known novel. As Hibbard puts it, "There would be no *Naked Lunch*, at least not in the form we know it, without Burroughs' sojourn in Tangier."[70] Hemmer takes the importance of Tangier as given, but he remains less optimistic than either Hibbard or Edwards about the possibility of reconciling the novel's ambivalence toward Morocco's nationalist aspirations. "Although Burroughs might not have been completely hostile to Moroccan nationalism," writes Hemmer, "*Naked Lunch* does not make a sustained stand against colonialism and often does not resist the arrogance of imperialism."[71] Further, while Hibbard and also Edwards acknowledge the importance of the Composite City vision and note its origin in *Yage*, they believe it finds its proper place, so to speak, in *Naked Lunch*. Hibbard writes, "Although Burroughs may have had a notion of the 'composite city' before he landed in Tangier, the dream-like quality of the North African city provided an ideal place for the vision to blossom" (61). And, according to Edwards, "Burroughs's vision of a zone of potential, of larval possibility, would crystallize in [Tangier]—imagined before arrival during his yagé expeditions in South America (and maintaining his prophetic descriptions of a Composite City from Peru in 1953) but developed and finding its form after Burroughs's experience with the Zoco Chico" (166).

I am reminded of the opening chapter of Slavoj Žižek's *The Sublime Object of Ideology* and the distinction Žižek makes between analyzing the content of dreams and the dream form itself.[72] That is to say, I don't wish simply to replace *Naked Lunch* with *Yage* or Morocco with Mexico as the key to unlock the final significance of Burroughs work; rather, I am interested in how the *very form* of these transpositions (whether of times, topographies, genres, identities, etc.) gives rise to a worlded panorama of radical possibility throughout his oeuvre. To read *Naked Lunch* solely as depicting Tangier in the waning days of its international status is to be confounded by Burroughs's seeming unwillingness or inability to confront the realities of Moroccan independence. Reading the novel alongside and *through* Burroughs's oeuvre taken as a whole—which the palimpsestic nature of his work encourages us to do—brings into view a complex reckoning with colonialism and decolonization.

Postprandial Reading: Burroughs after Naked Lunch

Burroughs's career as a writer tends to get read in a very un-Burroughsian manner: that is to say, a linear progression from the straightforward, naturalistic prose of *Junky* and *Queer* to the explosion of the routines in the antinarrative of *Naked Lunch* to the radical experimentation of the cut-up period and beyond. After the *Nova* trilogy, however, Burroughs largely abandoned the cut-ups that had defined him as a postmodern writer in the tradition of Beckett, Stein, and Joyce.[73] And his return to the routine form as the major organizing principle of his work parallels another return that actually began in *Nova*. Even if *Naked Lunch* can still properly be called his "Tangier novel," the next work to be published, *The Soft Machine* (1961), will take readers right back to Mexico. Ian MacFayden writes of *Naked Lunch* that "Mexico is all but lost in the shuffle and cut" and yet still exists in "spectral" form; in *Soft Machine* the author supplies that specter with flesh and bone.[74] Burroughs will continue to produce challenging and innovative prose for decades to come, much of it again centering in Latin America, and tracing this post–*Naked Lunch* itinerary opens up paths first staked out in Burroughs's earliest work.

New editions of *Soft Machine*, *The Ticket That Exploded*, and *Nova Express* introduce still more textual, thematic, and geographic links; Harris even cites a letter from Paul Bowles to Lawrence Ferlinghetti, suggesting that Burroughs had intended for the bulk of his "In Search of Yage" material to appear in *Soft Machine*.[75] The first of the three "cut-up novels," *Soft Machine* picks back up with Agent Lee, who is soon marching through Mexico with a gang of wild boys—"I picked thirty of the most likely and suitable lads all things considered and we moved South up over the mountains and down the other side and into the jungle"—and battling against the forces of Trak.[76] The Latin American setting suggests that Burroughs has imperial power and anticolonial rebellion specifically in mind. Before long, they arrive at what is clearly an iteration of the Composite City: "Up a great tidal river to the port city stuck in water hyacinths and banana rafts—The city is an intricate split-bamboo structure in some places six stories high overhanging the street propped up by beams and sections of railroad track and concrete pillars, an arcade from the warm rain that falls at half hour intervals" (36). And with the return to a familiar landscape comes a huge shift in emphasis from individual to collective action. At this particular moment, it is the "Vagos Jugadores de Pelota, *sola esperanza del mundo*," who can call forth "a million adolescents shattering the customs barriers and frontiers of time, swinging out of the jungle with Tarzan cries, crash landing perilous tin planes and rockets, leaping from trucks and banana rafts, charge through the black dust of mountain wind like death in the throat" (37). Their literally *transgressive* acts ("shattering the customs barriers and frontiers of time") give rise to an entire "Wild Boys" mythology in Burroughs's work post–*Naked Lunch*. Still in a "larval state" in *Soft Machine*, this mythology bursts forth in *The Wild Boys* (1969), which also begins in Mexico, and grows ever more elaborate with the oppositional and queer communities of Burroughs's *Red Night* trilogy.

When Burroughs revised *Soft Machine* for publication in the United States in 1966, the entirely new narrative episode "The Mayan Caper" became the centerpiece of this second edition. Harris actually dates the chapter to late 1962, which is when Burroughs was also finishing up *Yage*.[77] In it, Lee receives a body transplant and is sent back in time to destroy the Maya "control calendar," and his preparations turn out to be a reiteration of Burroughs's yagé experiences. (The author *has* described them as "space time travel," and *Soft Machine* is replete with images from *Yage*.) The "Mayan Caper" chapter is made up of composites—composite words, composite images, composite bodies—as Burroughs allegorizes the transition from the yagé experience to the cut-up experience, the development of the cut-ups out of earlier textual experiments centering on the Composite City vision.[78] When Lee infiltrates the temple and sabotages the "control machine" with "sound and image track rebellion," the machine dismantles itself (in a scene reminiscent of Kafka's "In the Penal Colony") with these words: "Cut word lines—Cut music lines—Smash the control images—Smash the control machine—Burn the books—Kill the priests—Kill! Kill! Kill!—" (96–97). (These last exclamations echo Lear late in Shakespeare's play.) With the immense performative energy of the cut-ups acting as catalyst, yagé does indeed become the "final fix."

In "William S. Burroughs and the Maya Gods of Death," Paul Wild writes, "Burroughs had many valid reasons to cast Maya priests as emblems of control and death even though he contradicted the mid-century archaeological view of the Maya as a benevolent theocracy. In recognizing the violence in Maya culture Burroughs was remarkably prescient."[79] Wild is generally sympathetic to Burroughs's reading of the Maya, although he takes the author to task for certain inaccuracies and misrepresentations. On the whole Wild is being overly positivistic. As he himself suggests, the most important question to ask is how Burroughs is *using* the Maya in *Soft Machine* and elsewhere. One thing he is not doing is romanticizing; the Maya have built up a control society on par with anything produced by the West. Burroughs's vilification of the priestly class—misplaced, according to Wild—allows him to voice a downright populist point of view that actually has a lot in common with his attitude toward the Moroccan situation (sympathy with the people of Morocco, mistrust of party leaders, etc.).

In *Yage* Burroughs expressed outright solidarity with the Liberals, also a populist gesture if we believe him that "the majority of Colombians are Liberals" aligned against the Conservatives and thus the "dead weight of Spain." At the heart of Burroughs's work, whether it be *Yage* or *Naked Lunch* or *Nova* or the later novels, is a singular concern with imperialism and control in all its forms, and not merely in an abstract sense but in response to a very long and very real history of colonial oppression in Latin America and across the globe. *Cities of the Red Night*, a beautiful and important book that Burroughs worked on through much of the 1970s, tells the story of a loose confederation of outlaws bent on toppling Spanish and British colonial rule in the Americas. The novel's parallel plots unfold both in the sixteenth century and in what Brion Gysin calls "Present Time," where a shadowy organization plots world domination from its South American headquarters, and one is again reminded of Artaud, who explains his imagined production *The Conquest of Mexico* by saying, "The subject of the Conquest has been chosen because *it concerns the present*." Poised on the great world-historical moment of decolonization—the "present" of Beat writing—Beat writers are perfectly positioned to launch a postcolonial critique, and the suggestion that there exists something that might accurately be called "postcolonial Beat literature" will come to the fore in the next chapter on Gysin's novel *The Process*.

5

FOR AFRICA . . . FOR THE WORLD: BRION GYSIN AND
THE POSTCOLONIAL BEAT NOVEL

"Hear My Voice"

In the spring of 1960, seven years after Burroughs's yagé experiments in South America, Allen Ginsberg set out on his own quest for the fabled hallucinogen. In Pucallpa, Peru, Ginsberg met a local *curandero* and participated in a yagé cure session that lasted through the night. The following day he wrote a letter to Burroughs, describing his profound and harrowing experience with the drug: "The whole fucking Cosmos broke loose around me, I think the strongest and worst I've ever had it nearly," telling him, "I was frightened and simply lay there with wave after wave of death-fear, fright, rolling over me till I could hardly stand it."[1] Ginsberg pleaded with his friend and former lover for guidance: "I do want to hear from you Bill so please write and advise me whatever you can if you can. I don't know if I'm going mad or not and it's difficult to face more. . . . I'm no Curandero, I'm lost myself, and afraid of giving a nightmare I can't stop to others" (65).[2] Both Ginsberg's letter and Burroughs's reply appeared in the "Seven Years Later" section of *Yage Letters* when the book was finally published by City Lights in 1963, after years of effort by Ginsberg to see it into print.

Given the evident despair of Ginsberg's letter from Pucallpa, Burroughs's cryptic reply may seem rather callous and willfully obscure. He began with an equivocal bit of wordplay, "There is no thing to fear," before providing these instructions:

> Take the enclosed copy of this letter. Cut along the lines. Rearrange putting section one by section three and section two by section four. Now read aloud and you will hear My Voice. Whose voice? Listen. Cut and rearrange in any combination. Read aloud. I can not choose but hear. Don't think

about it. Don't theorize. Try it. Do the same with your poems. With any poems any prose. Try it. You want "Help." Here it is. Pick up on it. And always remember. "Nothing is True. Everything is permitted" Last Words of Hassan Sabbah The Old Man Of The Mountain." (70)

Although Ginsberg later admitted that he had been looking for more "handholding," taken as a marker of the distance Burroughs has traveled, literally and figuratively, since his 1953 journey in search of yagé, his enigmatic reply is quite revealing indeed. Above all, it marks the growing influence of painter and fellow writer Brion Gysin. Burroughs and Gysin had met in Tangier in the mid-1950s, but it was not until they both found themselves living in Paris a few years later at 9 rue Gît-le-Coeur, the famed "Beat Hotel," that they became friends and began their intense artistic collaboration. What Burroughs offered Ginsberg in the letter is, of course, a version of the cut-up method, which he and Gysin had been working with extensively at the time.[3] His reply makes it clear that *cut-up-thought* had now supplanted *yagé-thought*. Yet insofar as the yagé experience is, as Harris suggests, primarily a textual experience, perhaps Burroughs's instructions to Ginsberg do make a certain sense.[4]

Now that the cut-up technique pointed him and Gysin toward a conception of language and linguistic production that radically decenters the speaking subject, Burroughs had little patience for anything as personal as Ginsberg's crisis of conscience and ego-concern. Burroughs's "Voice" in the letter is *produced* as a textual effect, not its source, and any authorial stability is immediately undercut when he asks, "My Voice. Whose voice?" These performative gestures on Burroughs's part are further complicated by the fact that the epistolary form generally relies on a mutually legible notion of sender and receiver. Gysin's influence is again signaled by the figure of "Hassan Sabbah The Old Man of the Mountains." The legendary Hassan-i Sabbah was leader of the twelfth-century military society and hashish cult known as the Assassins, or Hashashin. Sabbah is a central figure in Gysin's personal mythology, acting at times as a spiritual guide and at times an alter ego. Burroughs closely associates the two of them as well, especially in relation to the occult power of the cut-ups. In Gysin's 1969 novel, *The Process*, a modern-day "Brotherhood of the Assassins" is of immense narrative and thematic significance, and Sabbah's "last words," "Nothing is true. Everything is permitted," become a refrain in the novel. Furthermore, the concept of "Present Time"—Burroughs dates his letter to Ginsberg: "June 21 1960 Present Time Pre- Sent Time" (70)—is vital for understanding Gysin's representation of history and politics in *The Process*.

I begin with this story of Burroughs and Ginsberg in a chapter focused on Gysin because it showcases the dense intertextuality typical of so much Beat Generation writing. Mapping these transnational text-networks, to again use Gillman and Gruesz's term, requires a reading practice attentive to the structures of Dimock's deep time, which in turn requires a planetary, or worlded, perspective to be grasped in its spatial totality. The *Yage–Naked Lunch* text-network, to take our example from the previous chapter, stretches across no fewer than four continents; when Gysin's novel gets added to the mix, the network grows more expansive still. Through a complex and highly inventive set of tropes and tactics, Gysin attempts in *The Process* to figure the world as such. He also manages to create a prime example of what I am calling "postcolonial Beat literature." I say this knowing readers may balk at the idea of Beat Generation writing as postcolonial, but it is exactly this kind of unconventional, even anachronistic, linkage that my work on the Beats seeks to activate.[5] Worlded Beat writing designates in part a body of texts that present a sustained postcolonial critique: in previous chapters, this critique was operative in the Pan-Africanist/black nationalist rhetoric of Ted Joans and Amiri Baraka and in *Yage*'s sardonic assessment of Cold War neo-imperialism; likewise, Gysin's novel persistently interrogates orientalist discourses and engages imaginatively with colonial legacies in a decolonizing world.

Purists may also question the choice to include a chapter on Gysin at all. Was he really a Beat? His presence at the birth of the cut-ups and collaboration with Burroughs on all manner of textual, visual, and psychic experiments at the Beat Hotel alone warrant his presence here, it seems to me. Gysin anchored Burroughs's immensely fertile year in Paris, just as he had helped shape Tangier's expatriate scene during the final years of the International Zone. Through his relationship with the Jajouka musicians of Morocco, he helped introduce a Western audience to what would come to be known as "world music" or "worldbeat," later popularized by the likes of Paul Simon and Peter Gabriel.[6] It is rather the case that one really can't write a book about the World Beats *without* including Gysin. The present chapter puts into practice one of the more promising trends from the new Beat studies and a motivating principle behind my project: to open up the study and understanding of the Beat movement in as many ways as possible. The Beats bled into the New York School, the Black Mountain group, the San Francisco Renaissance, and the New American Poetry and have direct ties to the surrealists and other international avant-gardists. Beat writers learned from bebop musicians, Zen masters, and radicals of all stripes. In the end, the best way to describe the Beat movement—or perhaps any literary or artistic school or movement—is how Anne Waldman describes it: as an "open system," or like Diane di Prima: as a "jam session."[7]

For every Marinetti or Breton, nervously policing the borders of their reified "-ism," dissidents and defectors like Mina Loy or Antonin Artaud smuggle something across. Gysin rejected the Beat label, it is true, but so did Burroughs. If public disavowal were enough, we might have to strike Kerouac's name from the record too. Even he equivocated, or inflated the meaning of "Beat" *ad absurdum*. All this pushing back against labels is the flipside of the avant-garde impulse to name, and by naming to create. It is the necessary obverse of the performativity of the manifesto, which is "negatively" generative insofar as it conditions and fixes what it breathes life into. The Beats' refusal to be pinned down is part and parcel of a familiar avant-garde rhetoric, which, especially after World War II, becomes a critique of affiliation as such (leading finally to Tim Leary's "turn on, tune in, drop out.") But as this and other chapters try to show, absolute insistence on a Beat politics of *dis*association is untenable. What is needed is a more fluid conception of affiliation and more permeable definitions of "Beat," "American," "literature," and the rest.

"Naked Brion"

Gysin's years with Burroughs at the Beat Hotel, however productive, are only one chapter in a long and multifarious career. He had spent the better part of the 1950s in Morocco, after an initial invitation from Paul and Jane Bowles to join them at their Tangier villa. It was Paul who introduced Gysin to the Master Musicians of Jajouka, who would figure so largely in Gysin's life in Morocco. In 1954 Gysin opened the 1001 Nights restaurant in Tangier to showcase the Jajouka musicians. It was the hottest club in town before closing down after Tangier joined an independent Morocco in 1956. In "Cut-Ups Self-Explained" (1964), Gysin argues that "writing is fifty years behind painting," a charge made all the more trenchant by the fact the Gysin was himself a prolific painter who continues to be known today primarily as a visual artist.[8] During an earlier stay in Paris in the mid-1930s to attend classes at the Sorbonne, Gysin instead fell in with the surrealist group. He was invited to show his work at a group exhibition that included such luminaries as Picasso, Miró, Magritte, and Dalí but was devastated to find, on the day of the opening, his pictures being removed by order of André Breton on murky grounds of "insubordination."[9] The same gallery would later hold a solo exhibition of Gysin's work, which was beginning to move away from overtly surrealist influences and would become increasingly complex and innovative over the next several decades. By the late 1950s at the Beat Hotel, Gysin was producing canvases that overlaid gridlike patterns with Eastern calligraphic scripts and sought to liberate language in ways analogous to his and Burroughs's cut-up experiments.

Jason Weiss has noted that Gysin's multigenre, mixed-media approach, which seems to vacillate or occupy a kind of middle ground between visual art and the written word, has led to both his unfortunate obscurity and his enduring significance "in this age when scholars and readers are eager to think across the disciplines, to find connections between cultures, to discern the underlying matrix of an artistic moment beyond fixed horizons of identity or traditional expectations."[10] The hybrid identities (formal, linguistic, cultural, and otherwise) that Weiss views as central to Gysin's oeuvre are in many ways the obverse of a loss, even a refusal, of personal identity that becomes equally important to Gysin's mythos and worldview.[11] He once confessed, "I have never accepted the color or texture of my oatmealy freckled skin: 'bad packaging' I thought. Certain traumatic experiences have made me conclude that at the moment of birth I was delivered to the wrong address," adding, "I have done what I could to make up for this."[12] This last statement could apply to Gysin's incessant travels—a self-imposed exile or a pilgrimage with no known destination—and to the sum of his creative endeavors. But it is in *The Process*, where shifting identities and itineraries mirror the ceaselessly shifting sands of the Sahara, that Gysin launches his most profound attempt at "making up" for the very fact of his birth.

The creative detours that cut a meandering path across Gysin's novel add up to something more than an accidental masterpiece by a "peripheral" Beat writer or a relic of late sixties psychedelia. With *The Process* Gysin has made a significant contribution to Beat discourses on race, gender, ethnicity, and religion, as they offer an alternative, even a corrective, to familiar depictions of the "exotic" in Beat writing or the standard fare of what Brian Edwards has dubbed "hippie orientalism."[13] The cross-cultural aesthetics and wildly innovative narrative and figurative strategies that Gysin employs throughout the novel enable him to comment on racial and ethnic difference in a particularly complex and nuanced manner, and Hanson's willingness to "go native" in Morocco, perhaps unsettling at times, is but one highly performative means of counteracting the relentless *othering* that has always been an orientalist hallmark.[14] My reading of *The Process* as thoroughly worlded in scope and decidedly antiorientalist in outlook is grounded in the novel's presentation of personal identity and group affiliation as multiple and mutable and yet firmly rooted in local soils and histories, achieved in the novel through a highly wrought set of tropes and images revolving around the nexus of language and landscape. The linguistic and geographic permutations that become the text's most striking feature amount to nothing less than an active "process" of postcolonial world making. The novel, in fact, contains *many* worlds. Changes in perspective, shifts in consciousness, and other like phenomena are consistently described in terms of leaving one "world" for another, and Gysin's novel demands a constant reorientation on the reader's part to account at each step for new horizons, new vistas, and a new relation to an immanent and heterogeneous totality made radically expansive through its profound and paradoxical rootedness in space and time.

Gysin began composing the novel, his first, in 1965 and would spend the next several years in Tangier completing it. The events detailed therein generally take place about a decade earlier, but it is a roman à clef only in the broadest sense. Gysin clearly has something more ambitious in mind, and his novel works on its source material in highly inventive and challenging ways. These transformative operations—some of which are recognizable to anyone familiar with the curious genre of Beat "fiction," some distinctly Gysin's—form the basis of our discussion in what follows. A long opening chapter introduces our protagonist, Ulys O. Hanson III, an African American professor of history trekking through the Sahara to research his next book, which he plans to call "The Future of Slavery." To this end, Hanson has received funds from an obscure group called the Foundation for Fundamental Findings, although he makes it only as far as Adrar, Algeria, before being turned back by French troops—"the Heavy Water Police"—guarding the nuclear test site just to the south. The insidious presence of these and other agents of what Burroughs would call the "control society" permeates the desert, setting the tone for a series of uncertain crossings that structure Gysin's novel. Back in Tangier, having failed to reach "my Black Africa," Hanson is abruptly snatched away be Hamid, his "Moroccan mock-guru." The two of them escape the violently escalating anticolonial unrest brewing in the city and flee to the home of Hamid's uncles, none other than the Master Musicians of Jajouka.

As Gysin's narrative grows increasingly fractured and hallucinatory, the demands of what the novel figures as "Present Time" begin to assert themselves more forcefully. Hanson meets the ghostly Thay Himmer, "last White Rajah-Bishop of the Farout Isles" (204), at a Tangier café, and it turns out that Thay and his wife, Mya, have been bankrolling

Hanson through their Foundation for Fundamental Findings. They mean to embroil him in Mya's plot to take over the entire African continent. Hanson and Thay rendezvous with other members of the Himmer's organization at Mya's seaside citadel, Malamut, and when Hanson learns what the Himmers truly have in store for him, he is faced with a critical decision. The novel ends with one last set of narrative *permutations* (a watchword throughout) and a coda that returns us to a nearly identical scene from the opening chapter, leaving readers to ask whether this whole business has been, as Hanson suggests more than once, "a trap well-enough woven of words."

Whether or not one agrees that Paul Bowles's complaint to Ginsberg about the novel ("an awful lot of naked Brion in there") is cause for disapprobation, Bowles does have a point.[15] In spite of their obvious differences, Ulys Hanson can, and should, be read as Gysin's alter ego. Like Hanson, Gysin once wrote a book about the slave trade in Canada, and like Hanson, Gysin became one of the first "Fulbrighters" on the strength of that book.[16] Hanson's "mock-guru," Hamid, is closely modeled on Moroccan painter Mohamed Hamri, who was instrumental in bringing the Jajouka musicians to Tangier and the 1001 Nights. Hamri first met Paul and Jane Bowles, who recognized his talent as an artist, in 1950. He met Gysin a year later, and in 1952 they mounted a joint exhibition of their paintings in Tangier's Rembrandt Hotel. In his efforts to promote Hamri, Gysin is like Bowles, who championed the work of local artists and storytellers: among them Mohamed Mrabet, Ahmed Yacoubi, and Mohamed Choukri. Brian Edwards has written about his complicated relationship with Choukri in particular and the politics of Bowles's many translation projects.[17] For his part, Hamri offered Gysin a way in (a "passport," as it will be figured in *The Process*) to Moroccan life that would have remained hidden to him, hence the emphasis on initiation in Gysin's novel.[18] The Himmers bear a strong resemblance to John and Mary Cooke, a wealthy American couple and early boosters of Scientology and LSD. Gysin became close with John in particular, and when he got enmeshed in the Cookes' extravagant and tangled affairs in Morocco and Algeria, it ended up costing him his restaurant. This handful of major characters in *The Process* are at least clothed in pseudonyms; "naked Brion" does indeed appear at various points in the novel, as when Gysin refers, by name, to a litany of former lovers.

Compelling though such personal revelations may be, they pale in comparison with the subtle (and not-so-subtle) ways in which the novel's immediate cultural and political context—in particular, the context of African decolonization—percolate through the book. There are references to the Algerian War and to the demonstrations and riots that erupted across Morocco in the run-up to Independence: in particular, the 1952 Tangier riot that, as Paul Bowles would later write, "presaged the end of the International Zone of Morocco."[19] The March 30 riot marked the fortieth anniversary of the Treaty of Fez, creating the French and Spanish protectorates in Morocco. Characters include versions of anticolonial torchbearers Mehdi Ben Barka and Frantz Fanon, whose name in the novel, Francis-X. Fard—"world-famous psychiatrist and the internationally Prize-winning author of *Paleface and Ebony Mask*" (175)—also evokes not only Nation of Islam founder Wallace Fard Muhammad but also Malcolm X, the Nation's most controversial former member. This recombinatory gesture on Gysin's part is typical of the author's method and has the effect of linking both Fanon and Fard to a larger history of Pan-Africanism and black power swirling around the novel. (Ben Barka's name becomes "Ben Baraka" and is probably also an allusion to Beat poet LeRoi Jones, who had recently changed his name to Imamu Amiri Baraka and helped found the black arts movement.) There are additional references to poet Senegalese poet-cum-president Léopold Sédar Senghor and his former surrealist colleague Aimé Césaire, or "the Nabobs of Negritude" (181), to Claude Lévi-Strauss, aka "Professor Levy-Levant," leader of "the Paris school of social anthropology," and, for those more keen on waging a revolution of the *mind*, to psychedelic icons Aldous Huxley and Albert Hoffman (Mya's mentor, "Dr. Forbach of Basel").[20]

Along with these markers of its contemporary sociohistorical context, Gysin's novel weaves together a more remote, even mythic, history. Such is the tale of Persian military and religious leader Hassan-i Sabbah and his band of eleventh-century Assassins. The name "Assassins" is derived from the hashish rituals that adepts are alleged to have performed at Alamut, their mountaintop fortress. The group would inspire the nineteenth-century Club des Hashischins, whose members included Charles Baudelaire, Théophile Gautier, and Gérard de Nerval. Gysin was captivated by the mythology of the original Assassins, and in *The Process*, they are figured as a loose-knit "Brotherhood" of Sufi mystics and ritual keef smokers whom Hanson seems to meet everywhere he goes.[21] They are also closely associated with Hamid and the ritual performances of the Master Musicians, and their presence in the novel forms a circuit of reciprocity and mutual respect that exerts a countervailing pressure on the network of colonial authority following Hanson like a shadow across the desert.

"A Trap Well-Enough Woven of Words"

In the end, the strength of Gysin's novel resides not in its verisimilitude but in its willful departure from any one version of reality, and *The Process* differs from a lot of Beat fiction in its sheer narrative complexity, which includes no fewer than eight narrators and extensive transcriptions of tape recordings, journals entries, and computer files. The main narrative is threaded together with interstitial chapters by Hanson, but even his identity is multiple and grows increasingly elusive. Among whites and Europeans, he is Professor Ulys Hanson. To Hamid and other North African Berbers and Arabs, he is Hassan Merikani. Mya takes to calling him Ulysses-Hassan, and the foundation wants to name him "The Ghost of Ghoul" as they enlist him in the wild conspiracy that drives the novel to its conclusion. Gysin's novel describes a proliferation of identities that is also a *loss* of identity, and in the face of this personal and narrational slippage, Gysin's novel organizes itself mainly along geographic lines. Geography and identity become closely aligned; the novel's opening paragraph makes these alignments clear and is worth quoting in full:

> I am out in the Sahara heading due south with each day of travel less sure of just who I am, where I am going or why. There must be some easier way to do it but this is the only one I know so, like a man drowning in a sea of sand, I struggle back into this body which has been given me for my trip across the Great Desert. "This desert," my celebrated colleague, Ibn Khaldoun the Historian, has written, "This desert is so long it can take a lifetime to go from one end to the other and a childhood to cross at its narrowest point." I made that narrow childhood crossing on another continent; out through hazardous tenement hallways and stickball games in the busy street, down American asphalt alleys to paved playgrounds; shuffling along Welfare waiting-lines into a maze of chain-store and subway turnstiles and, through them, out onto a concrete campus in a cold gray city whose skyscrapers stood up to stamp on me. It has been a long trail a-winding down here into this sunny but sandy Middle Passage of my life in Africa, along with the present party. Here, too, I may well lose my way for I can see that I am, whoever I am, out in the middle of Nowhere when I slip back into this awakening flesh which fits me, of course, like a glove. (1–2)

One could easily imagine this scene cinematically. The narrator's voice-over accompanies the film's opening credits as a long, aerial shot finds the tiny specks of a desert caravan. The camera slowly zooms in while the narrator recounts his "childhood crossing," which is itself set in terms of a bleak urban desert, until it fixes a close-up of Hanson as he "slips back into this awakening flesh." The motion of the camera would parallel the incessant motion of Hanson's childhood, described in formulations like "out through," "down . . . to," shuffling along . . . into," and so on; it would also foreground the thematics of movement and travel that shape the novel.

Considering the gap between author and narrator, a statement like the glib "It has been a long trail a-winding down here into this sunny but sandy Middle Passage of my life in Africa" may be off-putting, but it is reflective of the willfully flippant approach to language in the novel. The hackneyed image of something fitting "of course, like a glove," further belabored by its ironic self-awareness, suggests that the narrator goes about his figuration with at least some ambivalence. Perhaps it is entirely fitting that an African American professor of the history of slavery would map out his own life in terms of a "Middle Passage," Hanson's skin— and the question of embodied identity—remains a major preoccupation throughout the novel. The Middle Passage reference, coming as early as it does, evokes the opening lines of the *Inferno* as well: "Midway upon the journey [*nel mezzo del cammin*] of our life" (Hamid, then, becomes Hanson's Virgil.) Like the name Ulys/Ulysses ("of Ithaca, N.Y."), the echoes of Dante, Homer, and Joyce reinforce, in splendidly ham-fisted fashion, the notion of Hanson as exile or wanderer. However self-reflexive and *constructed* Gysin's novel may be, none of this is meant to suggest that it bears no relation to a world outside of its own creation. Gysin's novel is firmly grounded in the world of history and politics, and unpacking its dense layers of reference and allusion will be essential to our reading.

The distance between author and narrator enables Gysin to imagine scenes that perhaps could not have been presented otherwise. A few years after the novel was published, Gysin would reflect, "I've lived the best years of my life in Morocco and [my 'lousy oatmeal skin'] can't take the sun. When I'm with Africans, I forget that I'm white. But they can't forget it. I stick out like a sore thumb. From miles away across the deserts or mountains, I look like a colonial cop or a mercenary. What side am I on?"[22] Whatever one may think of these pronouncements, it is clear that Hanson, black and able to "pass" as Muslim and African, fulfills a deep-seated desire on Gysin's part to escape his "lousy oatmeal skin." In *The Process*, the idea of passing is thematized, with characteristic facetiousness, in regard to Hanson's career in academia. From his bath in Alger's posh Hotel Saint-Georges, he explains,

I have taught: I have published. . . . My book could have made me a full professor; with tenure, what is more, in almost any good school in the East, and would have, I think, if I had only been white. As I ponder on this, I play with myself in the suds and stand up, creaming my body all over with soap in front of the full-length mirror. . . . When I applied for my Fulbright fellowship, I sent them this very white photograph of myself. When we all passed muster at a cocktail party before sailing, I thought some members of the board were surprised to see me in the old flesh, as we call it. . . . I laughed and saluted my white sponsors in the mirror, waving my cock at them all, before I rinsed off and became my black self again. (15)

The thematics of passing fit into a larger pattern of disguise and loss of identity in the novel. A few pages later, in a recognizable attempt at "going native" (a variation on passing), Hanson trades his "GI boots, field jacket and worn Levis for sandals, baggy *sarouel* pants . . . and this fine black burnous which has made me feel invisible, here, since it first dropped over my shoulders." From this point on, Hanson is largely assumed by others to be African and Muslim as he goes "more and more deeply disguised" (21). Later on, when he attempts a letter back to Fundamental Funds detailing his progress and need for more cash, he even "considered enclosing a street photographer's shot of me taken in the thick of [Tangier's] Socco Chico crush and scrawling across it, perhaps: '*Which one is me?*'" (121).

Hanson remains the protagonist, but each chapter of Gysin's sprawling novel is narrated by a different character (Hamid, Thay, Mya, several of Mya's associates and operatives) and becomes a world unto itself—complete with its own history, its own language, its own point of view. Chapter titles like "I" and "Thou," "He" and "She," "You (Fem.)" and "You (Masc.)" are a first clue to the novel's polyvocal desire to thematize and to interrogate the very process of subject formation. The narration of illiterate Hamid is recorded "almost by accident" (81) on Hanson's prized UHER reel-to-reel (a favorite of Gysin's as well). Like Hanson, Hamid is adept at passing between worlds, and when he recounts his youth in Tangier as a streetwise hustler and smuggler, it stands in sharp contrast to the idyllic scenes of time spent with his Master Musician uncles in the hills of Jajouka. The centerpiece of Hamid's narration is his depiction of the mysterious Bou Jeloud festival, which Bowles had first taken Gysin to see in the early 1950s and in which Gysin recognized the same Dionysian energies as those which had once animated the ancient Rites of Pan. The next long chapter, narrated by "Cheshire Cat" Thay Himmer, provides an account of the burgeoning subculture within Tangier's expatriate scene that, with its distinctive mix of spirituality and hedonism, presages the later influx of "hippie orientalists" inspired in large measure by the presence of Gysin, Burroughs, and Bowles.

Mya Himmer's narration, a rush of ellipses and italics, is extemporaneous and performative and looks very typically "Beat" on the page. Her section also serves as an important corrective to the phallocentric narratives of the male characters that make up the first half of the novel. Her telling allows for a very different history of events to emerge, particularly in the account of her Native American upbringing in Canada, surrounded by strong women and the magic of storytelling. In Mya's chapter—and in the final sections of the novel, which involve increasingly experimental narrative tactics (e.g., fragments from a journal; a transcribed computer archive; a pair of chapters from the Africanus twins, brother and sister who speak to and for one another as they merge voices and even sexes)—readers can discern a very deliberate strategy on Gysin's part to attempt to give voice to the Other, whether figured in terms of gender, race, indigeneity, or, finally, as blurring the line between human and nonhuman (the tape recorder, the computer, etc.). This highly fraught enterprise is recognized as such in the novel and made visible through its seemingly endless succession of revisions and reversals.

The apparent chaos of Gysin's method is belied, however, by a surprisingly limited vocabulary of repeated images, metaphors, and verbal formulas. The novel's use of repetition and doubling, and its relatively small cast of characters, all manage to create the illusion of vast space in what turns out to be a rather hermetic, self-contained textual universe. One set of verbal and *tactile* formulas favored by Hanson deals precisely with this idea of a world in miniature and thematizes the correspondences between "big world" (the world out there) and "small world" (his own private world). In the opening scene of the novel, Hanson is able to "slip back into" himself by performing the detailed, well-practiced ritual of fitting his keef pipe together, filling it with keef (the "green passport" Hamid has given him), and lighting it. He explains, "I make these moves not just out of habit but with a certain conscious cunning through which I ever-so slowly reconstruct myself in the middle of your continuum; inserting myself, as it were, back into this flesh which is the visible pattern of Me." This meticulous process, which recurs throughout the novel, is described in terms of an intimate connection Hanson shares with the objects he manipulates. The match and matchbox are limned in especially vivid detail: "Each match is a neat twist of brown paper like a stick dipped in wax, with a helmet-shaped turquoise-blue head made to strike on the miniature Sahara of sandpaper slapped onto one side of the box" (3). Calling the strip of sandpaper a "miniature Sahara" is not simply a clever metaphor. It becomes a reversal of the synecdochic relationship in Gysin's novel between desert and world, whereby an object in Hanson's immediate consciousness stands in for the desert as whole, renders it legible in its totality.

The matchbox, however, still contains a profound mystery, and one that gets at the core of how language functions and exerts its strange power in the novel:

> I know this whole business is a trap which may well be woven of nothing but words, so I joggle the miniature matchbox I hold in my hand and these masterpiece matches in here chuckle back what always has sounded to me like a word but a word which I cannot quite catch. It could be a rattling Arabic word but my grasp of Arabic is not all that good and no one, not even Hamid, will tell me what the matches say to the box. . . . If I remember correctly, Basilides . . . reduced all the Names proposed by the Gnostics into one single rolling, cacophonic, cyclical word which he thought might well prove to be a Key to the heavens: "*Kaulakaulakaulakaulakau* . . ." Can the matches match that? (3).

What Hanson means by "this whole business" is not yet clear in these opening pages. It most immediately refers to his elusive sense of self, and the notion of language as constitutive of both self-perception and objective reality is a major concern of Gysin's novel. He plays ceaselessly on the homology of "word" and "world," and as the narrative begins to take shape, one begins to suspect that the "trap woven of words" refers to the novel itself. This early passage also raises important issues of communication, of the ability or inability of various characters to communicate with one another, with the landscape, and so on. These appear with increasing frequency as the novel progresses, crystallizing in Hanson's difficulties of translating and transcribing his various narrators, in Thay and Mya's occult study of "grammatology," in Thay's subsequent vow of silence, in Freeky Fard's brother, Amos Africanus, his tongue mutilated at the hands of French colonial troops, and other equally resonant instances. Most significant in this passage is its final reference to the Egyptian Gnostic Basilides, whose "*Kaulakaula*" foreshadows the novel's central conceit and plot device. The *zikr*, or ritual recitation of the names and attributes of God (*Allahu Akbar, Subhan'Allah, La ilaha ilallah*), is depicted at several points in the novel—with Hanson and the Assassins, with Thay and the Hamadcha Sufi brotherhood. In Thay's final exhortation to Hanson that he "permutate the *zikr*" (187), which Hanson accomplishes in truly postmodern fashion with splices and loops on his reel-to-reel tape recorder, is the climactic event on which the entire narrative hinges. The act of permutation thus becomes a dominant trope in *The Process*, and just as Sufi initiates cycle through the many names of God, Gysin's novel cycles through its various narrators, tropes, and language games.

Allegorical permutation in the realms of history and politics—especially in relation to colonial history and postcolonial politics—is a tactic that gives *The Process* much of its critical charge. The novel's polyvalent allegories allow untold stories and marginalized voices to be heard in all their unsettling complexity. Readers learn, for example, that Mya was born Jackie Mae Bear Foot, a Native American princess, lending a degree of gravitas and historical significance to her otherwise monomaniacal and seemingly capricious plan to take over Africa—perhaps now on behalf of all the world's dispossessed, of those victimized by all forms of colonialism. The novel offers no easy answers to Mya's motives, yet it complicates them enough for us to imagine multiple possibilities. Mya's chapter also recalls a poignant scene of indigenous female knowledge and community—a world unto itself. She recalls, elliptically,

> In winter, it could be sixty degrees below zero . . . Fahrenheit, of course . . . and we'd all sit in the kitchen in front of the fire . . . all my grannies and me . . . and we'd wait for the mushroom tea to work and, when it did, why it was *true!* . . . we used simply *fly* away to another land that all those poor white people outside . . . those palefaces, never knew. [. . .] Home was another world. We were seven generations of women . . . believe it or not. [. . .] There were no men of *any* kind around our house . . . *ever*. Greatest Granny, as I called her, insisted that men were bad for the mushrooms . . . and she knew *all* about *them*. Dream-mushrooms always came up out of the ground when she called them by name, she said.[23]

This scene, and the magic it contains, provides an antidote to the patriarchal knowledge proffered to Mya by one Aldous Huxley, and with its claim that "men were bad for the mushrooms," the wisdom of Mya's grandmother neatly reverses the usual shamanic line that women's magic is sure to spoil a spell or potion.

The gender dynamics surrounding magic and ritual in Gysin's novel are reminiscent of a scene from an early draft of *Yage Letters*, where women are very much present at an ayahuasca ceremony. This is in spite of the fact that, as one *brujo* tells Burroughs, "if a woman witnesses the preparation the Yage spoils on the spot and will poison any who drinks it or at least drive him insane."[24] Burroughs is led to conclude that "evidently the taboo on women does not apply [everywhere]" (95). Mya's Borbor sounds remarkably similar to another substance described in *Yage* called *ololuiqui*: "Women are said to put this drug secretly in a man's food with the result that he loses all will power and becomes a helpless slave to the woman. Why the use of *ololuiqui* should be a monopoly of the female sex I don't know" (93). Burroughs, like Gysin, was clearly fascinated by the thematic possibilities of these psychotropic power differentials.

Borbor is described in the novel as a potent magic and a "mysterious substance" that allows women to control the men around them, and Mya is adept at its use.[25] (She calls herself Calypso.) Its intoxicating effects, plus the verbal slippage between Borbor and "bourbon" on more than one occasion, are also telling. Given the politics of keef versus alcohol use in *The Process*, Borbor/bourbon becomes yet another example of the novel's keen negotiations of language, gender, and religion. For a time the novel itself was to be named after Mya's "mysterious substance." According to Gysin biographer John Geiger, "'Bor-Bor' was the favored choice of Doubleday, the publisher interested in the book."[26] Burroughs, too, understood that Mya and her magic potion lay at the heart of Gysin's novel, explaining in 1973, "The basic message of the book is too disquieting to receive wide acceptance as yet . . . for the book is concerned with rubbing out the word as the instrument of female illusion. The Himmer empire is based on the use of Bor-Bor, the drug of female illusion." "After seeing some of the first drafts of *The Process* in 1967," writes Geiger, "Burroughs used the Bor-Bor idea himself in [the novel] *The Wild Boys*."[27] Disquieted or not, readers can discern, especially in Gysin's rendering of Mya's childhood, a fascination with indigenous practices and a respect for female empowerment; this becomes all the more interesting, and unexpected, considering Burroughs's and Gysin's persistent and well-documented misogyny.

It is from Mya that we learn the history of her husband, Thay, as well, and his family saga turns out to be a revision of the white god myth. Mya tells Hanson, "I'm sure you think you know the rest of the story . . . but, *no!* The Himmers were different. In the next generation, the family went native to conform with some local prophecy which allowed them to crown themselves rajahs with full native pomp" (205). Mya overall depiction of Thay's upbringing provides an image of a post/colonial network oriented away from the United States and toward an autonomous and heterogeneous Pacific Rim: "The Himmers were always *very much* of the East. They shopped in Singapore instead of San Francisco, for example . . . things like that. Black sheep of the family, like Thay's queer Uncle Willy, fled to Hong Kong and Macao before settling down on a remittance in some super-civilized place like Peking. Girls of the family were rather more spartan. They ran away to spin in an ashram in India with Gandhi . . . or took vows as Buddhist nuns at the court of the Queen of Siam" (205). Mya's itinerary posits a deorientalized East that is dynamic, multiple, and modern. Like her provocation—"you think you know the rest of the story"—it reminds us that colonial histories are as contingent as they are mutable, an idea reinforced by Gysin's overall strategy of narrative fragmentation and by the final incommensurability of the novel's many points of view.

Verbal transmutations like "Borbor/bourbon" and especially "word/world" point to profound correspondences between language and landscape in Gysin's novel. An additional permutation returns us to the desert, the organizing principal and a constant presence in the text. One possible referent of the titular process is the ceaseless transformations of the Sahara's substance as rocky plains of *reg* become sandy *erg*, great dunes that in turn proceed to "'colonize' broad expanses of flat *reg*" (290). Portraying the desert as dynamic, as a living, breathing, speaking organism, is a major impulse in *The Process*. The "landscape as body" metaphor could certainly fit in with the kind of shopworn figuration that Gysin's seems to revel in, although something more significant is going on here as well. Much of this trope has to do with *reading* the landscape, making a potentially threatening or aliening place more legible. Hanson is able to "slip back into" himself with the hypersensitive manipulation of his *own* body and relationship with the "miniature Sahara of sandpaper" on his "masterpiece matchbox" (2–3). Farther along, his desert caravan looks into the "watering eye of the mirage [which] is the great Show of the World" (47).

Hanson had tried to convince his friend Hamid to be his guide into the Sahara, but it was Hamid who required "a bout of instruction in the map." Spreading out a map of the North African Maghreb, Hanson explains it in corporeal terms to Hamid: "On this map, one handspan to the right along the Mediterranean shore lies Woran. With your thumb on Woran, your little-finger lands on Algut. If you pivot due south from that white city on the cliffs, your thumb will fall on Ghardaïa, the mysterious desert capital of the Dissident Mozabites." But, as always, the mapping process is fraught with the danger of illegibility, of losing one's way: "The trouble with this map is that it has two big insets of Woran

and Algut . . . and these effectively obscure the desert trails to the south"
(8). Hamid, mostly bemused by Hanson's entire project, reads his own
meaning in the map: "He pointed out that the Great Desert is in the
shape of a camel stretching its neck right across Africa. . . . He laughed
like a lunatic to see that the western butt-end of his camel was dropping
its Mauretanian crud on the Black Senegalese. . . . The head of Hamid's
camel drinks its fill in the sweet waters of the Nile. The eye of the camel,
naturally enough, is that fabled city of Masr, where the Arab movies are
made and all the radios ring out over streets paved with gold. Us poor
Nazarenes call the place Cairo, for short" (9). This conceit continues for
several more lines and indicates the novel's overall strategy of depicting
geographic space through a process of imaginative remapping. Hamid's
benighted attitudes toward the "Black Senegalese" and "poor Nazarenes"
also fits into a larger pattern in the novel—a friend of Hamid's, for example, asks the telling question, "why can't [Hanson] be a Muslim like
everyone else in the world?" (86)—and are meant not to so much to elicit
our censure as to turn the tables on the Christian West and its own uni-
versalizing rhetoric. Like so much in Gysin's novel, its discourse on race
and religion is characterized by an awareness of their geographic and
historical contingency.

A similar passage is worth citing for its even richer geopolitical dimensions. Describing a building style he likes to call "Sudanese Flamboyant,"
Hanson explains that it is "Mesopotamian in origin, surely, linking this
desert with that other called Arabia Felix—not called Felix because it is
happy but because it lies *al limine* (the Yemen), to the lucky right hand
when you look back east across the Tigris and the Euphrates, east to the
Gobi from whence all the palefaced freaklinas of history have always
swept down on us poor Africans" (66–67). Depicting a landscape that
bears the inscriptions of history is an essential component of worlded
geographies in Beat writing and elsewhere.[28] Hanson's evocative descriptions present a worlded vision of connection and collectivity in the face of
colonial oppression. A common substance and a common history "links"
the Sahara and its inhabitants with far-off places and peoples. The novel
repeatedly raises questions of the meaning and status of various racial,
ethnic, and cultural identities (Muslim, Arab, Berber, African, black,
white, Christian, European, American, etc.) and, in particular, Hanson's
identity in the eyes of his interlocutors. For his part, Hanson casts a very
wide net in asserting a shared community of all Africans, whereby what
is lost in the strategic erasure of difference among Africans is gained in
the assertion of a shared history and dedication to a common cause (al-

though the novel is at pains to show diverse, often incommensurable, visions of a united Africa.)

In the worlded multiplicity of Gysin's novel, the world itself emerges as a powerful organizing trope and topos. The novel continuously seeks out apprehensions of a "world-horizon come near." Preparing to meet for the first time with representatives from the Foundation for Fundamental Findings, Hanson muses, "One thing I forgot to tell the Foundation when I applied is that I have left not one foot back in *their world*, as they think, but a mere fading footprint. This foot I put forward into the Sahara is already firmly implanted in *this African world*, where my guide so far has been Hamid."[29] And farther into the desert, he describes, "Here on the desert as out on the sea, the round swell of the Earth is your rise in the road. . . . The watering eye of the mirage is the great Show of the World. On its dazzling screen you assist at the creation and destruction of the world in flames" (47). Eventually Hanson reaches the shrine of Hassan-i Sabbah, with its elaborately decorated mosaic floor, whose effect is not unlike that of Gysin's dream machine. Hanson explains, "These magic carpets in tile can catch up the soul into rapture for hours. They begin with mere optical illusion in which colors leap and swirl but the effect goes in developing to where pattern springs loose as you move into the picture you see. You step from this world into a garden and the garden is You" (61).

The will to transcendence—the sublime sameness of the world as unmarked *global* space—implied in Hanson's world-visions is strategically undercut by their baroque profusion, which occurs in other characters' narrations as well. Thay Himmer, for example, describes his initiation into the Hamadcha brotherhood as "land[ing] in a new world" (138). Leaving the Medina for the Socco Chico is like "leaving one world for another" (140), and Thay later admits, "Living between two worlds, as I did, I got provoked by Mya into doing the one thing one should never do—introduce one world to the other" (152). Sometimes, Africa and the Sahara are synecdochically connected to "the world," as when Mya tells Hanson that she and Thay "would both be happy if you would accept to come with us to 'Malamut' [her desert fortress]. . . . where we have some great plans under way . . . for Africa . . . for the world" (233).[30] Fard's wife and one of Mya's associates, Affrica "Freeky" Fard (née Africanus), writes about the desert's "hostile" fauna in her journal: "They would contend, I suppose, that they fight for water but I see their innate hostility as just one more example of the extreme nature of the Sahara; of the world" (286). Finally, internal and external worlds are linked metonymically in the figure of the market.[31] A train conductor with whom Hanson shares his keef tells him, "Beyond this town lies Oujda and the border. If you have no baggage [Hanson has none] you can easily go around it. The World is a Market" (72). And soon afterward, Hamid tells him, "We say about people like you: He can walk in the *souk* of my head, the market-place all Arabs live in" (82).

In topographical terms, the world that Hanson and the others most often confront is a desert one, yet when one might reasonably expect the desert in Gysin's novel to be presented as a void place: barren, unchanging, inscrutable—in short, orientalized—it instead presents the desert as full of dynamism and energy, marked by history and eminently legible. Hanson and other characters are able to "read" the desert at every turn. The silence of the desert is a pervasive "humming" silence; in Hanson's words, "All this ululating emptiness aches in my ears like the echo of a shell." He goes on to say, "When I listen down even further into myself, I contact something else which shakes my whole intimate contact with Me. When I try to tune out the constant moaning roar of the wind, my whole being vibrates to a sound down below the threshold of hearing." This is not to say the "voice" of the desert is always benevolent. Often, it is the voice of Ghoul, "the Djinn of the Desert, Keeper of the Land of Fear" (6), who leads travelers astray to madness and death. Other times, however, the voice of the Sahara consists of the "sibilant" sounds of its inhabitants:

> When desert-dwellers meet, they stand off a few paces to whisper sibilant litanies of ritual greeting, almost indistinguishable in sound from the rustling of stiff cloth, as they bare a long arm to reach out and softly stroke palms. They exchange long litanies of names interwoven with news and blessings until a spell of loosely knit identity is thrown over all the generations of the Faithful like a cloak. . . .
>
> Everything crackles with static electricity as if one were shuffling over a great rug. Everyone in the Sahara is very aware; tuned-in to the great humming silence. (21–22)

This poignant image evokes a deep resonance between the "desert-dwellers" and the landscape they inhabit. A hostile place is made hospitable by their rituals and the communities those rituals create and sustain. Hanson has been sensitive to the "voice of the desert" from the outset, but a more complete immersion in the landscape and a corresponding diminution of his identity as American, even as human, are required for a more profound participation to occur. At several points, Hanson will liken himself or another to the "winsome jerboa" or to the fennec, "that odd desert fox" who hunts it: "My ears are . . . bristly antennae that pick up and tingle with the silky sound of the sand sighing across the Sahara" (120)—in another set of formulas that indicate, with ritual repetition, a renewed ability to apprehend the vibrations and energies suffusing the Sahara.

Language and landscape, sense and signification work together in complex and unexpected ways throughout Gysin's novel to convey a singularly performative conception of community that pulls together the individual and the environment, native and foreigner, human and nonhuman, language and the ineffable. Waiting outside in the rain at a desolate train station early in the novel, Hanson hears "ranked choruses of bullfrogs recit[ing] the interminable Word they were set a long time ago, now, as their *zikr*: '*Kaulakaulakaulakaulakaulakau* . . .' it sounded like," while "bats looped about the lamps they lit along the track, presently: '*Train coming!*' The bats squealed up into their ultra-sonic radar frequencies like the brakes on distant steel wheels" (12). These are not instances of mere anthropomorphism but rather an initiation into deeper mysteries that exceed classification.

The Brotherhood of the Assassins, which becomes the prime exemplar of the novel's vision of subterranean community and connectivity, stages an impromptu initiation for Hanson when, aided by Hamid's "passport of keef," he appears at their compound with a young adept and hears in a "coded" knock on the door: "the same chuckling word the masterpiece matches say to the box" (30). The loose-knit community of Assassins, which refers us back to the eleventh-century cult of Hassan-i Sabbah, conjures a much longer history of transgression and intrigue. The exact nature and status of their Brotherhood is hard to pin down at any point in the novel, but this is very likely by design. In his usual cryptic manner, Hamid often tells Hanson, "We are all Assassins," and it is as if the Brotherhood must be created anew with each performance of its rituals, just as new worlds are created in the novel with each permutation of the Word. Upon his first night spent in their company and sharing in their rituals, Hanson has this revelation: "There is no friendship: there is no love. The desert knows only allies and accomplices. The heart, here, is all in the very moment. Everything is bump and flow; meet and good-by. Only the Brotherhood of Assassins ensures ritual continuity, if that is what you want and some do; for the lesson our *zikr* teaches is this: *There are no Brothers.*"[32]

All of this may appear far too insular or esoteric to have any real bearing on a world outside the text's own making, and with characteristic shrewdness Gysin's novel seems to endorse exactly such a conclusion. Very near the end, in a supremely self-reflexive gesture, Hanson once again muses that "this whole business is, of course, just a trap well-enough woven of words" (317), yet nothing could be further from the truth. Despite Hanson's demurrals, the novel is never merely a formal exercise, and certainly not, as John Geiger asserts, "a cut-up of memory and pure invention."[33] Earlier, I pointed out just a few of the ways in which the historical imperatives of "Present Time" enter the picture, and it is entirely possible to read the novel—especially its latter sections, where Mya's plans "for Africa . . . for the world" unfold and then unravel—as nothing less than a major work of postcolonial fiction. Gysin's postcolonial critique, launched alongside subtle, quasi-deconstructive gender and queer critiques, allows for a distinctive kind of politics to emerge in *The Process*.

"Fresh Meat and Roses"

Insofar as Gysin's text is committed to the relationship it consistently demonstrates between geographic and historical emplacement and interpersonal connection, readers are presented with a vision of cross-cultural communication and understanding very much at odds with what readers find in Bowles's *The Sheltering Sky* (1949) or *Let It Come Down* (1952) or Albert Camus's *Exile and the Kingdom* (1957), all of which deal with ill-fated encounters between East and West in the colonial Maghreb. For his part, wider philosophical commitments notwithstanding, Camus's response to the "Algerian question" remained strongly colored by his *pied-noir* background. In "The Guest," the best known of the six stories published as *Exile and the Kingdom*, the interactions between Daru the French schoolteacher and the unnamed Arab prisoner, who are undoubtedly meant to stand in for the larger colonial and native populations in French Algeria, are characterized by an almost utter inability to communicate. Their isolation from each other is reinforced by the desert landscape in which Daru and the Arab find themselves. Seemingly always frigid and relentlessly inhospitable, the desert looms large in the *Exile* stories. But whereas the Sahara in Gysin's novel is a dynamic place, full of signs to be read, words to be heard, and energies to be received, in "The Guest" the desert lies under an "unchanging" sky that "shed[s] its dry light on the solitary expanse where nothing had any connection with man [*rien ne rappelait l'homme*]."[34]

Camus's story presents a situation much closer to what Burroughs derides as "this inscrutable oriental shit like Bowles puts down."[35] My aim is not to scapegoat Camus or Bowles on behalf of a recuperated set of Beat writers. But with such writers—Gysin, to be sure, but also Kerouac, Ginsberg, even Burroughs—determined to maintain precisely that "connection" which remains (mostly) foreclosed in Camus's and Bowles's texts, there is a very different conception of one's relation to the Other and to the world at large. *The Process* is in many ways a rewriting of *Let It Come Down*, one that seeks to resolve its intractable questions concerning cross-cultural engagement. Bowles and Gysin were traveling through North Africa together while Bowles was composing his second novel (the first to be set in Morocco), and from the beginning Gysin took a strong, almost proprietary interest in Bowles's work in progress. He lobbied hard for Bowles to change the name, and in late 1951 Bowles even wrote to publisher, John Lehmann, asking, "Do you prefer Fresh Meat and Roses to Let It Come Down as a title? Brion Gysin has been insisting for so many months that a change should be made that I no longer have so strong a faith in my judgment."[36] (Bowles would end up using Gysin's suggestion as the title of his novel's pivotal third section.) Bowles's protagonist, New York bank teller Nelson Dyar, has left for Tangier to escape the "motionlessness" and "dead weight" of his life or, as Dyar imagines it, "to exchange one cage for another."[37] Before long, he becomes enmeshed in the crime and intrigue of international Tangier, and, on the run late in the novel, Dyar stumbles into a crowded café, where ritual Sufi music and dance are being performed. The scene crescendos with a Sufi dancer's self-mutilation, and what Dyar witnesses there affects him deeply, opening up a space of understanding and participation that had been previously unavailable to him. This is how Bowles describes the scene:

> Although the room shook with the pounding of the drums, it was as if another kind of silence were there in the air, an imperious silence that stretched from the eyes of the men watching to the object moving at their feet . . . and always the spasms that forced his body this way and that, in perfect rhythm with the increasing hysteria of the drums and the low cracked voice of the flute, seemed to come from some secret center far inside him. . . . Dyar stole a glance around at the faces of the spectators. The expression he saw was the same on all sides: utter absorption in the dance, almost adoration of the man performing it. A lighted kif pipe was thrust in front of him. He took it and smoked it without looking to see who had offered it to him. (506)

The scene crescendos:

> The music had become an enormous panting. It had kept every detail of
> syncopation intact, even at its present great rate of speed, thus succeeding
> in destroying the listeners' sense of time, forcing their minds to accept the
> arbitrary one it imposed in its place. With this hypnotic device it had gained
> complete domination. . . .
>
> Dyar was there, scarcely breathing. It could not be said that he watched
> now, because in his mind he had moved forward from looking on to a kind
> of participation. With each gesture the man made at this point, he felt a
> sympathetic desire to cry out in triumph. The mutilation was being done
> for him, to him; it was his own blood that spattered onto the drums and
> made the floor slippery. (507–8)

In his reading of this scene, Barry Tharaud underscores the "silence"
evoked at the outset and serving as a kind of connective tissue that links
observer and observed, subject and object. For Tharaud, this silence
stands in direct contrast to the "noise" that has predominated in Dyar's
experience of Tangier and has signaled Dyar's inability to communicate
at any level with the Moroccan world around him. Describing his "move
forward" from observation to participation, Tharaud writes, "This is
Dyar's ultimate escape from isolation and disconnectedness. . . . His new
mode of reality has penetrated to the core of existence, which includes
the kind of connectedness and openness that Dyar experienced at the religious ritual." However, as Tharaud also notes—and as is made evident
by the tragic events that conclude the novel—this so-called new mode of
reality is only fleeting.[38] Dyar's comprehension soon breaks down utterly,
and Bowles's novel seems, finally, to foreclose any possibility of the kind
of direct, unconditioned cross-cultural communication that it has just
offered us a glimpse of.

The silence emphasized by Tharaud is the antidote to the "meaning-
less noise" Dyar usually hears all around, which for Tharaud signals the
foreclosure of communication and connection (29). I would like to suggest that something more ambiguous and productive is going on in this
scene that mirrors the complexities of Bowles's own relationship with
Morocco. There is a way in which one can read the "noise" that shapes
Dyar's experience of Tangier as the only legitimate, ethical way to present
cultural difference as such. Dyar's "imperious silence," then, is a bad faith
gesture that must be rectified, and he is punished by novel's end. In this
case, Bowles's distancing strategy—between Dyar and the new world he
finds himself in, between reader and text—would be analogous to that

which Edwards sees operating in *Sheltering Sky*, where Bowles's inclusion of untranslated Arabic produces a similarly alienating effect.[39] For Edwards, this allows Bowles to escape, to a certain extent, Cold War discourses of cultural transparency, the United States as the measure of all things, and so on. In such a reading, Dyar's silence would be analogous to Port Moresby's desire, in *Sheltering Sky*, to wash away cultural difference in the name of a totalizing existential blankness.

But perhaps by reading Bowles *through* Gysin we can manage to locate, in Dyar's openness, connectedness, and participation, the kernel of a genuine, meaningful experience of transcultural engagement and interaction that *does* manage to escape its immediate foreclosure in the text. Bowles's novel hints at the path forward, but his gesturing toward the Other will find its full expression in Gysin's novel. I want to suggest that *The Process* exists entirely in the space opened up by Dyar's epiphany in the café scene. The action of *Let It Come Down* may turn on Dyar's experience there, but large swaths of Gysin's sprawling plot in *The Process* are, in fact, structured by a series of similar encounters between Hanson and the Assassins. Hanson, armed with his "green passport of keef," takes part in the Assassins' ritual dancing on several occasions. There are other significant points of crossing—narratively, thematically, biographically— between Bowles's text and Gysin's future novel. Hamid's character, for example, is clearly a version of Moroccan painter and writer Mohamed Hamri, who lived with Gysin at the Bowleses' first house in Tangier and became Gysin's link to the Jajouka musicians who would figure so largely in Gysin's life in Morocco.

It is Hamid who, in *The Process*, provides Hanson with his "passport" to see him through his travels through the desert. The scene in Gysin's novel, however, where Hamid "borrows" Hanson's suit and radio actually transpired in real life between Hamri and Bowles, making Gysin's protagonist an even more complex amalgamation. In a sense, Bowles enters Gysin's text by way of the suit and radio episodes, and Hamid's catalyzing presence at key moments in the novel reminds us that Gysin has *Let It Come Down* in mind. In his manner and narrative function, Hamid very much resembles Thami Beidaoui in Bowles's novel. Both are smugglers who frequently steal away from the city to stay with their families (in Hamid's case, his uncles the Master Musicians of Jajouka) in the hills above Tangier. Both are incessant keef smokers who act as unsolicited guides and initiators for their new American friends. Both allow local histories to enter into the narrative: Thami is the black sheep of a prominent Tanjawi family whose association with Moroccan nationalists points the way to Bowles's third novel, *The Spider's House* (1955), and Hamid vividly recounts to Hanson the violence that swept across Morocco in the years prior to independence.

In addition to the presence of this history in each novel, the most relevant point of comparison between them has to do with the role and status of indigenous music and the rituals surrounding it. Bowles had been a musician and composer who studied under Aaron Copland and Virgil Thomson and had a successful career in New York before he moved to Tangier and began writing fiction in earnest. His love of traditional Moroccan music is in large part what kept him there. Considering Bowles's description of his earliest encounter with the music of North Africa, of its accordance with his "infantile criteria" for beautiful sound (repetitive, "non-thinking," etc.), it is tempting to assume that Bowles prizes such music precisely for its timeless, even primitive, quality.[40] But as his knowledge and appreciation grew deeper and more nuanced, and certainly by the time Bowles embarked on the Library of Congress recording project, the historical and political nature of Moroccan music was inseparable from its rhythmic and harmonic textures. Publishing an account of his trek through the Rif Mountains, recording what indigenous music could still be found there, Bowles situated that music within a much larger social and historical context: "The most important single element in Morocco's folk culture is its music. . . . Instrumentalists and singers have come into being in lieu of chroniclers and poets, and even during the most recent chapter in the country's evolution—the war for independence and the setting up of the present pre-democratic regime—each phase of the struggle has been celebrated in countless songs."[41]

"Folk music," according to Bowles, has played and continues to play a role in documenting a long history of struggle and rebellion. Morocco's indigenous music is not at all timeless or unchanging but rather dynamic and adaptive, able to meet new needs and record new phases of a living history. In other words, we are *not* dealing here with Kerouac's "fellahin orientalism." Or if we are, it has been tempered with a strong awareness of historical contingency and geographic specificity. A major aim of Bowles's recording project was to show the great diversity among tribal musics and to assert the richness of indigenous Berber culture that has persisted *and developed* through centuries of Arab and Muslim hegemony. In his travel account, Bowles singles out the Moroccan Rif, a region with a particularly intense history of anticolonial resistance.[42] He again emphasizes the consciousness-altering action of its music, writing, "The Berbers developed a music of mass participation, one whose psychological effects were aimed more often than not at causing hypnosis."[43] The political content of this "music of mass participation"—which, according to Bowles, "celebrates each phase of the struggle"—is manifested for and through a collective body, which serves as both agent and repository of oppositional energies. In his novel Gysin will foreground the subversive and communal aspects of Berber music to an even greater extent, figuring the Jajouka musicians as the modern-day Assassins.

Shortly after Gysin's arrival in Tangier in 1950, he and Bowles attended the Bou Jeloud festival at Sidi Kacem, which is where Gysin declared, "I want to hear that music every day of my life."[44] It is true that Bowles would later admit, "For me Jajouka never had a great musical interest but Gysin went mad about it."[45] In general, the two men seem to have cultivated very different relations to Morocco and Moroccan culture, and these differences become apparent in their respective oeuvres. At one end of the spectrum is Bowles, who, after four decades in Tangier, remained unambiguously Western in his manner of dress and highly critical of the "Rousseauesque" fantasy of "going native."[46] At the other end is Gysin, who often wore a *djellaba* and was considered by Bowles to have "gone native with a vengeance."[47] Each represents an opposing aspect of the "orientalist trap." In the former, cultural difference tends either to be reified and insurmountable; in the latter, such difference is all too easily overcome. So, on one hand, there are Port Moresby in *The Sheltering Sky* and Nelson Dyar in *Let It Come Down*, unwilling or unable to read their surroundings or engage meaningfully with cultural difference, and, on the other hand, Ulys Hanson in *The Process*, the African American professor of history who delights in traveling "in disguise" as African and Muslim. In Gysin's novel, the distance between protagonist and author is clearly marked, suggesting the possibility of inhabiting otherness through and in the act of writing.

Through the world-conjuring power of traditional music, a final uncanny echo of Gysin (and now Bowles) resounds in Burroughs's *Yage Letters*. In the letter dated January 30 [1953], but in fact not composed until early 1955—that is, *after* he had met Bowles and Gysin in Tangier[48]—is where Burroughs first recounts his experience of entering a Colombian cantina and hearing "Shepherd music played on a bamboo instrument like a panpipe" (14). Burroughs' evocative description of "music played on bamboo like a *panpipe*" might very well refer to the annual Bou Jeloud festival, which culminates in the appearance of a boy dressed in goatskins. (Gysin somewhat spuriously interprets this figure as a manifestation of the Greek god Pan.)[49] It is true that Burroughs did not become close with Gysin until Paris, but he did visit the 1001 Nights from time to time, and the possibility of a connection is tantalizing. For Burroughs to gather Pan and Bou Jeloud into his Pasto vision, attributing to the Colombian "mountain music" an "Altantean" origin carried by "phylogenetic" memory, would be typical of the author's figurative assemblages. Such configurations—along with the geographies, communities, and identities they imply—are radically generative: dynamic and multiple yet deeply rooted in time and place.

The representation of history and politics in Gysin's novel requires a concept of worlded time that exceeds, but must also account for, historical time. One of the most pressing, if often submerged, concerns of Gysin's novel is how to represent the folds of worlded immanence that exist within the positivist telos of historical time as "Present Time." So where, and what exactly, *is* history in Gysin's novel? "Present Time" in the novel most often refers to Mya Himmer's plans "for Africa . . . for the world," which, as the narrative progresses, we begin to understand are a response to and continuation of the Moroccan independence movement. An attempt to spark a much broader African insurgency, one "phase" of the Himmers' plot is to free members of the "First Revolutionary Government," including Ben Baraka, in exile at "Fort Tam." The presence of Baraka/Barka and Fard/Fanon among them suggests even larger third worldist ambitions. Thay and Mya continually beseech Hanson to "snap into Present Time" and assume the role of "The Ghoul," leader of their new Africa, which is to say that, for the Himmers, Hanson's usual keef fog clouds out the present moment and would be only a hindrance to their designs. But there is much in Gysin's novel to suggest that keef, and its corresponding "keef time," is the name for another, more radical conception of history and politics. This is made clear enough in a telling passage earlier in the novel, where Hamid describes the forced exile of Morocco's Mohammad V and its aftermath in characteristically keef-inspired language:

> In my little café, I heard Radio Cairo saying our sultan was the prisoner, now, of Mademegascar. Through the keef in my head, I could see this Madame Gascar with her yellow hair and her little yapping white dog she had trained to bite Arabs. If any real French madame had passed through the market right then, I'd have spat on her. And at that very moment, I heard the Whale blow, down below in the Old Town. . . . A voice in my head said; "This Whale is the Whale that's going to eat Tanja!" And it did. It flushed

up from the port, flooding into the Socco, our little plaza framed with cafés, where it began flailing the flukes of its tail in a spray of plate-glass. . . . If you stopped to pick up a thing, you were lost. Money-changers tossed their bills into baskets and were still scooping up change in their hats when they burst into flames from the blast from a hundred, a thousand! hot Arab faces all bellowing: O! (114–15)

The rioting is met with the familiar response: "The policemen popped in and popped out again but, this time, with guns. Their captain screamed: "*Fire!*" In one minute, there were so many people kicking and twitching or dead on the ground that it looked like a movie" (116). The chaos and bloodshed is not restricted to urban Morocco; the Sahara itself has become a police state administered by a series of forts and outposts and their commanders. The captains have authority over Hanson's movements through the desert, but their control is in turn deterritorialized by Hanson and the Assassins he meets, for whom the desert is a space composed of chance encounters and fortuitous connections.

As Mya's officers make their way from Tam to the final rendezvous at Malamut, "present time" and "keef time" seem to converge in a series of increasingly bizarre locations and occurrences. These highly ambivalent scenes are at once the most surreal and the most tightly bound up with North African history and politics. The ruins of the recent colonial past have been occupied by newer, more dubious forces, a shabby amalgamation of imperialist vestiges, Marxism, and Arab nationalism; at Tam, which has the appearance of a "tiny, crenellated white toy fort," the Himmers' secretary, Olav, reports, "We have all been quartered in the Officers' Mess, which was obviously built back in colonial days. Nearby, another unlikely relic lies awash in the sands. It is a long building in concrete built in the form of a transatlantic tanker and is said to have been a brothel whose rooms were the cabins in the superstructure. There was a bar on the captain's bridge. The well-deck was a swimming pool surrounded by walls like the prow of the ship. Today, this astonishing structure has the Cuban flag painted on its side" (267–68). The beached whale of European imperialism lies exposed and desiccated, and history repeats itself as farce as the travelers are questioned by a bearded captain dressed like Fidel Castro. The brothel in the form of an oil tanker is an unambiguous metaphor for colonial exploitation, while the Cuban flag now painted on its side points to a very real history of third world solidarity, yet there is also something rather pathetic about the second-hand nature of the iconography and perhaps even the cause.

Leaving Tam, the party catches a ride atop a "cargo of mattresses" and is driven to the coast, where Olav continues,

> We are in the newly ruined Spanish capital city which must once have been shining white; perhaps, only a year ago. Unless someone catches this place pretty quick, it is going to go back to the desert. Only the barracks are well kept, while private houses and the hotel have been boarded up or have already fallen into ruin since they were broken into and looted. A few Arab fisherman in anonymous rags slouch through the streets and along the abandoned *avenidas* of shut shops. I noticed them hanging their nets from the marquee of a dilapidated movie house down by the beach. (269)

In these final images of a "dying colonialism," to use Fanon's very apt term, the ruined capital becomes a lesson to the well-kept barracks. The nationalist officers, like the captain in Tam with the Castro beard, are using borrowed forms of colonial power and are thus doomed to failure; they are as useless and incongruous as the word *avenida* made to describe rows of pillaged and shuttered shops. The town—and, by extension, the entire colonial-cum-nationalist enterprise it represents—has two sources of possible redemption. One is to "go back to the desert," which, as the novel instructs us, is not a death wish but rather an opening up to the unpredictable but ultimately affirmational energies that permeate the desert landscape. The other source of hope resides in the "Arab fisherman in anonymous rags." Uncanny reminders of a much longer colonial history in the Maghreb, they also suggest the possibility of a lived, material futurity in their improvisatory repurposing of the "dilapidated movie house," where one can still almost imagine the dim flickering of Hollywood dream images on a torn silver screen.

This entire discussion of Gysin's novel began in cinematic terms with a camera tilting down on Hanson's desert caravan. Hamid describes the traumas of "the Whale" as being "like a movie," and a movie house features in the previous passage. It seems appropriate, then, to close with the suggestion that the novel's images of colonialism in ruins anticipate the more surreal moments of a film like Coppola's *Apocalypse Now* (screenplay begun in 1969), especially the scene, restored to the 2001 *Redux* version, in which Willard and his crew chance upon a French plantation, and the spectral imperialism implied by this final outpost of Western civilization. The surreal, hallucinatory temporalities of "keef time"—full of gaps and distortions but also unexpected juxtapositions and sudden revelations—represent not an evasion of "present time," not a disavowal of the past's demands on us in the present, but rather their more profound apprehension in accordance with a worlded sense of history's multiplicity and nonlinearity, of the past's immanence within the present moment.

Thinking about the filmic qualities of Gysin's novel, I am again reminded that genre is a notoriously tricky business in Beat literature. Kerouac's highly constructed works of literary fiction, for instance, have long been read as pure autobiography.[50] But it is Kerouac the *poet*, especially in the 1959 collection *Mexico City Blues*, who is the source of some of Beat literature's most profoundly worlded insights and innovations. Previous chapters have looked at Kerouac's memoir-fiction and the "jazz chorus" sketches of *Mexico City Blues*, the genre of travel writing and Beat travelogues, the manifesto and "manifesto art," and the epistolary form. Gysin's novel is clearly a work of fiction—one of the most overtly fictional works in the entire Beat canon—yet it relies on a very real set of historical, political, and cultural contexts on which it works its textual permutations. With its multiple sites of narration (including a tape recorder and a computer file), rapid jumps in time and space, unaccountable repetitions, and massive self-referentiality ("a trap well-enough woven of words"), Gysin's novel is characteristically postmodern; it shares in another important tradition as well. At least since Sartre and Lukács, fiction—novelistic fiction in particular—has been understood as the privileged category for representing history in literature. This privileging of the novel is doubly true of postcolonial literature; prominent writers from Chinua Achebe to Salman Rushdie and Maryse Condé have often exploited the possibilities within the novel form to recover lost histories or to imagine alternative ones. Reading Gysin within such a lineage allows readers to reevaluate a whole range of Beat texts, whether prose or verse, fiction or memoir, overtly political or not, as also engaged with post/colonial history. Gysin's novel helps us reassess the tangled web of interests and interactions that binds Beat writing to the wider world.

[6]

COLUMBUS AVENUE REVISITED: MAXINE HONG
KINGSTON AND THE POST-BEAT CANON

The Post-Beat Moment

To world the Beats is to wager that their significance, then as now, cannot be reduced to a singular, unified movement among so many others or to what has been called the "Beat Generation," which has been so easily assimilated into the commodity spectacle, thoroughly depoliticized, and packaged as a now-globalized notion of American counterculture. A worlded view of the Beats demands that one seek out the remainder, what gets left out of the always partial and impure affair of assimilation. When one considers the significance, for example, of the surge in readers of *On the Road* in China in the 1990s, of the landmark "Beat Meets East" conference held in Chengdu in 2004, or of Chinese poet Liao Yiwu—a "reluctant dissident," according to Elaine Sciolino of the *New York Times*, "nourished on Beat Generation literature"—it becomes tempting to shape these events into a parable of democracy, consumerism, and the reawakening of spiritual values in a deracinated global culture that nonetheless privileges the American perspective: in short, "to let only the West serve as a vantage point on the world."[1] The response to Beat Generation literature across the globe over the course of the last half century has reframed Beat writing in terms of its transformative potential as well as its blind spots, especially where racial and ethnic difference is concerned.

Can we talk about a post-Beat present? Is there a cohesive, identifiable post-Beat movement out in the world? The Beats saw themselves as members of a cohesive group with a party platform à la Breton and the surrealists or Marinetti and the futurists before them. In this concluding chapter I want to take seriously, however, the possibility that the term "post-Beat" might be able to do some interpretive work. I want to define it provisionally as both a body of texts and a mode of thought. On one hand, it shares with Beat writing a concern for thinking the world as such and, to achieve this, employs a similar set of world-making tactics. On the other hand, post-Beat describes later works that critique, and in some cases "correct," the Beat canon. In the same way that Allen Ginsberg and Gary Snyder draw parallels between their worlded itineraries and Whitman's transnational imaginary in "Passage to India" and elsewhere, actuating the outernational potential at the heart of U.S. literary history (and drawing a line from the so-called American Renaissance of the 1850s to the San Francisco Renaissance), contemporary writers and artists who "talk back" to the Beats can help clarify the significance of Beat legacies today.

In tracking these legacies, what quickly emerges is the fact that moving forward in time means moving outward in space. As signaled by the Chengdu conference, the Beats have made a mark globally. Even before the U.S. counterculture, practically unthinkable absent the Beats, became a hot commodity, supremely exportable, writers, artists, and activists the world over had begun to seize on the Beat movement's transgressive, liberatory energies. Beat writing, in fact, played a larger role in what scholars call the "global sixties" than has generally been acknowledged. References to Beat culture appear throughout Timothy Scott Brown's new book on 1960s-era West Germany, for example. In a particularly telling discussion of poet Rolf Dieter Brinkmann, who "played a major role in first importing literature such as the work of the Beats into West Germany," Brown writes, "For Brinkmann, Beat literature corresponded to deep personal and aesthetic-artistic longings. . . . Yet here *the global was very much prescribed by the needs of the local.* The foreign was, for Brinkmann, an answer to the impasse in which the artist found himself at home."[2] Here the "prescription" is the whole point, the point being that groups and individuals such as Brinkmann have been able to adapt the meanings and significance of Beat writing to fit their immediate needs, contexts, and circumstances. The Beats are being *put to use* in the same way that Beat writers were constantly putting other traditions, other languages, other literatures to use in their own writing.

Along the space-time continuum of literary influence and linkages, a great source for information about the oppositional movements and individual writers who took inspiration from or were otherwise involved with the Beats is *The Transnational Beat Generation* (ed. Grace and Skerl) The volume features several essays about the Beats and their reception in places ranging from Central America to Europe to East Asia. Michele Hardesty writes about Nicaragua under the Sandinistas, when poet-priest Ernesto

Cardenal was minister of culture and drafted the "Declaration of Three" (1982) along with Allen Ginsberg and Soviet poet Yevgeny Yevtushenko. Two decades earlier Cardenal had translated Beat poetry for his 1963 *Antología de la poesía norteamericana*, which he coedited with fellow poet and former politician José Coronel Urtecho. (Their 1979 translation of Ezra Pound contained an afterword by Lawrence Ferlinghetti, who would visit Nicaragua in 1984.) Hardesty concludes, "These projects were predicated on the principle that U.S. poetry was a not a force of cultural imperialism, but rather that poets and poetry were forces that could transcend political borders."[3] Ginsberg and Cardenal's plea for solidarity among the poets of the world is at the same time a pledge of solidarity *with* the world.

Jaap van der Bent writes about the Schule für Dichtung (School for Poetry), which opened in Vienna in 1991. Its founder, Ide Hintze, "had come into contact with Ginsberg the year before. The school was partly a result of their meeting." Van der Bent compares the Schule für Dichtung to the Jack Kerouac School of Disembodied Poetics established at the Naropa Institute (now University) in 1974, and he notes that Ginsberg, Anne Waldman, and other Beat writers have all taught there at time or another.[4] Analogous examples from other locales could be elaborated here, but the bottom line continues to be that at each nodal point of the post-Beat network, local writers, artists, and agitators were adapting the Beat example to fit their own time and place: in other words, *worlding* the Beats. Ginsberg's imagined community of poets transcending nationality and political commitments turns out to be very real, but this community is only made manifest—and "also more *true*," as Hardesty writes—when it is firmly rooted in local soils and local histories.[5] With contributors writing from Japan and across Europe and the United States, *The Transnational Beat Generation* demonstrates, moreover, the extent to which the study of Beat literature has itself become more transnationally situated. In 2013 an English translation of Jorge García-Robles's 1995 book *La bala perdida: William S. Burroughs en Mexico* was published by the University of Minnesota, yet another indication of the broadening geographic scope of Beat studies today. Critics such as García-Robles bring new perspectives to the study of Beat Generation writing and its place in U.S. cultural history and the wider world. In 2010 the European Beat Studies Network was founded and has since held conferences in the Netherlands, Denmark, and Morocco.

Post-Beat writers talking back to the Beat canon, especially from a worlded or transnationalist perspective, are often able to confront head-on the thorny issue of Beat representations of racial and ethnic difference.

They interrogate what a number of critics have called, and not without reason, "Beat orientalism," and what Manuel Luis Martinez describes as the Beat Generation's uncritical reproduction of the American ideology of individualism and mobility: so insidious for Martinez because predicated on keeping minorities "in their place." But perhaps Robert Bennett has a point when he responds that Martinez does not adequately explain "the revolutionary energy that Beat culture *did* unleash."[6] Post-Beat writers have grappled with both the power and the perils of the worlded Beat writing that precedes them. Literary "inheritance" is always a tricky business—Marx and Engels famously abolish hereditary rights in the *Communist Manifesto*—whether that inheritance is along the lines of Harold Bloom's psychic struggle with "the father" or something more akin to Lautréamont's "plagiarism is necessary."[7] The Beats' legacy is clearly multiple, and those who would claim it must sometimes proceed with caution.

Avant-garde groups like the futurists and surrealists, who performatively (and selectively) rejected the cultural inheritance of the West, were singularly concerned about their own future estates. In Marinetti's "Founding and Manifesto of Futurism," Marinetti fantasizes his destruction, writing, "The oldest among us are thirty; so we have at least ten years in which to complete our task. When reach forty, other, younger, and more courageous men will very likely toss us into the trash can, like useless manuscripts. And that's what we want! Our successors will rise up against us, from far away, from every part of the world."[8] How different are the Beats: in particular Ginsberg, who was very much concerned with the futurity of the Beat movement. Interestingly enough, for Ginsberg the Beats' legacy is bound up with a worlded view of culture and connectivity. In Martin Scorsese's 2005 Bob Dylan biography, *No Direction Home*, an elderly Ginsberg describes his first experience listening to Dylan's music: "When I got back from India and got to the West Coast, there's a poet, Charlie Plymell, at a party in Bolinas played me a record of this new young folk singer, and I heard 'Hard Rain['s A-Gonna Fall],' I think, and wept—because [Ginsberg holds back from crying] it seemed that the torch had been passed to another generation, from earlier bohemian or Beat illumination and self-empowerment."[9] The same desires that manifest themselves in the form and function of the manifesto further urged Marinetti and Ginsberg to recognize their heirs, to (either violently or lovingly) pass the torch to the next generation. But most telling is the manner in which Ginsberg seems to conflate his recent experiences abroad, including more than fourteen months spent in India, with the power and emotional intensity of just one Dylan song, as if Dylan had been able to channel all that worlded energy, recognizable at once to the older poet.

No matter its limitations and provisional nature, the concept of the post-Beat brings to the fore the fact that any reconception of space necessarily entails a corresponding reconception of time. Susan Gillman and Kirsten Silva Gruesz have argued, in fact, that the worlded space of the "hemispheric text-network" requires thinking about time in similarly worlded ways, that periodicity is as unstable and multiple as nationality, for example. Space and time, along with Gillman and Gruesz's third term, language (or translation), become the coordinates by which one might plot the intricate paths taken by a text, an author, or an event as it travels within and among cultures. They cite the work of critics and theorists such as Wai Chee Dimock, for whom the structures of deep time and planetarity incorporate both spatial and temporal elements. Tyrus Miller's *Time-Images* is similarly invested in plotting the "alternative temporalities" that have given shape to the world-historical system under modernity and postmodernity.[10] While *Time-Images* echoes Deleuze alongside Henri Bergson and his radical thinking of time as *la durée*, Miller's evocatively titled edited collection *Given World and Time* harks back to Marvell and his coy mistress (*carpe diem* becomes *carpe mundum*), as it charts the dual horizons of space and time across a range of historiographic moments.[11] Likewise, an implicit, but still very operative, claim throughout the preceding chapters has been that to expand the geographic domain of Beat writing is also to expand our sense of the Beat movement's temporal boundaries. In terms of the *subterranean* thought that has grounded this investigation, time itself becomes immanent, multiple, and heterogeneous within the space of the subterranean rhizome. Furthermore, this rhizomic temporality is what allows Beat writing to gather disparate influences, transforming the past from the present moment and remaining open and available to an unforeseen future-to-come.

An earlier chapter made the paradoxical claim that one might begin to determine the transnational dimensions of Beat writing by looking at the Beats in relation to *U.S.* literary traditions. Comparing the San Francisco Renaissance of the 1950s and 1960s to the American Renaissance of Emerson, Whitman, and Thoreau a century earlier, I have suggested that members of that later cohort were following their nineteenth-century predecessors in asserting that U.S. geography and history—the nation's past as well as its present and future—are thoroughly worlded in all the ways I have been attempting to describe. And by looking at how Emerson and company helped shape the worldview of their Beat successors, who actively sought them out as models, one can apprehend the "truth" of those earlier writers' own worldview. Considering the operations of influence as a multidirectional network or assemblage and following a Deleuzian conception of the subterranean rhizome as immanent and multiple, in "Renaissance America" the past is reborn in the unfolding of its often contradictory claims on the present moment. The past is *presenced* in this surplus of transformative potential.

Then, as Beat writing opens out onto the world at large, the temporality of what I have called at times "Beat syncretism" comes to the fore. In contrast to the kind of "fellaheen orientalism" so tempting to ascribe to a work like *On the Road*, where Kerouac sees the entire history of "the fellaheen people of the world" reflected in the eyes of a Mexican peasant girl, the syncretic consciousness of Burroughs's *Yage Letters* or Snyder's *Earth House Hold* or Gysin's *The Process* understands the past not as static and eternal but as alive and dynamic and able to transform and be transformed in the present. The marker of this presence is the radical multiplicity that Burroughs extols throughout *Yage Letters*, especially in the image of the Composite City, with its vast market where all cultures, all races, all forms of real and imagined life are brought into contact with one another. Here, Burroughs's utopian reverie is condensed in the figure of the *transaction*, whether brought about by travel, drugs, writing, sex, camaraderie, or by means as yet undetermined. And what catalyzes all such syncretic visions in Beat writing is an intimation of history or a glimpse of world-historical processes that most likely occurs in some obscure, elliptical, or unexpected ways. This is certainly the case in Gysin's novel, where the violence of anticolonial struggle erupts within Hamid's keef-vision of a whale swallowing Tangier and then reappears in ruins of empire witnessed on the road to Malamut (the beached ship-brothel, the desert/ed ghost town draped with fishing nets, etc.). In *The Process* Gysin repeatedly opposes Hamid's "keef-time" (performative, eruptive, the time of the Assassins) to Mya's "present time" (teleological, logocentric) in a manner not unlike Michel de Certeau's spatial dyad of *lieu* (place: fixed, gridlike) and *espace* (space: open, democratic). And Kingston begins *Tripmaster Monkey* with this disclaimer: "This fiction is set in the 1960s, a time when some events appeared to occur months or even years anachronistically."[12]

Finally, the post-Beat moment raises important questions about the Beats' own place in literary and cultural history. The Beat movement *as such*, rethought along expanded temporal as well as spatial lines, appears—or rather *dis*appears—within a nexus of international avant-garde trajectories. This "disappearing act," as Michael Davidson has figured the nebulous forces and shifting alliances of the San Francisco Renaissance, is the necessary result of rhizomic assemblage at the level of the individual as well as the collective. In Chapter 2 the tortuous temporality of the avant-garde manifesto sets the stage for a number of Beat permutations. In Jacques Derrida's reading of the archetypal *Communist Manifesto*, the deconstructive futurity of the *à-venir* is called on by the manifesto, whose performative energy clears a place for an unconditioned, indeterminate future-to-come. Janet Lyon and other theorists of the manifesto form see its oppositional force residing in the ability to call on and stand in for an entire history of commitment and struggle. The manifesto exists in what Walter Benjamin calls "redemptive time," where present struggles redeem prior ones. Beat writers have engaged with this history in complex ways. The work of Amiri Baraka, for one, suggests that surrealism has been redeemed by the civil rights movement and then by black nationalism. Baraka, along with Joans and Kaufman, taps into and amplifies surrealism's latent anti-imperial, antiracist power.

Maxine Hong Kingston and the Beat Canon

Maxine Hong Kingston is without a doubt best known as the author of *The Woman Warrior* (1975), the mythic recasting of Kingston's "girl-hood among ghosts"—that is to say, her Chinese American upbringing in Northern California. Kingston has also written what I consider to be the quintessential work of post-Beat writing: the 1989 novel *Tripmaster Monkey*. In this novel Kingston talks back, but lovingly, to the Beats. Her novel critiques certain blind spots in Beat writing dealing with race, gender, and ethnicity, but at the same time, her novel redeems the Beats by recognizing and then transforming their transgressive, liberatory spirit to suit the author's own purposes. Kingston's protagonist is Wittman Ah Sing, a fifth-generation Chinese American and belated beatnik who wrestles with the ghost of Kerouac in 1960s San Francisco as he attempts to find his voice and make his way in life. The title, *Tripmaster Monkey* refers in part to Sun Wukong, the monkey king (or monkey god) who assists Xuanzang on the monk's voyage to India to collect Buddhist scriptures and take them back with him to Tang Dynasty China.[13] Their pilgrimage is depicted in *Journey to the West*, a late sixteenth-century tale of travel, adventure, and transculturation that Kingston also makes use of in her novel.

This literal journey westward to India foreshadows the later waves of Chinese emigration "west" to California: the obverse of the *traveling west to reach the East* paradox that so captivated Thoreau as well as Wittman's namesake (*Journey to the West* as another "passage to India"). Buddhism is a traveling religion that truly flourished far from home, and the Beats, of course, have played an important role in popularizing Buddhism in the United States. In *Tripmaster Monkey* Wittman Ah Sing becomes Kingston's 1960s avatar of Sun Wukong: the shapeshifting trickster god now disguised as a North Beach beatnik. Wittman's name is tellingly hybrid, or "mongrel," as Rob Wilson might phrase it. His father "tried to name him after" Walt Whitman, poet of journeys to America's farther shores.[14] While "Ah Sing" is a convincing enough family name, it should also be read it as Whitman's characteristic "I sing." Examples such as these of linguistic error multiply throughout the novel and become quite generative of meaning and critical force. Whitman sought to renew the English language and poetic diction, and this involved many a strange and idiosyncratic neologism; "mistranslations" like the wonderful *camerado*, which the poet uses to describe simultaneously the most intimate connections between men and the most worldly democratic communities, run parallel to the kinds of linguistic minoring and deterritorialization that occur in *Tripmaster*. A similar thing happens with Kerouac and his mangled Spanish in *Mexico City Blues* and elsewhere (e.g., "Do you know what I p a l a b r a").

One can dismiss Kerouac's verbal tourism outright or take a more sympathetic view; the latter, though, requires really grappling with both the good and the bad. These are the choices Wittman wrestles with in Kingston's novel, and in a way Wittman's struggle is akin to James Baldwin's in *Notes of a Native Son*. Both Baldwin and Wittman have to choose between, as Baldwin puts it, "amputation" and "gangrene."[15] One is the dismissal, the giving up on "ghosts" (as Kingston's family calls white Americans), and the other is the (often painful) grappling. Wittman certainly considers himself a "native son" and boasts about the fact that his family has been in California longer than many of the Anglos who still see them as foreigners. And at several points in the novel he reveals his disdain for more recent arrivals from China: "What had he to do with foreigners? With F.O.B. émigrés? Fifth-generation native Californian that he was. Great-Great-Grandfather came on the *Nootka*, as ancestral as the *Mayflower*" (41). In addition to calling himself Go-sei (meaning "fifth generation"), he envies Japanese Americans their term "Americans of Japanese Ancestry," saying "the emphasis is right—'American,' the noun in front, and 'Japanese,' an adjective, behind" (326).

This close attention to language by Wittman and by the novel high-lights again and again the peculiar relationship between language, place, and (personal and group) identity. In Kingston's hands Wittman becomes a postmodern flaneur, and *Tripmaster* opens with a situationist-style dérive that has the effect of deflating the whole Kerouac mystique and its orientalist assumptions. In fact, the opening chapter of the novel unites dérive and détournement in very canny ways. As he wanders through San Francisco, Wittman continually, obsessively, remaps the city; he acts upon the city as a text to be detourned. Such scenes are a singular example of influence that has become spatialized, or influence, *as* geography. The very first lines introduce the city as a character in its own right, a driv-ing force behind the action of Kingston's novel: "Maybe it comes from living in San Francisco, city of clammy humors and foghorns that warn and warn—omen, o-o-men, o dolorous omen, o dolor of omens—and not enough sun, but Wittman Ah Sing considered suicide every day" (3). The author's receptivity to location and climate (which gives rise to her protagonist's own desire to "let it all in") also brings to the fore the dense web of reference and allusion that shapes the novel. "Omen, o-o-men" is unmistakably Kerouac, and the baleful atmosphere of San Francisco, driving Wittman to contemplate suicide, is suffused with literary history, which Wittman, who searches desperately for an authentic self, finds as stifling and oppressive as the fog. His thoughts of suicide are themselves mediated by the literary past; he resolves to shoot himself through the temple, musing, "Hemingway had done it in the mouth. Wittman was not el pachuco loco."[16] The very fact that Wittman wants "the mouth part of his head [to] remain attached" speaks to his desire for liberated expression via a symbolic death and rebirth. He imagines those jumping from the Golden Gate Bridge are giving their final answer to the question "To be or not to be?" (3).

Fortunately, Wittman merely "entertains" such thoughts, but as he strolls through the city in Kingston's opening chapter, he continues to be visited by literary spirits. When he sees "a pigeon and a squatting man" in the park, "both puking," he decides, "This walk was turning out to be a Malte Laurids Brigge walk. There was no helping that" (4). A few pages later, we learn that Wittman indeed carries with him a volume of Rilke, "for such gone days" (8), which he proceeds to read aloud for the delec-tation of his fellow passengers on a crowded city bus. Kingston quotes the famously peripatetic poet verbatim for over a page, and the way that Rilke's words take on new shades of meaning in transit, as well as en-dowing the moving city with new meaning, is exactly what I mean by dérive and détournement combined in the novel. Kingston writes, "None of the passengers was telling Wittman to cool it. It was pleasant, then, for them to ride the bus while Rilke shaded and polished the City's greys and golds" (9). Just as Wittman overlays Rilke onto the city, he begins to imagine a reading program that would have similar effects on the state of California as well, launching into an inventory that becomes both a cartography and an ethics of reading:

> Will one of these listening passengers please write to the Board of Supe[rvisor]s and suggest that there always be a reader on this route? Wittman has begun a someday tradition that may lead to job as a reader riding the railroads throughout the West. On the train through Fresno—Saroyan; through the Salinas Valley—Steinbeck; through Monterey—*Cannery Row*; along the Big Sur ocean—Jack Kerouac; [and so on]. . . . What a repertoire. A lifetime reading job. And he had yet to check out Gertrude Atherton, and Jack London of Oakland, and Ambrose Bierce of San Francisco. And to find "Relocation" Camp diaries to read in his fierce voice when the train goes through Elk Grove and other places where the land once belonged to the A.J.A.s. He will refuse to be a reader of racist Frank Norris. He won't read Bret Harte either, in revenge for that Ah Sin thing. Nor *Ramona* by Helen Hunt Jackson, in case it turned out to be like *Gone with the Wind*. . . . Wittman's talent was that he could read while riding without getting carsick. (9–10)[17]

Wittman's bibliography serves as a critique of xenophobic and orientalist depictions of Asian and Asian Americans in literature, and the ways in which such representations are embedded in a cultural geography. The same goes for film—Wittman avoids the Steinhart Aquarium: "Remember *The Lady from Shanghai*," and so on—and place names in general: "No Oriental Tea Garden, either. 'Oriental.' Shit" (5). And not least, performance as such is vital to Wittman's mapping procedures, as when he reads "in his fierce voice" the diaries of interned Japanese Americans while in the vicinity of the former camps.

The opening lines, so evocative of Kerouac, also set a tone for the liberating deformation of language that occurs throughout the novel. The paranoia evident in the example cited earlier leads to an intensely creative activity. The protagonist's name, Wittman Ah Sing, is obvious enough; the Eastern multitudes his namesake so loved to "sing" are now speaking back and, in Deleuze's formulation, putting a major language to a minor use. On the bus Wittman thinks, "Here we are, Walt Whitman's 'classless society' of 'everyone who could read or be read to'" (9). Likewise, Wittman loves to intone the names of San Francisco sights and streets in a Chinese pronunciation, as if echoing his own name and forging a linguistic connection between himself and the city, as in: "'Fu-li-sah-kah Soo.' He said 'Fleishhacker Zoo' to himself in Chinatown language, just to keep a hand in, so to speak, to remember and so to keep awhile longer words spoken by the people of his brief and dying culture" (6). Such renaming is figured as a creative activity, as when Wittman tries to impress a college crush at a North Beach coffee shop: "I'm an artist, an artist of all the Far Out West. 'Feh-see-no. Soo-dock-dun,' he said, like an old Chinese guy bopping out a list poem. 'Gi-loy. Wah-lay-ho. Lo-di'" (19).[18]

In Wittman's hands, language becomes a weapon. He is fiercely proud of his Chinatown heritage, which extends back over a century and, as he is keen to point out, makes him and his family more native than the white racists who consider him a foreigner. Wittman's rage is often misdirected, though, as when he passes a Chinese family in the park "taking a cheap outing on their day offu. Immigrants. Fresh Off the Boats out in public. . . . So uncool" (5). Wittman's deep-seated ambivalence toward his place in society and direction in life motivates his erratic, self-destructive behavior, but it also liberates his creative spirit. Consider these early passages, notable for this very ambivalence, along with their thick irony: "Whose mind is it that doesn't suffer a loud takeover once in a while? . . . He was not making plans to do himself in, and no more willed these seppuku movies—no more conjured up that gun—than built this city" (3). And just a couple pages later, at the onset of his "Malte Laurids Brigge walk," we hear, "There was no helping that. There is no helping what you see when you let it all come in; he hadn't been in on the building on any city" (4). Through his extreme openness, however, he is now "in on" unmaking and *re*building it—just as Rilke "shaded and polished the City's greys and golds," through naming, through the echoes of "the Chinamen built the railroads." Wittman is in on a very active process of assemblage and world making: through the dérive and détournement, through his intense receptivity, through his minor use of language, through the peculiar pathways of influence, and so forth.

Wittman saves his sharpest critique for "King Kerouac," whose presence Wittman feels most acutely throughout his walk and at several points later in the novel. On one hand Wittman clearly idolizes Kerouac and reads the city through him, but on the other hand he is deeply troubled by the condescension, if not outright racism, present in Kerouac's work. In some sense, Wittman's struggle epitomizes the task of the post-Beat writer or critic. What to make of the less-than-savory depictions of otherness (in terms of race, ethnicity, gender, sexuality) always cropping up in Beat writing? Kingston's novel suggests some powerful tactics: renaming, remapping, simply talking back, among others. Wittman does not blacklist Kerouac—his Big Sur is included on the reading railroad bibliography/itinerary—as he does Norris and Bret Harte, but he does make his qualms known. And this even as he relishes strolling through North Beach with his "beautiful almost-girlfriend" Nanci Li, "the two of them making the scene on the Beach, like cruising in the gone Kerouac time of yore" (20).

As Wittman and Nancy pass City Lights Bookshop, he thinks about the *Howl* trial and how Shigeyoshi "Shig" Murao was "the one charged with selling an obscene book." He then recalls, "There had been a Chinese-American guy who rode with Jack and Neal. His name was Victor Wong, and he was a painter and an actor. . . . All this written up in *Big Sur*, where Jack calls Victor Wong Arthur Ma ('Little Chinese buddy Arthur Ma.' Shit.) . . . It would have been better if Victor/Arthur had been a writing man like the rest of them, but anyway he talked a lot and was good at hallucinations. 'Little Arthur Ma (yet again 'little'!) who never goes anywhere without his drawing paper and his Yellowjacket felt tips of all colors'" (21).

Wittman is dismayed by Kerouac's characterization of "Little" Arthur Ma and feels a need to recuperate him and his role in the novel, stressing how he "talked a lot and was good at hallucination" (ideal Beat traits) and how Kerouac was impressed with his drawing skills and stamina during an all-night drinking and bellowing session at Big Sur. Wittman reserves his most trenchant and highly pitched critique for a little later on in the narrative. Walking downtown, regretting that one cannot be a proper "boulevardier" on sooty Market Street (68), he recalls a poem of Kerouac's describing a Beat city scene, fixating, of course, of the line describing "the twinkling little Chinese" (69). Devastated by the thought that if Kerouac were there, that's how he would see Wittman, he then proceeds to rail:

"Refute 'little.' Gainsay 'twinkling.' A man does not twinkle. A man with balls is not little. As a matter of fact, Kerouac didn't get 'Chinese' right either. Big football player white all-American jock Kerouac. Jock Kerouac. I call into question your naming of me. I trust your sight no more. You tell people by their jobs. And by their race. And the wrong race at that. . . . Listen here, you twinkling little Canuck. What do you know, Kerouac? . . . I'm the American here. I'm the American walking here. Fuck Kerouac and his American road anyway. Et tu, Kerouac. Aiya, even you." (69–70)

Readers may object to the chauvinistic terms of Wittman's quarrel with Kerouac, but his critique is startlingly trenchant nonetheless. It is important to unsettle Beat writing in this way. Wittman points to the same pitfalls under discussion throughout the proceeding chapters, and even as readers relish the power and beauty of Kerouac's world-visions, it is more important to account for what they distort or occlude.

Juliana Spahr is another Bay Area writer who has absorbed and reworked Beat legacies and influence. Like Kingston's novel, the central questions of Spahr's work revolve around a similar nexus of language, place, and identity. Living and teaching in Hawaii for some years, her critical work turned to the politics of language and the fraught linguistic choices facing indigenous writers. Given Hawaii's not too distant colonial past—and the slow pace of its demilitarization—the relationship between language traditions and territorial sovereignty is still very active in the minds of writers there. The flippant title of Spahr's 2001 collection, *Fuck You–Aloha–I Love You*, registers the importance of indeterminacy and multiplicity (linguistic and otherwise), place and performance, in her work. The opening poem, "*localism, or t/here*," begins in Steinian fashion—declaring, "There is no there there anywhere. / There is no here here or anywhere either. / Here and there. He and she. There, there"—and then moves through a series of permutations that bind person and place ever more tightly together.[19] In other poems, Spahr incorporates both Hawaiian and pidgin words that have the effect of both estrangement and intimacy. The text of "*gathering: palolo stream*" is followed by a note that reads, "*Public Access Shoreline Hawai'i vs. Hawai'i County Planning Commission*, 1995 WL 515898 protects indigenous Hawaiians' traditional and customary rights of access to gather plants, harvest trees, and take game." The court decision expressly acknowledges the fact that "the western concept of exclusivity is not universally applicable in Hawai'i," and Spahr's work, taken as a whole, attempts to counteract this foundational "western concept of exclusivity" (31). Like *Aloha*, the collection *This Connection of Everyone with Lungs* seeks out ever new tactics of forging "this connection" between person and place, person and person, person and otherness.

Writing in the wake of the Beats, what both Spahr and Kingston seem to be responding most to is the inseparability of writing, the act of writing, its performance, and *location*. Also motion and movement are included in the name of a creative errancy, whether in Wittman's paranoid *dérive* through San Francisco and the "gone Kerouac time of yore" or in the speaker who asserts in Spahr's "*localism*":

Oh yes. We are lost there and here.
And here and there we err.
And we are that err.
And we are that lost.
And we are arrows of loving lostness
    gliding, gliding, off, and off, and off,
    gliding. (3)

Here again is the image of the flaneur, or perhaps now the *flâneuse*. Anne Friedberg has asserted that there can be no such thing as a flaneuse since, for Friedberg, *flânerie* always implies a subject position of relative dominance and the power to stand apart and remain unmarked.[20] In responding to and critiquing certain less-than-inclusive tendencies among the Beats, post-Beat women writers are also responding to the whole tradition of flânerie in modernity (which involves to power to remap, rename, etc.). In *Tripmaster Monkey* Kingston asserts these rights through Wittman Ah Sing, who is marked racially and ethnically, if not by gender. Anne Waldman, an originary "post-Beat" (alternately, "second generation Beat," "baby Beat"), has also staked a claim on the flaneur tradition. Her 2005 book *Fleuve Flâneur* (in collaboration with Mary and David Kite) changes the already fraught position of the flaneur even more radically by asserting its geographic provenance. The title is a complex formulation, especially considering that, grammatically, the "proper" gender agreement should render it *Fleuve Flân*-euse. It is as if the river (geoconsciousness) works to dissolve gender (grammatical, cultural, or otherwise), and the *fleuve* becomes the image of the errant poet.

Poet Javier Huerta has likewise been described as "post-Beat."[21] His bilingual collection of poetry, *Some Clarifications y otros poemas*, opens up a space for the two languages to deform and transform each other. His 2012 mixed-genre work, *American Copia: An Immigrant Epic*, is, like all epics before it, a "traveling" poem. It opens with a preface that immediately registers the ideological work done to and with language; Huerta tells the story of the day he and his *abuelita* had their naturalization interviews with the Immigration and Naturalization Service: "Then the agent asked her to write the following sentence in English: 'I love America.'"[22] Huerta goes on to say, "By the time of my INS interview, I was an English major at the University of Houston. . . . I wanted to tell the INS agent that I could do things with the English language that she could never imagine." He settles for showing her that his test sentence—"Today I'm going to the grocery store"—"scans as iambic pentameter" and telling

her, "One day . . . I will write an epic starting with that line." This moment
of mastery, however, belies a deeper lesson for the writer: "My mistake
was to think I or anybody else could master this or any other language. I
have since learned of the abundance of language" (xiii). This abundance
of language (the "American *copia*") is a form of jouissance, which destabilizes language and forms as well as the subject, whether a national
subject, an ethnic or racial subject, a gendered subject, and so on. There
will always be a remainder. In Althusserian terms, one can never be fully
reduced to one's ideological image.

Barbara Jane Reyes is a final poet interested in Beat legacies and
whose work explores similar terrain. Reyes was born in the Philippines
and raised in San Francisco, and her poetry combines English, Spanish,
and Tagalog to map a psycho-linguistic terrain overlaying everyday San
Francisco in history, memory, language, and identity. It is always possible
to get lost within such linguistic and historical complexity and transgressive abundance (as against overdetermination), and, like Rebecca Solnit,
Reyes foregrounds and thematizes this potential disorientation (mark of
the modern—likewise, the *poeta* is at large in the city). Her 2005 volume, *Poeta en San Francisco*, where location is everything, comprises
three major sections: *orient, dis-orient*, and *re-orient*, with new valences
of *orient* as "the Orient," or "orientalism." The flipside of an abundant
landscape (Huerta's *copia*) is cultural amnesia and spiritual violence. The
2003 invasion of Iraq looms silently but still felt over *Poeta en San Francisco*. Violence, like language and identity, is layered and omnipresent,
and Reyes's poems conjure that violence to exercise it. In these lines for
example, she conjures California's colonial past:

> we find ourselves retracing the steps of gold
> hungry arrogant spaniards. walking on knees
> behind their ghosts, could we ever know how
> much blood has seeped into the soil—
> this church, a prison. here, tongues
> severed and fed to wild animals.
>
> en esta ciudad we have forgotten how to speak
>
> aquí, en esta ciudad sin memoria.[23]

Silencing is a form of violence ("tongues / severed"), and we in the present must honor the past by giving it voice. Linguistic and cultural displacement becomes physical displacement in a still unfolding history of
conquest, genocide, internment, and now gentrification. Yet San Fran-

cisco has always harbored fugitive, liberatory possibilities and the potential to build new communities from the ground up. Reyes in fact points to Lawrence Ferlinghetti as a classic DIY publisher who started out by "publishing his friends" and has impacted "not just . . . Beat Poetry or San Francisco Poetry, but . . . World Poetry."[24]

Columbus Avenue Revisited: The Post-Beat Umwelt

Descending into the basement of City Lights bookstore, one finds, among sections on feminism and "stolen continents" and stacks of Howard Zinn, a set of shelves marked "Radical Topographies." Here are descendants of a recognizable canon that includes, on the poetico-performative side of the street, Baudelaire's flaneur and Gérard de Nerval's *Promenades et Souvenirs*, the surrealist wanderings of Breton's *Nadja* and Aragon's *Paysan de Paris*, and the lettrist/situationist dérive, and, on the critico-theoretical side, Simmel's urban sociology, Lefebvre's "spatial triad," Bourdieu's *habitus*, and Certeau's dialectic of *lieu* and *espace*. (Benjamin and the *Passagenwerk* seem to me to occupy the middle ground between theory and practice.) The Occupy Wall Streeters, borrowing equally from the Paris Commune and Tahrir Square, remind us that social struggle necessarily involves a struggle over social space. Or as Henry Miller once said, "What is not in the open street is false, derived, that is to say, *literature*."[25] To clarify the Beats' relationship to the history of thinking critically about social space is the aim of these closing pages, and in this regard the errant and uncanny paths of time and space are such that only by reflecting on the contemporary "post-Beat" moment can one determine the final significance of Beat writers as theorists and practitioners of their own "radical topographies."

Near the base of Columbus Avenue, just down the street from City Lights, stands the recently rebuilt International Hotel. Once the heart of San Francisco's Manilatown, the I-Hotel fell victim to the "Manhattanization" of the city during the 1970s and 1980s. Manilatown, located on the northern edge of the Financial District, was swallowed up in the frenzy of high-rise construction. Karen Tei Yamashita has written about the hotel's demise; her *I Hotel* is a polyvocal tale comprising ten interwoven novellas that all converge with the struggle to save the International Hotel. Yamashita gives voice to California's dense history of Asian and Asian American struggle, resistance, and empowerment. The fight for the I-Hotel galvanized an even more diverse constituency; as James Sobredo writes, "The I-Hotel symbolized the Filipino American struggle for identity, self-determination, and civil rights. It was a struggle that involved not only Filipinos but other Asian Americans, African Americans, Latin Americans, student activists, religious groups and organizations, gays and lesbians, leftists, and community activists" (among them the Weather Underground and Jim Jones's Peoples Temple).[26]

At the same time, these *local* stories and struggles over place (one's home, one's place in society: the fate of Manilatown involved both) are also tied to global flows and America's imperial past. Broadly speaking, at the turn of the twentieth century, U.S. imperialism comprised two theatres: Latin America/the Caribbean and the Pacific, with the latter being commanded from San Francisco. Writers and critics from Mark Twain to Gray Brechin have noted that the splendor of the city and its rise as an imperial power center is unthinkable without the trade and militarism of U.S. interests in the Pacific. The city itself is deeply marked by the shocks and juxtapositions of its competing histories. Sobredo points out that San Francisco's Union Square and its centerpiece, the 1903 Dewey Monument, which commemorated Adm. George Dewey's victory over the Spanish in the Battle of Manila Bay, is located just blocks away from Manilatown. Sobredo sums up the view that "that day marked the beginning of the United States as a world superpower" (275). After the United States' subsequent annexation of the Philippines, Filipinos began emigrating to Hawaii and then California in increasing numbers, and Manilatown was born.[27]

The Dewey Monument crowns what Gray Brechin has termed "Imperial San Francisco." And yet, in the end, the city's imperialist history also set in motion countervailing trends: the city's potent blend of anarchism and bohemianism, the labor movement, its openness to spiritual flows from Asia and the Pacific Rim, appreciation of the fierce natural beauty so close at hand—a whole host of factors and forces that would give rise to the San Francisco Renaissance and the West Coast Beat movement. Wilson has described the "warp zone" effect that seems to draw in and transform all these disparate energies. California, and the West in general, has so long served as a repository for clashing ideologies—manifest destiny, the pioneer, U.S. expansion into the Pacific, but also countervailing forces of iconoclasm and pacifism—it would be difficult to find a more overdetermined site than this so-called Bagdad by the Bay. It should not be surprising that writers and artists of all stripes, the occupy movement, gay rights and antimilitarism activists, and all the rest, coupled with the new gold rush of Internet IPOs, continue to spark such creativity and critical thought today or that the "radical topographies" on sale at City

Lights include the work of so many Bay Area thinkers. In a manner not unlike David Pike, who is keenly interested in the cultural history of urban undergrounds, Brechin, a historical geographer based in Berkeley, excavates the political economy of California's subterranean spaces.

For Brechin, the history of San Francisco is the history of empire; accordingly, he appropriates a term from the Roman world—the *contado* —to describe how San Francisco, an imperial city that still controls an enormous amount of wealth, draws in resources from the surrounding hinterlands and repays them in the form of air and water pollution, deforestation, and ecological destruction on a massive scale.[28] Most relevant to the present discussion, however, is Brechin's image of the "inverted pyramid," which shows how the huge wealth generated by California's gold and silver mines ultimately supported a West Coast empire in its own right. This empire's reach now extends much further, drawing in natural resources, labor, and capital from the developing world across the Pacific. In its own way, Brechin's work is another corrective to the Beats' romanticized subterranean, revealing it as a site of power whose occulted nature renders it all the more insidious. But even if it is true that the underground is thoroughly colonized by power, perhaps Brechin does not consider fully enough the antihegemonic potential of Ginsberg's "view from below."

The flipside consists of works and deeds like those recounted in the City Lights collection *Reclaiming San Francisco*: the 1934 general strike, Harvey Milk and the gay rights movement, the racially and ethnically overdetermined history of "urban renewal" in Western Addition and the Fillmore District, the fight to save the International Hotel, and so on. But in recent years, no single writer has seemed more committed to unearthing a subterranean archive of "lost causes" (*lost* yet still vital in the messianic Benjaminian sense) in the name of taking the city back than Rebecca Solnit. Her 2005 paean to errancy, *A Field Guide to Getting Lost*, figures losing one's way as a process of discovery and *recovery*. Taken as a whole, Solnit's work is dedicated to unearthing hidden pathways and giving voice to those whose unsanctioned itineraries have been marginalized by official history. The earlier *Wanderlust: A History of Walking* discusses the power of such an act—both literal and figurative—either to reify or disrupt dominant ideologies.[29] Elsewhere, Solnit also posits the existence of the *flâneuse*, a disruptive presence that troubles imperial space.[30]

In *Hollow City* Solnit and photographer Susan Schwartzenberg document a familiar story of gentrification in San Francisco's Mission and South of Market Districts during the 1990s dot-com boom, the latter neighborhood having been depicted with such loving attention in Kerouac's prose poem "October in the Railroad Earth." ("There was a little alley in San Francisco back of the Southern Pacific at Third and Townsend.")[31] The familiar trend of demolition and displacement has forced out many of the already marginalized residents of South of Market's single-resident occupancy hotels, as well as portions of the Mission's traditionally Latino population. To use Certeau's dyad of fixed, hierarchical "place" and open, heterogeneous "space," Solnit's most recent work seeks to recover the latter within the former. The visually stunning *Infinite City: A San Francisco Atlas* (like its 2013 follow-up, *Unfathomable City: A New Orleans Atlas*) was written and illustrated in collaboration with an array of local artists and activists. The resulting "atlas" remaps and rewrites the terrain of Brechin's *contado*, drawing together heterodox visions of the city's landscape, celebrating alternative histories and positing alternative ecologies.

The radical cartographies that make up Solnit's oeuvre reveal the too-often veiled power dynamics (involving race, class, gender, sexual identity, environmental havoc, flows of capital and desire) that have inscribed themselves on the physical landscape. These are the same histories, inscribed on the city itself, that Wittman Ah Sing tries to deconstruct, performatively, linguistically, as he wanders the city. Kingston's protagonist in *Tripmaster Monkey* is a postmodern flaneur, rewriting the city as he strolls along. It is fitting that he should drawn toward the Tenderloin, where "depressed and unemployed, the jobless Wittman Ah Sing felt a kind of bad freedom" (67). It is fitting that he should ask, "How am I to be a boulevardier on Market Street?" with its "tangles of cables on the ground and in the air, open manholes, construction for years" (68). Wittman's San Francisco is a city in flux, as was Baudelaire's Paris a century earlier. Broke and beatific, in danger of being swallowed up by the street's "open manholes," he is in a perfect position to do his work as a flaneur-critic. Amid the detritus of late capitalism and the byproducts of urban renewal, Wittman unearths signposts pointing the way to revolution. The flaneur's efficacy as a mobile critic and roving dialectical image comes from standing astride two worlds, with those worlds joined *in stride*. Kristin Ross's work on Arthur Rimbaud and the Paris Commune reminds us of the very high stakes of transgressive conceptions of urban, "social" space and its transformative potential under modernity.[32] During the 1870 insurrection, not long after Baron Haussmann's urban renewal projects in the name of an ascendant bourgeoisie, the street *as such* becomes a site and object of proletarian struggle. (*Aux barricades!*) Ross's bold gesture—asserting politically revolutionary origins for the profane illuminations of a supremely apolitical poet (so it goes) like Rimbaud—should have profound implications when thinking about Breton's *révolution surréaliste* and for a broader consideration of avant-garde (which is also to say Beat) politics.

In many ways Walter Benjamin set the terms of critical theory's viewing urban space as revolutionary ("messianic") space. For Benjamin the city's revolutionary potential has to do with the dense layers of history that overlay one another, giving rise to the "shock" of epiphanic juxtaposition. In "Paris, Capital of the Nineteenth Century," he writes,

> Corresponding in the collective consciousness to the forms of the new means of production, which at first were still dominated by the old (Marx), are images in which the new is intermingled with the old. . . . In addition, these wish-fulfilling images manifest an emphatic striving for dissociation with the outmoded—which means, however, with the most recent past. These tendencies direct the visual imagination, which has been activated by the new, back to the primeval past . . . that is, of a classless society. Intimations of this, deposited in the unconscious of the collective, mingle with the new to produce the utopia that has left its traces in thousands of configurations of life, from permanent buildings to fleeting fashions."[33]

Here and in the unfinished *Arcades Project*, Benjamin documents the conditions that gave birth to the Baudelairean flaneur and its later variations. These conditions include first and foremost the modernization and "rationalization" of Paris by Haussmann. The fragments of the old and "outmoded" that somehow managed to escape the city's transformation are precisely where Benjamin, pointing to Baudelaire and the surrealist flaneurs who followed his lead, attempts to locate the harbingers of a truly transformative future-to-come. Yamashita and Solnit and Kingston seem to have found an analogue of Second Empire Paris in late twentieth-century San Francisco, where postwar "urban renewal" led to the displacement of primarily low-income and minority residents. Ironically, in Western Addition and the Fillmore—the heart of the city's African American community—many of those same residents now being pushed out had replaced the Japanese Americans who had been interred during the war. The history of the Bay Area turns out to be a history of displacement, from the Ohlone, who were displaced by the first Spanish settlers, to poor and working-class residents pushed out during the first tech boom to current residents of the Tenderloin on the edge of eviction by the new Twitterhordes.

Finally, while my analysis of the Beat/post-Beat Umwelt owes much

to theorists of social space, from Marx to Benjamin to Pierre Bourdieu
and Michel de Certeau, no current is potentially richer, and more fraught,
than the one connecting Beat writers and the contemporaneous lettrist
and situationist internationals when it comes to both a theory and *practice* of radical topographies. Texts such as "Formulary for a New Urbanism" and "Theory of the Dérive" and the whole lettrist conception
of *psychogeography* were major updates on the flânerie tradition; the
practice of the dérive provided getting lost with a Marxian foundation.
The Beats and the lettrists/situationists not only represent nearly simultaneous manifestations of an avant-garde counterculture in the 1950s and
1960s, but several major Beat writers were living on the situationists' home
turf during the period of their most significant breakthroughs. In *The Beat
Hotel*, however, Barry Miles laments the fact that although Burroughs,
Gysin, Ginsberg, and Gregory Corso walked the same Left Bank streets as
Guy Debord (and probably shared the same hashish connections), nothing tangible ever materialized from these tantalizing near misses. Miles
concludes, somewhat spuriously, that Burroughs and company remained
mostly uninterested in anything that was going on outside the walls of 9
rue Gît-le-Coeur, and their indifference, it seems, was more than mutual.
Debord and the SI were openly hostile to the Beats, calling them "mystical
cretins" in the first issue of *Internationale situationniste*; they deplored the
vestiges of romantic obscurantism and the "rotten egg smell exuded by
the idea of God" in what the Beats stood for![34]

Miles's lament that nothing tangible came of the shared space-time
of these two groups is too literalist and short-sighted. Even if certain
elements of Beat "mysticism" are incompatible with Debord's situationist ideology, one can still think of these two groups together as well as
against one another. What shared conditions was each group responding
to? What kinds of tactics did they employ? What subterranean linkages
might exist between them, underneath their supposed differences? Despite Miles's protestations to the contrary, the Beats living in Paris were
keenly aware of not just the city's glorious past but also the current political and economic straits of the French Republic, inseparable from the
Algerian situation. Even Corso cannot help but figure these issues into
his poetry during the Paris years (e.g., "The Sacré-Coeur Café," "Bomb").
And Burroughs's and Gysin's cut-ups share clear affinities with the situationist practice of *détournement*. The situationists, like the surrealists before them, were motivated by fervently anticolonial sentiments (whether
in North Africa, Indochina, or the unconscious), and in a number of distinct contexts such sentiments are a thread connecting a wide array of

Beat writing, from *Yage Letters* to "Cuba Libre" to *The Process* to the *Black Manifesto*. Even Kerouac muses in *Mexico City Blues* that "the rewards of French Lettrism abide in heaven" (24) (presumably among his own manuscripts published there).

The dérive, like all iterations of modernist or avant-garde flânerie, is an *errance* (derived from the French *errer*, meaning "to wander," to—willingly—get lost, to lose oneself.) In this sense, "to err" is not a failure but rather a generative activity: of new desires, new potentialities, new connections, new communities. Reading *The Yage Letters*, or *The Process*, or Deborah Baker's account of the Beats in India, one can tally the number of times the Beats and others lose their way, fail to communicate, or fail to understand, but if we keep in mind the notion of a productive errancy that runs through Beat travel writing, such failures or limitations will be so only in the positive sense of delimiting as *de-limiting*: that is to say, unmaking boundaries, recognizing difference, and so forth. In the U.S. context, the flaneur that emerges in Beat writing is one interested in tracking down and documenting what might be the last vestiges of the "old, weird America" as it slips into the ever more totalizing global commodity spectacle.[35] Thus, even if the Beat movement began as a distinctly American form of restlessness—as John Clellon Holmes argues in "This Is the Beat Generation"—Beat flânerie, which mirrors and maps the increasingly global flows of late capitalism, must necessarily become a worlded phenomenon.

Today's "radical topographers" want to cure the historical amnesia of the *ciudad sin memoria*. Taken together, all these conceptions of radical topographies—sometimes competing, sometimes complementary—add up to a powerful theory of what I propose to call "nonrational space." Just as contemporary theorists of the *world* and *worlding* oppose themselves to the *globe* of *globalization*, the cartographers of nonrational space endeavor to pry apart the map's fixed grid: in the name of excavating the utopian dreams of past generations (Benjamin), unleashing new and unknown energies of desire in the present (Debord), or giving voice to those who have traditionally remained silent and whose histories have been forced to the margins (Solnit). I hope to have made some small contribution to this theory by suggesting that the subterranean spaces that permeate Beat writing are a vital part of the story that, in turn, offers a different view of Beat writers and their significance today. *This* is the Beat Generation—materially grounded, geographically diverse, historically aware, politically committed—whose legacy is alive and well in the twenty-first century.

NOTES

Introduction: Worlding the Beats

1. See Baker, *Blue Hand*, 155–208. Baker's account weaves together a number of published and unpublished source texts, including Ginsberg's *Indian Journals*.

2. Baker, *Blue Hand*, 162.

3. For Baraka's 1960 account of the trip for *Evergreen Review*, see "Cuba Libre," *Home*, 23–78. James Baldwin, Langston Hughes, and other notables were also scheduled to go, but, we are told, they backed out at the last minute (24). Baraka's "radicalization" is usually dated to 1965, when, spurred by the death of Malcolm X, he changed his name, left his wife and daughter, and moved uptown to Harlem to found the Black Arts Repertory Theatre and School. Tietchen, however, locates an initial break and shift in consciousness five years earlier during the Cuba trip.

4. See Tietchen's chapter on Baraka in *Cubalogues*, 69–97.

5. Miles, *Beat Hotel*, 160.

6. Corso, *Happy Birthday of Death*, 66.

7. Corso was the Beat Generation's *enfant terrible*, comparing himself to the likes of Rimbaud and Shelley. When he was eighteen years old, Corso did time for robbery at New York's infamous Clinton State Prison. He had been incarcerated for larceny and breaking and entering.

8. Skerl, introd. to *Reconstructing the Beats*, 2.

9. Grace and Skerl, "Transnational Beat," introd. to Grace and Skerl, *Transnational Beat Generation*, 11.

10. Damon has written about Bob Kaufman, Jack Spicer, Robert Duncan, and others in her book *The Dark End of the Street: Margins in American Vanguard Poetry*.

11. See Connery and Wilson, *Worlding Project*.

12. Adams, *Continental Divides*, 6; Gillman and Gruesz, "Worlding America," in Levander and Levine, *Companion*, 229. See also Seigel's "Beyond Compare" and Spivak's "Rethinking Comparativism."

13. Gillman and Gruesz, "Worlding America," in Levander and Levine, *Companion*, 229.

14. Muthyala, *Reworlding America*, 2.

15. Adams, *Continental Divides*, 7; Ramazani, *Transnational Poetics*, 17; Wilson, "*Worlding* as Future Tactic," afterword to Connery and Wilson, *Worlding Project*, 212.

16. See Buell, "Ecoglobalist Affects," in Dimock and Buell, *Shades of the Planet*, 227–48.

17. See Connery, "Worlded Pedagogy," in Connery and Wilson, *Worlding Project*, 3.

18. Wilson, "*Worlding* as Future Tactic," afterword to Connery and Wilson, *Worlding Project*, 212.

19. Edwards, *Morocco Bound*, 164.

20. Clifford and Ramazani are quoted in Ramazani, *Transnational Poetics*, 17.

21. Spivak, *Death of a Discipline*, 72, 101.

22. Pease, "Re-mapping the Transnational Turn," in Fluck, Pease, and Rowe, *Re-framing the Transnational Turn*, 1, 10.

23. Dimock, "Literature for the Planet," 175, 178.

24. Dimock, "Deep Time," 763–64.

25. Ibid., 770.

26. Giles, *Global Remapping*, 5.

27. Bercovitch, *Rites of Assent*, 85.

28. Berkeley, "Verses," 4:366.

29. Whitman, *Poetry and Prose*, 531. Subsequent references will be given in parentheses in the text.

30. A bit later Whitman rounds out the list with "the group of powerful brothers toward the Pacific, (destined to the mastership of that sea and its countless paradises of islands,) [which] will compact and settle the traits of America [into a] giant growth, composite from the rest, getting their contribution, absorbing it, to make it more illustrious" (976). Ambiguous, to say the least.

31. Thoreau, *Week*, 94.

32. Thoreau, *Portable Thoreau*, 61, 66–67.

33. Ibid., 603–4.

34. Matthiessen, *American Renaissance*, 84.

35. Thoreau, *Portable Thoreau*, 604.

36. His transcendentalist sense of correspondence might explain the shift from Berkeley's "course" to Thoreau's "star," as well as his conviction that the sun "is the great Western Pioneer whom the nations follow. . . . The islands of Atlantis, and the islands and gardens of Hesperides . . . appear to have been the Great West of the ancients, enveloped in mystery and poetry" (ibid., 605).

37. Thoreau, *Portable Thoreau*, 538–59.

38. Matthiessen, *American Renaissance*, 117–18 (emphasis added).

39. Trotter, "Techno-Primitivism."

40. Emerson, "Ode," 477.

41. Ibid., 478–79. Matthiessen and others have detailed Nietzsche's acute interest in Emersonian philosophy, and we see in these lines that it is only a short leap from "over-god" (or "over-soul") to Übermensch. The "prating" voice in Emerson's poem, however, serves to deflate not just the *translatio imperii* as manifest destiny but the entire rhetoric of "Right" and "Might" that Nietzsche's concept implies. Doris Sommer is right that the imperialist gaze, which she associates with Whitman in particular but which can be said to be characteristic of Thoreau and Emerson as well—it was Emerson, after all, who imagined himself a transparent eyeball, subsuming difference

and appropriating the otherness of the Other—is but the poetico-philosophical counterpart of and, ultimately, the justification for the very real appropriations of manifest
destiny. But Emerson, for one, clearly imagines his spiritual expansiveness to be the
proper antidote to the distinctly American grasping that he decries with such uncharacteristic venom in his "Ode" to Channing; and even Thoreau, for all of his walking,
remains one of America's great homebodies, who projects his world-visions from a
hermit's cabin on the shores of Walden Pond.

42. Berkeley, "Verses," 4:365.

43. Wallerstein, *World-Systems Analysis*, 98.

44. Bürger, *Avant-Garde*, 51 (more on Bürger in chapter 2).

45. Uexküll, *Foray*, 43, 70 (emphasis added).

46. Leibniz, "Principles of Philosophy," 220.

47. Orwell, *Inside the Whale*, 40.

48. Ibid., 42–43.

49. Ibid., 11.

50. Perse, *Selected Poems*, 72 (more on Perse and what Burroughs calls "yage poetry" in chapter 4).

51. Williams, *Paterson*, 100 (punctuation and spacing in the original).

52. Ibid., 43.

53. Ibid., 173, 211.

54. See Derrida, *Rogues*; and Agamben, *State of Exception*. Both books are responding in part to the permanent state of exception created by the United States'
"war on terror."

55. Davis, "Global Resistance."

56. In truly Derridean fashion, Artaud is "supplementing" *himself*. James Clifford has written about "ethnographic surrealism," particularly in relation to Georges
Bataille and the Documents group. More on Artaud and the Tarahumara in chapters
3 and especially 4.

1. A World, a Sweet Attention: Jack Kerouac's Subterranean Itineraries

1. Kerouac, *On the Road*, 276.

2. Kerouac, *On the Road: The Original Scroll*, 381.

3. Kerouac, *Desolation Angels*, 341.

4. Grace, *Literary Imagination*, 145.

5. Kerouac, *Lonesome Traveler*, 23–24.

6. Wilson, "Masters of Adaptation," 197–98, 201–2.

7. Kerouac, *On the Road*, 98.

8. Lawrence, *Classic American Literature*, 151.

9. See Sommer's chapter on Whitman: "Freely and Equally Yours," in *Proceed with
Caution*, 35–61.

10. Adams, *Continental Divides*, 7.

11. Ibid., 26.

12. Kerouac, *Subterraneans*, 3.

13. Melehy, "Exile and Return," 592. See also Melehy, "Nomadic Cartographies,"
in Grace and Skerl, *Transnational Beat Generation*, 31–50.

14. See, for example, Deleuze and Parnet, "On the Superiority of Anglo-American Literature," in *Dialogues II*, 58.

15. In Barry Miles's recent biography of William Burroughs, Miles cites Kerouac's refusal to disavow his mother's attitude toward Ginsberg as the final straw leading to the estrangement between Burroughs and Kerouac, which lasted from 1958 to the end of Kerouac's life. *Call Me Burroughs*, 336–37.

16. For an account of the novel's genesis and evolution, see chapters 3 and 4 of Gewirtz, *Beatific Soul*.

17. Kerouac writes to Donald Allen from Tangier about the need to preserve his "rush of lowdown confession," telling him evocatively, "I want to blow as deep as I want," March 19, 1957, in Kerouac, *Selected Letters*, 17–18.

18. Charters, introd. to "Spontaneous Prose," in Kerouac, *Portable Jack Kerouac*, 481.

19. Ginsberg, dedication to *Howl and Other Poems*.

20. Considerations of the dual nature of Beat writing as both contestatory and community building take very different forms, from the queer cultures of Davidson's *San Francisco Renaissance* and *Guys Like Us* and Ellingham and Killian's *Poet Be Like God* to Yu's more recent *Race*, which again speaks to the reciprocal nature of transpacific and worlded Beat influences. The implications of their readings, especially as they pertain to Beat writing as collective and, above all, political, are developed in the chapters that follow.

21. It is actually Baker in *Blue Hand* who provides a rare glimpse of who the real "subterraneans" were and how their paths intersected those of Ginsberg, Kerouac, and Corso in the crucible of the Village. She does this through her "recovery" of the largely unknown Hope Savage, a Greenwich Village poet and muse who became a world traveler and then disappeared altogether. Baker makes her a central figure in her account of the Beats in India.

22. Dylan, interview by Cameron Crowe.

23. This last claim is derived from Derrida's lengthy discussion of *Hamlet* in *Specters of Marx*.

24. This refrain provides the title of Worden's documentary on Kerouac in Big Sur, *One Fast Move*.

25. Kerouac's triad can be compared with Uexküll's classic formulation of the *Umwelt*: the life-world of the tick consisting only of the odor, warmth, and skin feel of the potential host animal. It can also be compared with Whitman's "When Lilacs Last in the Dooryard Bloom'd," with its determining elements of flower, star, and bird.

26. Kerouac, *Big Sur*, 9–10.

27. Deleuze and Parnet, *Dialogues II*, 36; Lawrence, *Classic American Literature*, 9.

28. Deleuze and Parnet, *Dialogues II*, 36.

29. Lawrence, *Classic American Literature*, 9.

30. Deleuze and Parnet, *Dialogues II*, 36–37.

31. Baraka, "Preface to a *Twenty Volume Suicide Note*," in *Preface*, 3. I am referring to William Harris's categories in his introduction to Baraka's *Reader*, which include "The Beat Period," "The Transitional Period," "The Black Nationalist Period," and so on (see xxii–xxx). The following chapter concerning African American Beat

writing attempts to complicate these categories through the subterranean linkages that connect rather than separate the various phases of Baraka's long career.

32. Ginsberg, quoted in Raskin, *American Scream*, xiv.

33. Kaufman, *Solitudes Crowded with Loneliness*, 11.

34. Dylan, "Subterranean Homesick Blues," 141.

35. Ginsberg, "Howl," in *Collected Poems*, 126.

36. Deleuze and Guattari, *Capitalism and Schizophrenia*, 7, 9.

37. See Deleuze and Parnet, *Dialogues II*, 30. The quote is from Henry Miller's *Hamlet Letters* (1936).

38. Damon's work is particularly instructive with regard to "margins" in American literature. See in particular her chapter on Kaufman in *Dark End*, 32–76.

39. Both quotes are taken from Green and Siegel's film *Weather Underground*.

40. Waldman, *Outrider*, 40.

41. Pike, *Subterranean Cities*, 1. For an account of this history that precedes Pike's by a decade or so, see Lesser, *Life below the Ground*. Ackroyd offers another take on subterranean London in *London Under*. See also Wark, *Beach beneath the Street*, named for the wonderfully resonant situationist slogan from May 1968: *Sous les pavés, la plage*.

42. Pike, *Passage through Hell*, xi. In this particular book, Pike draws heavily from Walter Benjamin and his *Passagenwerk*.

43. Pike, *Subterranean Cities*, 8.

44. Deleuze and Guattari, *Kafka*, 13. Like the Deleuzian "rhizome," their conception of "minor literature" has proven very useful in relation to Kerouac's writing.

45. Dostoevsky, *Notes from Underground*, 36–37.

46. Ellison, *Invisible Man*, 4.

47. Ibid., 7.

48. Nietzsche, *Thus Spake Zarathustra*, 3–4.

49. Lamantia, "Intersection," in *Collected Poems*, 101.

50. See in particular "The Mayan Caper" in Burroughs's *Soft Machine*, 79–92.

51. In *Literary Imagination*, Grace has written at length about Kerouac's conflation of Buddhism and Catholicism. See especially her chapter on *Some of the Dharma*, 133–60.

52. Kerouac, *Tristessa*, 42.

53. Kerouac, *Visions of Cody*, 251. (It's the return of "Jack Iroquois.")

54. Kerouac, *Desolation Angels*, 385.

55. Ibid., 278, 261.

56. Jones, *Mexico City Blues*.

57. Kerouac, "Belief," 59. Davidson, *San Francisco Renaissance*, 21.

58. Kerouac, *Subterraneans*, 6.

59. Kerouac, *Mexico City Blues*, n.p.

60. Through her research into the textual history of *Mexico City Blues*, Grace reveals that, as is so often the case with Kerouac's compositions, there is more to the story than meets the eye (see in particular 173–76.) She notes that although Kerouac largely remained faithful to the constraints of his notebook method, the choruses did not go without strategic revisions, insertions, and emendations. The fiction of spontaneity, like the notebook form, becomes yet one more tactic at the poet's disposal.

61. Certeau, *Practice of Everyday Life*, 27, 117.

62. Wilson, "*Worlding* as Future Tactic," afterword to Connery and Wilson, *Worlding Project*, 212.

63. Certeau, *Practice of Everyday Life*, 115.

64. See Miles, *Call Me Burroughs*, 352.

65. Kerouac, *Lonesome Traveler*, 141.

66. Kerouac to Malcolm Cowley, March 8, 1957, Tangier, in Kerouac, *Selected Letters*, 15.

67. Kerouac, *Desolation Angels*, 346, 354.

2. *The Beat Manifesto: Avant-Garde Poetics, Black Power, and the Worlded Circuits of African American Beat Writing*

1. I am referring to Damon's chapter on Kaufman in *Dark End*, which is titled "Unmeaning Jargon/Uncanonized Beatitude: Bob Kaufman, Poet," 32–76.

2. Kerouac, *Good Blonde and Others*, 155–65.

3. Charters, "Variations on a Generation," xx.

4. Tzara, "Dada Manifesto 1918," 149.

5. Lyon, *Manifestoes*, 12, 16, 39.

6. Puchner, *Poetry of the Revolution*, 22.

7. In fact, the manifesto as a distinctly modernist form has had much to do with notions of the avant-garde manifesto as collage or découpage. See, for example, Carlo Carrà's *Manifestazione Interventista*, Wyndham Lewis's *Blast*, or any number of futurist, Dada, or lettrist works.

8. Puchner, *Poetry of the Revolution*, 89.

9. Bürger, *Avant-Garde*, 22.

10. Perloff, *Futurist Moment*, 7; Cendrars, "Prose," 26.

11. Perloff, *Futurist Moment*, 111.

12. Bürger, *Avant-Garde*, 20–27.

13. See Baudrillard, *Political Economy*, 164–84.

14. Sollors's major study of Baraka's work is titled *Amiri Baraka/LeRoi Jones: The Quest for a "Populist Modernism."*

15. Derrida, *Specters of Marx*, 101–2.

16. See also Winkiel, *Modernism, Race, and Manifestoes*.

17. See Yu, *Avant-Garde*, 19–37.

18. Ramazani, *Transnational Poetics*, 43–44.

19. Nielsen, "Hard Rain," 141.

20. Kaufman, *Solitudes Crowded with Loneliness*, 9.

21. At least one valence in Nielsen's essay is white Beat culture's fascination with the black body. In this regard, see also Sollors, *Amiri Baraka*. Most puzzling about Nielsen's essay on Kaufman is its title, which goes unremarked by the author. Why invoke Bob Dylan's "A Hard Rain's a-Gonna Fall"? Is Dylan's rain also Kaufman's *ancient* rain?

22. Lee, "Black Beats," 162.

23. Joans, "Ted Joans," 6.

24. See Sollors, *Amiri Baraka*, especially chs. 1 and 2.

25. Nielsen, *Black Chant*, 49. The full citation can be found in Oren, "Umbra Poets Workshop," 2:177–223.

26. Nielsen, *Black Chant*, 49.

27. Baraka, *Autobiography*, 243; Tietchen, *Cubalogues*, 87, 96.

28. Baraka, *Home*, 40–41.

29. See W. Harris, introd. to Baraka, *Reader*, xxi–xxiv; Breton, *Manifestoes of Surrealism*, 125.

30. Baraka, "BLACK DADA NIHILISMUS," 72–73.

31. Sollors, *Amiri Baraka*, 127

32. Baraka, *Home*, 238.

33. Artaud, *Theatre and Its Double*, 85 (translation modified).

34. Joans, *Black Manifesto*, 13.

35. Quoted, among other places, in Nicosia, "Lifelong Commitment," introd. to Joans, *Teducation*, iv.

36. Ted Joans, "I, Black Surrealist," unpublished typescript, 1989, Ted Joans Papers, Bancroft Library, Berkeley, CA, 36.

37. Fabre, *From Harlem to Paris*, 308–9.

38. Joans, "Bird and the Beats," 14–15.

39. "For Hip Hosts."

40. Joans, *Teducation*, 222–23.

41. Fabre, *From Harlem to Paris*, 314.

42. Joans, *Teducation*, 156–57.

43. Ted Joans to Allen Ginsberg, unpublished letter, May 3, 1968, Paris, Ginsberg Papers, Green Library, Stanford University, CA. My thanks go out to Rick Swopes for bringing this letter to my attention.

44. Kaufman, *Solitudes Crowded with Loneliness*, 43. James Smethurst writes in capacious terms about the nexus of Jewishness, blackness, and leftism in Kaufman's life and work in "When Indians Were Red," which appears in *Callaloo* in the 2002 special section on Kaufman edited by Maria Damon.

45. See Nicosia, "Lifelong Commitment," introd. to Joans, *Teducation*, iv.

46. Kaufman, *Solitudes Crowded with Loneliness*, 4.

47. Kaufman, *Ancient Rain*, 22, 28, 75–76.

48. Cf. Breton's first *Manifesto of Surrealism*, which also comprises several discrete sections with competing voices, demands, and even typographies.

49. Kaufman, *Solitudes Crowded with Loneliness*, 85.

50. *Abomunist Manifesto*, in *Solitudes Crowded with Loneliness*, 78.

51. See Nicosia, "Lifelong Commitment," introd. to Joans, *Teducation*, v.

52. Perloff, *Futurist Moment*, 90; Puchner, *Poetry of the Revolution*, 90–91.

53. Césaire, "Thoroughbreds," 91.

54. Damon, *Dark End*, 40–41.

3. A Multilayered Inspiration: Philip Lamantia, Beat Poet

1. Breton's praise is quoted, among many other places, in Charters, *Portable Beat Reader*, 317.

2. See, for example, Frattali, *Hypodermic Light*, a rare single-author study of a

Beat writer other than Kerouac, Ginsberg, or Burroughs. For Lamantia's own account of his surrealist involvement, see his interviews by Meltzer, in *San Francisco Beat*, and by Crowe, in "Philip Lamantia."

3. Wheatland, *Frankfurt School*. Adorno, Marcuse, and others eventually made their way to California, and we can pick up this story in Davis's *City of Quartz*, an intellectual history of Los Angeles that devotes a chapter to what I like to call "Frankfurt School West."

4. Meltzer's book of interviews, *San Francisco Beat*, is a treasure trove of information and insight.

5. Lamantia, interview by Meltzer, in Meltzer, *San Francisco Beat*, 134, 137. These and other linkages abound during the wartime period of New York's worlded horizons. Lamantia says it was Paul Bowles, for instance, who introduced him to "world music" during this time (135).

6. Lamantia, *Collected Poems*, 8.

7. Lamantia, interview by Meltzer, in Meltzer, *San Francisco Beat*, 136–38.

8. Bezzola, *André Breton*, 158.

9. Smith, *Utopia and Dissent*, 55.

10. Philip Lamantia, "Intersection," unpublished typescript, n.d., Lamantia Papers, Bancroft Library, Berkeley, CA.

11. Philip Lamantia, interview by John Suiter, December 11, 2000, transcript, Lamantia Papers.

12. Caples, "Note on *Tau*," 6.

13. Cf. Damon on Kaufman's "uncanonized beatitude" in *Dark End*, 32–76.

14. The poem appears in print for the first time in Lamantia's *Collected Poems*, 131–32. Before that, Lamantia's inimitable voice performing the poem was recorded and released on *Howls, Raps, and Roars*.

15. Apollinaire, "Zone," in *Selected Writings*, 117.

16. Caples, Joron, and Peters, "High Poet," introd. to Lamantia, *Collected Poems*, liv.

17. Lamantia, unpublished note, ca. August 1998, Lamantia Papers.

18. Ginsberg, "At Apollinaire's Grave," 180.

19. Miles, *Beat Hotel*, 160.

20. For a full history of the 1844 wall and the *zone non aedificandi*, see Cohen and Lortie, *Fortifs au périf*.

21. Benjamin, "Philosophy of History," 255.

22. Caples, Joron, and Peters, "High Poet," introd. to Lamantia, *Collected Poems*, xliv.

23. Caples, "Note on *Tau*," 6.

24. Wilson accounts for the complexities of conversion in *Be Always Converting*.

25. I refer to the Suiter interview, which became source material for the sections on Lamantia in Suiter's *Poets on the Peaks* (see especially 148–51).

26. Lamantia, interview by Suiter, 24.

27. Lamantia, interview by Meltzer, in Meltzer, *San Francisco Beat*, 142.

28. Lamantia, unpublished typescript, May 16, 1962, Lamantia Papers.

29. Quoted in Suiter, *Poets on the Peaks*, 151. See also Caples's "Note on *Tau*," 1–6.

30. Cf. Kerouac's final breakdown in *Big Sur*, which also ends with a vision of the cross.

31. Lamantia, interview by Meltzer, in Meltzer, *San Francisco Beat*, 138.

32. Carpentier, "Marvelous Real," in Parkinson and Faris, *Magical Realism*, 98.

33. Lamantia, interview by Meltzer, in Meltzer, *San Francisco Beat*, 144.

34. "Enabling fiction" is Davidson's term. It reminds me of what Jonah Raskin says about the night of the Six Gallery reading, after which Ginsberg, Kerouac, and company "went to The Place, a bohemian haunt in North Beach, where they drank, talked, and began to create the legend of the Six Gallery reading," in *American Scream*, 19. This pivotal night in Beat history was from the very beginning a myth, a "legend." Indeed, the Beat legend became their reality as well and cannot be excluded to form a pure literary or cultural historiography.

35. Davidson, *San Francisco Renaissance*, 2, 3.

36. The "pioneering work" I refer to is Matthiessen's *American Renaissance*.

37. Raskin, *American Scream*, 8.

38. Ibid., 19.

39. B. Morgan, *Beat Atlas*, 11.

40. Davidson, *San Francisco Renaissance*, 19.

41. See also Ellingham and Killian, *Poet Be Like God*. In a personal interview conducted in the summer of 2010 by Gabriel Chestnut-Finlay, one of my former Beat Lit students, Snyder similarly pointed to San Francisco's queer-friendly atmosphere and sexual permissiveness as a major early catalyst for the Renaissance.

42. Snyder, *Earth House Hold*, 93.

43. William Everson, interview by Meltzer, in Meltzer, *San Francisco Beat*, 30.

44. Nietzsche, *Thus Spake Zarathustra*, 6.

45. This material was collected and distributed as *Rolling Renaissance: San Francisco Underground Art in Celebration, 1945–1968.*

46. Meltzer, "Revolution Is Dead," in Finson, *Rolling Renaissance*, 33–34.

47. Albright, "San Francisco's Rolling Renaissance," in Finson, *Rolling Renaissance*, 3.

48. Rigney, "Creativity in Bohemia," in Finson, *Rolling Renaissance*, 12–13. Rigney and Douglas Smith researched their 1961 book, *The Real Bohemia: A Sociological and Psychological Study of the Beats*, by administering personality tests to North Beach beatniks. See also Lawlor, *Beat Culture*, 336–37.

49. Albright, "San Francisco's Rolling Renaissance," in Albright, *Rolling Renaissance*, 7.

50. Matthiessen, *American Renaissance*, 596.

51. Whitman, *Uncollected Poetry and Prose*, 1:236.

52. Whitman, "To a Foil'd European Revolutionaire," in *Poetry and Prose*, 497. The original 1856 title was "Liberty Poem for Asia, Africa, Europe, America, Australia, Cuba, and the Archipelagoes of the Sea."

4. Cut-Ups and Composite Cities: The Latin American Origins of Naked Lunch

1. I couldn't resist taking this from the colorfully titled *Rolling Stone* interview "Beat Godfather Meets Glitter Mainman: William Burroughs, Say Hello to David Bowie," by Craig Copetas.

2. Burroughs and Ginsberg, *Yage Letters Redux*, 50.

3. See especially "The Thing Itself," in O. Harris, *Secret of Fascination*, 95–100.

4. Burroughs, prologue to *Junky*, xli. For an extensive account of the novel's genesis and publication history, see Harris's introduction, especially xi–xxxi.

5. Burroughs, *Interzone*, 110–11.

6. Burroughs, *Red Night*, 332.

7. For Deleuze's view on Burroughs and the cut-up method, see *Dialogues II*, 10, 18; and Deleuze and Guattari, *Capitalism and Schizophrenia*, 6.

8. Burroughs, *Interzone*, 65–66.

9. Burroughs, *Queer*, 82.

10. This letter is also published as "Ginsberg Notes" in *Interzone*, 130.

11. The early trilogy refers to *Junky*, *Queer*, and *The Yage Letters*. For a time Burroughs had even conceived of publishing them together as "Naked Lunch, Parts I–III," although, as Harris points out, this "Naked Lunch" was evidently not the same as the text that would ultimately bear that name.

12. Vrbančić has recently written about the "phantasmic maps" of the later novel *Cities of the Red Night* ("Burroughs's Phantasmic Maps"), while Bolton is interested in how Burroughs "destabilizes and diffuses" setting in his novels (see *Mosaic of Juxtaposition*, esp. 80–110). Bolton's thesis is provocative, but I cannot follow him in his insistence on spatial reference in Burroughs as essentially abstraction or simulacrum.

13. The reference to the "sheer contingency" of Burroughs's oeuvre is from Harris's introduction to *Everything Lost*, xxi. Harris's editorial work in recent editions of *Junky*, *Queer*, and *Yage*, as well as the related essays "Virus" and "Final Fix," have all been invaluable.

14. O. Harris, introd. to Burroughs, *Everything Lost*, xxii.

15. On page xxii of his introduction to *Everything Lost*, Harris quotes, in full, spread 52 from Burroughs's 1953 notebook. In *Queer* Allerton is the fictionalized avatar of Lewis Marker, the reluctant lover who accompanied Burroughs on his first yagé journey in Ecuador and Panama.

16. O. Harris, introd. to Burroughs and Ginsberg, *Yage Letters Redux*, xii.

17. See, for example, "Dinner with Legs McNeil, James Grauerholz, Andy Warhol, and Richard Hell," in Burroughs, *Report from the Bunker*, 138–41. That evening, in fact, Burroughs was about to travel to Milan to present a paper at an international conference on psychoanalysis.

18. Burroughs, 1985 introd. to Burroughs, *Queer*, 135. Harris, however, isn't buying Burroughs's stated account of the genesis of his second novel. He thinks it's revisionist and oversimplifies or outright disavows the sexual politics of *Queer*. I agree with Harris in part: it's both/and. (For more on Burroughs, *Queer*, and the return of the repressed, see O. Harris, *Secret of Fascination*, 96–98.)

19. Ibid., 20.

20. One extremely telling example of this "return" is when Vollmer actually does appear to Ginsberg in a dream. See Ginsberg, "Dream Record," 132.

21. Burroughs to Ginsberg, June 24, 1954, Tangier, Burroughs, *Letters*, 217. In his chapter on Burroughs in *Morocco Bound*, Edwards makes much of this intriguing statement, although I believe it steers him off course when it comes to trying to place *Naked Lunch* so firmly (solely) in Tanjawi soil.

22. For the epistolary origins of *Queer*, see Harris, *Secret of Fascination*, 133–40.

23. Skerl, "Freedom through Fantasy," in Skerl and Lydenberg, *At the Front*, 192. Skerl specifically refers to his use of the routine form in *Wild Boys*, but the definition holds generally.

24. O. Harris, introd. to Burroughs and Ginsberg, *Yage Letters Redux*, xxxiii.

25. See ibid., xxiv–xxv.

26. Ibid., xxv.

27. [Ginsberg?], in Burroughs and Ginsberg, *Yage Letters Redux*, 42.

28. Burroughs to Ginsberg, May 23, 1953, Lima, Burroughs, *Letters*, 126. See also Harris's footnote to the letter.

29. See O. Harris, "Virus," 245–46.

30. Kesey's statement was, however, on a book cover blurb. See Burroughs, *Red Night*.

31. I am referring to the 1960 preface to *Naked Lunch*, "Deposition: Testimony Concerning a Sickness," where Burroughs writes, "I apparently took detailed notes on sickness and delirium. I have no precise memory of writing the notes which have now been published under the title *Naked Lunch*," xxxv.

32. Burroughs and Ginsberg, *Yage Letters Redux*, 18.

33. O. Harris, introd. to Burroughs and Ginsberg, *Yage Letters Redux*, xxxiii.

34. Burroughs to Ginsberg, July 10, 1953, Lima, Burroughs, *Letters*, 182.

35. O. Harris, "Final Fix," n.p.

36. Burroughs, *Naked Lunch*, 96. In their *Restored Text* edition of *Naked Lunch*, editors Grauerholz and Miles chose to remove the first instance of the repeated lines at the beginning of "The Market," a decision that Harris takes issue with, arguing that "the editors overlook the longstanding integrity of the 'Composite City' text as it had existed in its manuscript, magazine, and book publishing histories. The descriptive potentials of a socialized approach could have better guided the editors' decisions, even if they were framed by a traditional theory of final authorial intentions" ("Final Fix").

37. O. Harris, introd. to Burroughs and Ginsberg, *Yage Letters Redux*, xxiv.

38. O. Harris, "Final Fix."

39. Burroughs, *Junky*, 52–53, 63.

40. Burroughs, *Naked Lunch*, 4.

41. Burroughs, *Queer*, 65, 57.

42. O. Harris, "Virus," 246.

43. Copetas, "Beat Godfather," 25. Cf. Deleuze: "The only aim of writing is life, through connections which it draws" (*Dialogues II*, 6), and his and Guattari's take on Kafka's "burrow-maker"—an image of the writer and ceaseless creative activity.

44. Burroughs describes the fate of the Interzone material and his varying use of cut-ups in, among many other places, a 1972 interview by Robert Palmer. See Burroughs, *Conversations*, 71–72.

45. O. Harris, introd. to Burroughs and Ginsberg, *Yage Letters Redux*, xxviii.

46. Miles, *Beat Hotel*, 60.

47. Burroughs to Ginsberg, April 22, 1953, Quito; October 29, 1956, Tangier, both in Burroughs, *Letters*, 159, 339.

48. Burroughs and Ginsberg, *Yage Letters Redux*, 38 (emphasis added).

49. Cf. Benjamin's essay "On Hashish," 54, which uses the strange term *mêmité* (Benjamin's coinage) to denote the feeling of "sameness" often induced by the drug. He writes of his Marseille experiment: "Here, in the deepest state of intoxication, two figures passed me as "Dante and Petrarch." He then writes, "All men are brothers."

50. In Gysin's novel *The Process*, the market becomes a figure of world-belonging-ness and the affection between the two main characters, Hanson and Hamid.

51. Edwards, *Morocco Bound*, 174.

52. Kerouac, *On the Road*, 280.

53. Burroughs, *Junky*, 149.

54. O. Harris, *Secret of Fascination*, 123–24.

55. Burroughs, *Junky*, 149.

56. T. Murphy, *Wising Up the Marks*, 66.

57. O. Harris, introd. to Burroughs and Ginsberg, *Yage Letters Redux*, xxiv.

58. In *The Process* Gysin explores the effects of a similar condition brought on by the substance "Borbor." Note that Burroughs's emphasis in explaining Latah sounds remarkably similar to what Althusser will call *interpellation*.

59. Burroughs, *Everything Lost*, spread 41. Some of the earliest cut-ups were done with text from Perse's *Anabasis*: further evidence for the Latin American origins of the cut-up method. For more on the poet's role in shaping *Yage*, see O. Harris's introd. to Burroughs, *Everything Lost*, xiii–xiv.

60. The Artaud connection allies Burroughs with the surrealist anthropology most closely aligned with Georges Bataille and the *Documents* circle but extends to other figures associated with the surrealist movement at one time or another. See also Clifford, "On Ethnographic Surrealism."

61. Artaud, *Peyote Dance*, 12, 13.

62. Artaud, "Surréalisme et révolution," 147. The original text in French of this and other lectures and editorials from the Mexico trip have been lost and now exist only in Spanish translation. For a compendium of these translations, see Artaud, *México*.

63. Artaud, *Peyote Dance*, 28.

64. Artaud, "What I Came to Mexico to Do," 371–72.

65. Burroughs, *Interzone*, 66.

66. Hibbard, "Making of *Naked Lunch*," in Harris and MacFayden, *Naked Lunch@50*, 58–59.

67. Edwards, *Morocco Bound*, 171.

68. Burroughs to Ginsberg, January 23, 1957; October 29, 1956, Tangier, Burroughs, *Letters*, 349, 337.

69. Hemmer, "Natives Are Getting Uppity," in Harris and MacFayden, *Naked Lunch@50*, 69. Hemmer pushes his critique even further in "Aestheticizing the Revolution," in Hibbard and Tharaud, *Bowles/Beats/Tangier*, 99–106.

70. Hibbard, "Making of *Naked Lunch*," in Harris and MacFayden, *Naked Lunch@50*, 56.

71. Hemmer, "Natives Are Getting Uppity," in Harris and MacFayden, *Naked Lunch@50*, 66.

72. See Žižek, "Invent the Symptom," esp. 11–21.

73. Burroughs comments on his post-*Nova* moratorium on the cut-ups in a 1972

interview with Robert Palmer for *Rolling Stone*, republished in Burroughs, *Conversations*. See especially page 71.

74. MacFayden, "Dossier One," in Harris and MacFayden, *Naked Lunch@50*, 13.

75. O. Harris, introd. to Burroughs, *Soft Machine*, xxxi.

76. Burroughs, *Soft Machine*, 18.

77. Ibid., 238.

78. In an unpublished manuscript from this period, Burroughs uses the Composite City passage from *Yage*—which already approximates and anticipates the cut-up aesthetic—as raw material for further cutting up. See *Soft Machine*, xxxi–xxxii.

79. Wild, "Maya Gods of Death," 38.

5. For Africa . . . for the World: Brion Gysin and the Postcolonial Beat Novel

1. Ginsberg, "Seven Years Later," in Burroughs and Ginsberg, *Yage Letters Redux*, 60, 62.

2. Ginsberg uses similar language to describe the psychic aftermath of his 1948 "Harlem visions," which he also recalls in the letter to Burroughs. After hearing the voice of William Blake speak aloud to him and seeing a "blue hand" of divine intelligence stretched out over the city, Ginsberg begins to doubt his sanity and eventually receives treatment at Columbia Psychiatric Institute. In a letter to John Clellon Holmes from this period, Ginsberg wonders if he, "like Oedipus," is "the criminal that has been bringing on all the plague." June 16, 1949, Paterson, Ginsberg, "*Letters of Allen Ginsberg*, 46.

3. Because the cut-ups seem to be a natural extension of Burroughs's formal breakthroughs in *Naked Lunch*, they are often credited to Burroughs alone, but he would insist on calling it the "cut-up method of Brion Gysin." The fullest, most authoritative account of the Beats' Paris years remains that of Miles in *Beat Hotel*. For Miles's discussion of Gysin, see in particular chapters 6, 8, and 9. Gysin provides his own, characteristically transmutated, account of 9 rue Gît-le-Coeur in *The Last Museum*, a novel he had been working since the late 1960s but ended up being the final work he published before his death in 1986.

4. O. Harris, introd. to Burroughs and Ginsberg, *Yage Letters Redux*, xxiv.

5. A notable exception would be Edwards, whose *Morocco Bound* places Burroughs and *Naked Lunch* firmly in their colonial and postcolonial Moroccan contexts. For some, appealing to the postcolonial at all in a book that advertises itself as transnationalism might appear out of sync with current trends. I am thinking again of Pease and his claim in "Re-mapping" that the transnational turn has effectively (re)marginalized the fields of postcolonial studies, ethnic studies, and so on.

6. Gysin took Rolling Stones guitarist Brian Jones to Jajouka in 1968 and later provided the liner notes for Jones's *Pipes of Pan* recording, and jazz pioneer Ornette Coleman would also visit and perform with the Master Musicians.

7. Waldman, *Outrider*, 40; Di Prima, *Recollections*, 254.

8. Gysin, *Back in No Time*, 132. Gysin's article, with an accompanying demonstration of his and Burroughs's method, first appeared in *Evergreen Review* and was published later that year in *Brion Gysin Let the Mice In*.

9. Geiger, *Nothing Is True*, 45. Thus, Gysin's name can be added to the venerable

list of "dissident" surrealists that includes Georges Bataille, Antonin Artaud, Salvador Dalí, and Louis Aragon.

10. Weiss, introd. to Gysin, *Back in No Time*, ix.

11. Although it has since fallen out of critical favor, "hybridity" was once a powerful organizing concept within postcolonial studies. See in particular Bhabha, *Location of Culture*. The performance of hybridity is a central theme in Gysin's life and work.

12. Gysin and Wilson, *Here to Go*, xvii.

13. See Edwards, *Morocco Bound*, especially chs. 4 and 6.

14. At the other extreme of what Edwards calls the "orientalist trap" is the desire for total identification with the Other: for example, Sal Paradise's "wishing I were a Negro" (180) in *On the Road* or, earlier, "They thought I was a Mexican, of course, and in a way I am" (98).

15. Quoted in Geiger, *Nothing Is True*, 202.

16. While in the Canadian military, Gysin met the great-grandson of Rev. Josiah Henson, who had been the model for Harriet Beecher Stowe's "Uncle Tom." Gysin was inspired to write *To Master: A Long Goodnight* (1946) as an update to Stowe's novel (Geiger, *Nothing Is True*, 64–65). It was Gysin's long coda on "The History of Slavery in Canada" that earned him a Fulbright in 1949.

17. Edwards, "Moroccan Paul Bowles."

18. Geiger, *Nothing Is True*, 91–92.

19. Bowles, "Preface," 7. According to Bowles, "Tangier was never the same after the 30th of March 1952" (7).

20. Gysin, *Process*, 137–38. Given Lévi-Strauss's appearance in the text, plus the fact that Mya's organization calls itself "GRAMMA," a "splinter-group of something called 'Logosophy'" (207), and the novel's highly performative critique of logocentrism in general—Hanson's final mission is "*to rub out the Word*"—it becomes very tempting to posit at least some knowledge of Derrida and deconstruction on Gysin's part. Although Derrida's *Of Grammatology* was first published in 1967, just two years before Gysin's novel, these tantalizing allusions probably extend no further than the more immediate referents of the Himmers and Scientology.

21. After visiting Alamut in 1973, Gysin composed an account of his journey and a meditation on Sabbah's influence called "A Quick Trip to Alamut: The Celebrated Castle of the Hash-Head Assassins," published in Gysin, *Back in No Time*, 218–39.

22. Gysin, "Fire: Words by Day—Images by Night," in *Back in No Time*, 244.

23. Gysin, *Process*, 217, 218 (ellipses in the original).

24. Burroughs and Ginsberg, *Yage Letters Redux*, 28

25. Ibid., 146.

26. Geiger, *Nothing Is True*, 202.

27. Ibid., 201–2.

28. Within the orbit of Gysin's novel, I am thinking of the textual assemblage that includes Artaud's "Voyage to the Land of the Tarahumara" (*Peyote Dance*), where Artaud's paranoiac-anthropological methods drives him to read the Central American landscape palimpsestically, to unearth, from beneath the accreted layers of Western civilization, signs of an indigenous culture nearly destroyed by European colonialism and Mexican nationalism in turn. As we have seen, Artaud's "Tarahumara," like his

earlier manifestoes for the "Theatre of Cruelty," is a fiercely anticolonial text, and echoes of Artaud can be found in such disparate Beat writings as *Yage*, Lamantia's posthumously published *Tau*, and Baraka's "Revolutionary Theatre."

29. Gysin, *Process*, 17 (emphasis added).

30. Ellipses in the original.

31. One of the many affinities between Gysin's and Burroughs's work is this shared image of the market. The previous chapter looks closely at the crucial sequence from *Yage Letters*, reprised in *Naked Lunch*, where Burroughs writes of a "Composite City where all human potentials are spread out in a vast silent market" (50). For both writers, the market becomes a potent symbol of transgressive exchange and the liberatory promise of radically proliferating desires.

32. Gysin, *Process*, 35–36.

33. Geiger, *Nothing Is True*, 28.

34. Camus, "The Guest," 93.

35. Burroughs to Ginsberg, January 26, 1954, Tangier, Burroughs, *Letters*, 195.

36. Bowles to John Lehmann, Tangier, October 1, 1951, Bowles, *In Touch*, 239–40.

37. Bowles, *Let It Come Down*, 262; Bowles, *Sheltering Sky*, 260.

38. Tharaud, "Language, Noise, Silence," in Hibbard and Tharaud, *Bowles/Beats/Tangier*, 29–30.

39. Edwards, *Morocco Bound*, 113.

40. For an early take on North African music, see Bowles, "Bowles on Bowles," in Swan, *Paul Bowles Music*, 5–7.

41. Bowles, "The Rif, to Music," in *Their Heads Are Green*, 97–98.

42. A recent chapter in this long history of Berber intransigence was the Rif War of 1920–26. Spain's attempts at consolidating power in northern Morocco after the Treaty of Fez led to an escalation of violence across the region, and an independent (though short-lived) Republic of the Rif was created in 1923. The following year, French forces joined the Spanish in a redoubled effort to subdue the Berber insurgents, while in Paris the newly formed surrealist group rallied against French involvement in the Moroccan Rif.

43. Bowles, *Their Heads Are Green*, 98.

44. Gysin, "Hamri's Hands," in *Back in No Time*, 279. Compare Gysin's statement to Bowles's claim, "When I first heard Arabic music on records, I determined to go live where I could be surrounded by sounds like those" ("Paul Bowles," 38).

45. Quoted in Sawyer-Lauçanno, *Invisible Spectator*, 329.

46. Bowles, *Conversations with Paul Bowles*, 77.

47. T. Morgan, *Literary Outlaw*, 322.

48. See O. Harris, introd. to Burroughs and Ginsberg, *Yage Letters Redux*, 114n14.

49. Gysin, "The Pipes of Pan," 122–24.

50. For an extended discussion of Kerouac and the question of fiction versus memoir, see Grace, *Literary Imagination*.

6. Columbus Avenue Revisited: Maxine Hong Kingston and the Post-Beat Canon

1. Elaine Sciolino, "Poet's Nightmare in Chinese Prison," *New York Times*, April 9, 2013; Connery, "Worlded Pedagogy," in Connery and Wilson, *Worlding Project*,

7. For a broader account of these developments, see Wen Chu-an's entry, "Beats in China," in Lawlor's encyclopedic *Beat Culture*, 58–60.

2. Brown, *Global Sixties*, 139–40 (emphasis added).

3. Hardesty, "'Writers of the World," in Grace and Skerl, *Transnational Beat Generation*, 118.

4. Van der Bent, "Beating Them to It?," in Grace and Skerl, *Transnational Beat Generation*, 177.

5. Hardesty, "Writers of the World," 118.

6. For Beat orientalism, see, for example, Gray, *Gary Snyder*, 130. Martínez, *Countering the Counterculture*, 3–19; Bennett, "Deconstructing and Reconstructing," 181 (emphasis added).

7. Bloom articulates his well-known thesis in *The Anxiety of Influence* and elsewhere; for another take on influence, see Ducasse [Lautréamont]'s *Poésies*, esp. 67.

8. Marinetti, "Founding and Manifesto," 51.

9. Ginsberg, interview, in Scorsese, *No Direction Home*.

10. See T. Miller, *Time-Images*.

11. See T. Miller, *Given World and Time*.

12. Kingston, *Tripmaster Monkey*, n.p.

13. In the more immediate 1960s context, "tripmaster" refers to someone who, having him- or herself refrained, acts as a guide (and chaperone) to individuals who have taken LSD.

14. Kingston, *Tripmaster Monkey*, 161.

15. Baldwin, *Notes of a Native Son*, 112.

16. Kingston, *Tripmaster Monkey*, 3. "Pachuco" refers to the Chicano hipsters of the 1930 and 1940s who, as Mauricio Mazón, Anthony Macías, and others have argued, were forerunners of the beatniks.

17. The "Ah Sin thing" refers to Harte's satirical poem *The Heathen Chinee* (1870).

18. Fresno, Stockton (Kingston's hometown), Gilroy, Vallejo, and Lodi are outlying farm towns of northern California and the Central Valley, where migrant labor is absolutely essential to the crop production that takes place on such a massive scale.

19. Spahr, *Aloha*, 3.

20. See Friedberg on the "mobilized" and "virtual" gaze, in *Window Shopping*, 15–40.

21. I am referring to the publicity material for the Latino Literature/La literatura latina IV Conference organized by the Latino Literary Cultures Project/Proyecto Culturas Literarias Latinas at the University of California, Santa Cruz, November 30, 2012.

22. Huerta, *American Copia*, xi.

23. Reyes, *Poeta en San Francisco*, 19.

24. Reyes, "Indie Publishing."

25. H. Miller, *Black Spring*, 3.

26. Sobredo, "Manila Bay," in Brook, Carlsson, and Peters, *Reclaiming San Francisco*, 279.

27. Twain was moved to condemn the annexation in the strongest terms. The Spanish War was to him what the Mexican War was to Thoreau fifty years prior.

28. According to statistics from the International Monetary Fund, the San Francisco Bay Area ranked twenty-first among nations based on its 2012 gross domestic product of $594 billion, just below Switzerland and ahead of Sweden, Belgium, and Taiwan. "World Economic Outlook Database," *International Monetary Fund*, April 2015, www.imf.org.

29. Solnit's study *Wanderlust* reads a number of the figures (e.g., Thoreau, Baudelaire, Benjamin, Breton) who are central to this chapter and this book.

30. See, for example, Solnit's incisive chapter "Other Daughters, Other American Revolutions," in *Gates of Paradise*, 297–306.

31. Kerouac, *Lonesome Traveler*, 37.

32. See Ross, *Emergence of Social Space*.

33. Benjamin, "Paris," 148.

34. Situationist International, "Sound and the Fury," in Knabb, *Situationist International Anthology*, 47. It is as if a founding gesture of the SI was to distance itself from the Beats.

35. I take this phrase from Greil Marcus's evocatively titled study, *The Old, Weird America: The World of Bob Dylan's Basement Tapes*.

BIBLIOGRAPHY

Ackroyd, Peter. *London Under: The Secret History beneath the Streets*. New York: Doubleday, 2011.

Adams, Rachel. *Continental Divides: Remapping the Cultures of North America.* Chicago: University of Chicago Press, 2009.

Agamben, Giorgio. *State of Exception*. Translated by Kevin Attell. Chicago: University of Chicago Press, 2005.

Albright, Thomas. "San Francisco's Rolling Renaissance." In Finson, *Rolling Renaissance*, 5–10.

Andrae, Thomas, Bertrand Augst, and Trinh T. Minh-ha, eds. "The Silent Beat." Special issue, *Discourse* 20, nos. 1–2 (1998).

Anzaldúa, Gloria. *Borderlands/La Frontera*. 25th anniversary ed. San Francisco: Aunt Lute, 2012.

Apollinaire, Guillaume. "Zone." In *Selected Writings*, translated by Roger Shattuck, 116–27. New York: New Directions, 1971.

Aragon, Louis. *Paris Peasant*. Translated by Simon Watson Taylor. Boston: Exact Change, 1994.

Artaud, Antonin. *México*. Edited by Luis Cardoza y Aragón. Mexico City: Universidad Nacional Autónoma de México, 1962.

———. *The Peyote Dance*. Translated by Helen Weaver. New York: Farrar, Straus and Giroux, 1976.

———. "Surréalisme et révolution." In *Oeuvres complètes*, 8:141–50. 28 vols. Paris: Gallimard, 1971.

———. *The Theatre and Its Double*. Translated by Victor Corti. London: Calder and Boyars, 1970.

———. "What I Came to Mexico to Do." In *Selected Writings*, edited by Susan Sontag, 370–74. New York: Farrar, Straus and Giroux, 1976.

Austin, J. L. *How to Do Things with Words*. Edited by J. O. Irmson and Marina Sbisà. 2nd ed. Cambridge, MA: Harvard University Press, 1975.

Baker, Deborah. *A Blue Hand: The Beats in India*. New York: Penguin, 2008.

Baldwin, James. *Notes of a Native Son*. Boston: Beacon, 1984.

Baraka, Amiri [LeRoi Jones]. *The Autobiography of LeRoi Jones*. Chicago: Hill, 1997.

———. *The Dead Lecturer*. New York: Grove, 1964.

———. *Home: Social Essays*. New York: Akashi, 2009.

———. *The LeRoi Jones/Amiri Baraka Reader*. Edited by William J. Harris. New York: Thunder's Mouth, 1991.

———. *Preface to a Twenty Volume Suicide Note*. New York: Totem, 1961.

———. *S O S: Poems, 1961–2013*. Edited by Paul Vangelisti. New York: Grove, 2015.

Baudrillard, Jean. *For a Critique of the Political Economy of the Sign*. Translated by Charles Levin. Saint Louis: Telos, 1973.

Bauer, Ralph. "Hemispheric Studies." *PMLA* 124, no. 1 (2009): 234–50.

Benjamin, Walter. *The Arcades Project*. Edited by Rolf Tiedemann. Translated by Howard Eiland and Kevin McLaughlin. Cambridge, MA: Belknap, 2002.

———. *On Hashish*. Edited by Howard Eiland. Cambridge, MA: Harvard University Press, 2006.

———. "Paris, Capital of the Nineteenth Century." In *Reflections: Essays, Aphorisms, Autobiographical Writings*, edited by Peter Demetz, 146–53. New York: Schocken, 1986.

———. "Theses on the Philosophy of History." In *Illuminations: Essays and Reflections*, edited by Hannah Arendt, translated by Harry Zohn, 253–64. New York: Schocken, 1969.

Bennett, Robert. "Deconstructing and Reconstructing the Beats: New Directions in Beat Studies." *College Literature* 32, no. 2 (2005): 177–84.

Benston, Kimberly. *Baraka: The Renegade and the Mask*. New Haven, CT: Yale University Press, 1976.

Bercovitch, Sacvan. *The Rites of Assent: Transformations in the Symbolic Construction of America*. New York: Routledge, 1993.

Berkeley, George. "Verses on the Prospect of Planting Arts and Learning in America." In *Works*, edited by Alexander Campbell Fraser, 4:365–66. 4 vols. Oxford: Clarendon, 1901.

Bezzola, Tobia. *André Breton: Dossier Dada*. Ostfildern-Ruit, Germany: Hatje Cantz, 2005.

Bhabha, Homi. *The Location of Culture*. New York: Routledge, 1994.

Bloom, Harold. *The Anxiety of Influence: A Theory of Poetry*. 2nd ed. Oxford: Oxford University Press: 1997.

Bolton, Michael Sean. *Mosaic of Juxtaposition: William S. Burroughs' Narrative Revolution*. Amsterdam: Rodopi, 2014.

Bowles, Paul. "Bowles on Bowles." In *Paul Bowles Music*, edited by Claudia Swan, 5–7. New York: Eos, 1995.

———. *Conversations with Paul Bowles*. Edited by Gena Dagel Caponi. Jackson: University Press of Mississippi, 1993.

———. *In Touch: The Letters of Paul Bowles*. Edited by Jeffrey Miller. New York: Farrar, Straus and Giroux, 1994.

———. *The Sheltering Sky, Let It Come Down, The Spider's House*. Edited by Daniel Halpern. New York: Library of America, 2002.

———. *Their Heads Are Green and Their Hands Are Blue: Scenes from the Non-Christian World*. New York: Harper, 2006.

———. "Thirty Years Later." Preface to *Let It Come Down*, 7–14. New York: Harper, 2006.

Brechin, Gray. *Imperial San Francisco: Urban Power, Earthly Ruin*. Berkeley: University of California Press, 2006.

Breton, André. *Manifestoes of Surrealism*. Translated by Richard Seaver and Helen R. Lane. Ann Arbor: University of Michigan Press, 1969.

———. *Nadja*. Translated by Richard Howard. New York: Grove, 1960.

Brown, Timothy Scott. *West Germany and the Global Sixties: The Anti-authoritarian Revolt, 1962–1978*. Cambridge: Cambridge University Press, 2013.

Buell, Lawrence. "Ecoglobalist Affects: The Emergence of U.S. Environmental Imagination on a Planetary Scale." In Dimock and Buell, *Shades of the Planet*, 227–48.

Bürger, Peter. *Theory of the Avant-Garde*. Translated by Michael Shaw. Minneapolis: University of Minnesota Press, 1984.

Burroughs, William S. *Cities of the Red Night*. New York: Holt, 1981.

———. *Conversations with William S. Burroughs*. Edited by Allen Hibbard. Jackson: University Press of Mississippi, 1999.

———. *Everything Lost: The Latin American Notebook of William S. Burroughs*. Edited by Geoffrey D. Smith, John M. Bennett, and Oliver Harris. Columbus: Ohio State University Press.

———. *Interzone*. Edited by James Grauerholz. New York: Viking, 1989.

———. *Junky: The Definitive Text of "Junk."* Edited by Oliver Harris. New York: Penguin, 2003.

———. *The Letters of William S. Burroughs*. Vol. 1, *1945–1959*. Edited by Oliver Harris. New York: Penguin, 1993.

———. *Naked Lunch*. New York: Grove, 1990.

———. *Naked Lunch: The Restored Text*. Edited by James Grauerholz and Barry Miles. New York: Grove, 2001.

———. *Queer*. Edited by Oliver Harris. 25th anniversary ed. New York: Penguin, 2002.

———. *The Soft Machine: The Restored Text*. Edited by Oliver Harris. New York: Grove, 2014.

———. *The Wild Boys: A Book of the Dead*. New York: Grove, 1994.

———. *With Williams Burroughs: A Report from the Bunker*. Edited by Victor Bockris. New York: St. Martin's Press, 1996.

Burroughs, William S., and Allen Ginsberg. *The Yage Letters*. San Francisco: City Lights, 1986.

———. *The Yage Letters Redux*. Edited by Oliver Harris. San Francisco: City Lights, 2006.

Campbell, James. *This Is the Beat Generation: New York–San Francisco–Paris*. Berkeley: University of California Press, 2001.

Camus, Albert. *Exile and the Kingdom*. Translated by Justin O'Brien. New York: Vintage, 1986.

Caples, Garrett. "A Note on *Tau*." In Lamantia, *Tau*, 1–15.

Caples, Garrett, Andrew Joron, and Nancy Joyce Peters. "High Poet: The Life and Work of Philip Lamantia." Introduction to Lamantia, *Collected Poems*, xxi–lxiii.

Carpentier, Alejo. "The Baroque and the Marvelous Real." In *Magical Realism: Theory, History, Community*, edited by Lois Parkinson Zamora and Wendy B. Faris, 89–108. Durham, NC: Duke University Press, 1995.

Cendrars, Blaise. "The Prose of the Transsiberian and of Little Jeanne of France." In *Complete Poems*, translated by Ron Padgett, 15–29. Berkeley: University of California Press, 1993.

Certeau, Michel de. *The Practice of Everyday Life*. Translated by Steven F. Rendall. Berkeley: University of California Press, 1984.

Césaire, Aimé. "The Thoroughbreds." In *The Collected Poetry*, translated by Clayton Eshleman and Annette Smith, 90–103. Berkeley: University of California Press, 1984.

Charters, Ann, ed. *The Beats, Literary Bohemians in Postwar America*. Detroit: Gale, 1983.

———, ed. *The Portable Beat Reader*. New York: Penguin, 1992.

———, ed. *The Portable Jack Kerouac*. New York: Penguin, 1992.

———. "Variations on a Generation." Introduction to *Portable Beat Reader*, xv–xxxvi.

Chu-an, Wen. "Beats in China." In *Beat Culture: Lifestyles, Icons, and Impact*, edited by William Lawlor, 58–60. Santa Barbara, CA: ABC-CLIO, 2005.

Clifford, James. "On Ethnographic Surrealism." *Comparative Studies in Society and History* 23, no. 4 (1981): 539–64.

———. *Routes: Travel and Translation in the Late Twentieth Century*. Cambridge, MA: Harvard University Press, 1997.

Cohen, Jean-Louis, and André Lortie. *Des fortifs au périf: Paris, les seuils de la ville*. Paris: Picard, 1991.

Connery, Christopher Leigh. "Worlded Pedagogy in Santa Cruz." Introduction to Connery and Wilson, *Worlding Project*, 1–12.

Connery, Christopher Leigh, and Rob Wilson, eds. *The Worlding Project: Doing Cultural Studies in the Era of Globalization*. Santa Cruz, CA: New Pacific, 2007.

Copetas, Craig. "Beat Godfather Meets Glitter Mainman: William Burroughs, Say Hello to David Bowie." *Rolling Stone*, February 28, 1974, 24–27.

Corso, Gregory. *The Happy Birthday of Death*. New York: New Directions, 1960.

Damon, Maria, ed. "Bob Kaufman, Poet: A Special Section." *Callaloo* 25, no. 1 (2002): 105–231.

———. *The Dark End of the Street: Margins in American Vanguard Poetry*. Minneapolis: University of Minnesota Press, 1993.

Davidson, Michael. *Guys Like Us: Citing Masculinity in Cold War Poetics*. Chicago: University of Chicago Press, 2004.

———. *San Francisco Renaissance: Poetics and Community at Mid-Century*. Cambridge: Cambridge University Press, 1984.

Davis, Angela Y. "Global Resistance to Global Capitalism: Reformulating Race, Class, and Gender in the 21st Century." Lecture given at Central Washington University, Ellensburg, WA, May 6, 2005.

Davis, Mike. *City of Quartz: Excavating the Future in Los Angeles*. London: Verso, 1990.

Debord, Guy, and Gil J. Wolman, "User's Guide to Détournement." In Knabb, *Situationist International Anthology*, 14–21.

Deleuze, Gilles, and Félix Guattari. *Capitalism and Schizophrenia*. Vol. 2, *A Thousand Plateaus*. Translated by Brian Massumi. Minneapolis: University of Minnesota Press, 1987.

———. *Kafka: Toward a Minor Literature*. Translated by Dana Polan. Minneapolis: University of Minnesota Press, 1986.

Deleuze, Gilles, and Claire Parnet. *Dialogues II*. Translated by Hugh Tomlinson, Barbara Habberjam, and Eliot Ross Albert. New York: Columbia University Press, 2002.

Derrida, Jacques. *Rogues: Two Essays on Reason*. Translated by Pascale-Anne Brault and Michael Naas. Stanford, CA: Stanford University Press, 2005.

———. *Specters of Marx: The State of the Debt, the Work of Mourning, and the New International*. Translated by Peggy Kamuf. New York: Routledge, 1994.

Diderot, Denis. *Supplément au Voyage de Bougainville*. In *Political Writings*, edited by John Hope Mason and Robert Wokler, 31–76. Cambridge: Cambridge University Press, 1992.

Dimock, Wai Chee. "Deep Time: American Literature and World History." *American Literary Studies* 13, no. 4 (2001): 755–75.

———. "Literature for the Planet." *PLMA* 116, no. 1 (2001): 173–88.

———. *Through Other Continents: American Literature across Deep Time*. Princeton, NJ: Princeton University Press, 2008.

Dimock, Wai Chee, and Lawrence Buell, eds. *Shades of the Planet: American Literature as World Literature*. Princeton, NJ: Princeton University Press, 2007.

Di Prima, Diane. *Recollections of My Life as a Woman: The New York Years*. New York: Penguin, 2001.

———. *Revolutionary Letters*. San Francisco: Last Gasp, 2007.

Dostoevsky, Fyodor. *Notes from Underground*. Translated by Mirra Ginsburg. New York: Bantam, 1974.

Ducasse, Isidore [Comte de Lautréamont]. *Poésies and Complete Miscellania*. Edited and translated by Alexis Lykiard. London: Allison and Busby, 1978.

Dylan, Bob. *Chronicles*. Vol. 1. New York: Simon and Schuster, 2004.

———. Interview by Cameron Crowe. Liner notes. *Biograph*. New York: Columbia, 1985.

———. *Lyrics, 1962–2001*. New York: Simon and Schuster, 2004.

Edwards, Brian T. "The Moroccan Paul Bowles." *Michigan Quarterly Review* 50, no. 2 (2011): 191–209.

———. *Morocco Bound: Disorienting America's Maghreb, from Casablanca to the Marrakech Express*. Durham, NC: Duke University Press, 2005.

Edwards, Brian T., and Dilip Parameshwar Gaonkar, eds. *Globalizing American Studies*. Chicago: University of Chicago Press, 2010.

Ellingham, Lewis, and Kevin Killian. *Poet Be Like God: Jack Spicer and the San Francisco Renaissance*. Middleton, CT: Wesleyan University Press, 1998.

Ellison, Ralph. *Invisible Man*. New York: Vintage, 1980.

Emerson, Ralph Waldo. "Ode Inscribed to W. H. Channing." In *Selected Writings*, edited by William H. Gilman, 476–79. New York: Penguin, 1965.

Fabre, Michel. *From Harlem to Paris: Black American Writers in France, 1840–1980*. Urbana: University of Illinois Press, 1991.

Finson, Bruce, ed. *Rolling Renaissance: San Francisco Underground Art in Celebration, 1945–1968*. San Francisco: Intersection, 1968.

Fluck, Winfried, Donald Pease, and John Carlos Rowe, eds. *Re-framing the Transnational Turn in American Studies*. Hanover, NH: Dartmouth College Press, 2011.

"For Hip Hosts." *Time*, February 15, 1960.

Frattali, Steven. *Hypodermic Light: Philip Lamantia and the Question of Surrealism*. New York: Lang, 2005.

Friedberg, Anne. *Window Shopping: Cinema and the Postmodern*. Berkeley: University of California Press, 1994.

García-Robles, Jorge. *The Stray Bullet: William S. Burroughs in Mexico*. Translated by Daniel C. Schechter. Minneapolis: University of Minnesota Press, 2013.

Geiger, John. *Nothing Is True, Everything Is Permitted: The Life of Brion Gysin*. New York: Disinformation, 2005.

Gewirtz, Isaac. *Beatific Soul: Jack Kerouac on the Road*. London: Scala, 2008.

Giles, Paul. *The Global Remapping of American Literature*. Princeton, NJ: Princeton University Press, 2011.

Gillman, Susan, and Kirsten Silva Gruesz. "Worlding America: The Hemispheric Text-Network." In *A Companion to American Literary Studies*, edited by Caroline F. Levander and Robert S. Levine, 228–47. Malden, MA: Wiley, 2011.

Ginsberg, Allen. *Collected Poems, 1947–1997*. New York: Harper, 2007.

———. *Howl and Other Poems*. San Francisco: City Lights, 1956.

———. *Indian Journals*. New York: Grove, 1970.

———. *The Letters of Allen Ginsberg*. Edited by Bill Morgan. Cambridge, MA: Da Capo, 2008.

Grace, Nancy M. *Jack Kerouac and the Literary Imagination*. New York: Palgrave, 2007.

Grace, Nancy M., and Ronna C. Johnson. *Breaking the Rule of Cool: Interviewing and Reading Women Beat Writers*. Jackson: University Press of Mississippi, 2004.

Grace, Nancy M., and Jennie Skerl, eds. *The Transnational Beat Generation*. New York: Palgrave, 2012.

———. "Transnational Beat: Global Poetics in a Postmodern World." Introduction to Grace and Skerl, *Transnational Beat Generation*, 1–11.

Gray, Timothy. *Gary Snyder and the Pacific Rim: Creating Countercultural Community*. Iowa City: University of Iowa Press, 2006.

Green, Sam, and Bill Siegel. *The Weather Underground*. Washington, DC: Independent Lens, 2003.

Gruesz, Kirsten Silva. *Ambassadors of Culture: The Transamerican Origins of Latino Writing*. Princeton, NJ: Princeton University Press, 2001.

Gysin, Brion. *Back in No Time: The Brion Gysin Reader*. Edited by Jason Weiss. Middleton, CT: Wesleyan University Press, 2001.

———. *The Process*. Woodstock, NY: Overlook, 2005.

Gysin, Brion, and Terry Wilson. *Here to Go: Planet R-101*. San Francisco: Re/Search, 1982.

Hardesty, Michele. "'If the Writers of the World Get Together': Allen Ginsberg, Lawrence Ferlinghetti, and Literary Solidarity in Sandinista Nicaragua." In Grace and Skerl, *Transnational Beat Generation*, 115–28.

Harris, Oliver. "Can You See a Virus? The Queer Cold War of William Burroughs." *Journal of American Studies* 33, no. 2 (1999): 243–66.

———. Introduction to Burroughs, *Everything Lost*, ix–xxvi.

———. Introduction to Burroughs, *Junky*, ix–xxxiii.

———. Introduction to Burroughs, *Queer*, ix–l.

———. Introduction to Burroughs, *Soft Machine*, ix–liii.

———. Introduction to Burroughs and Ginsberg, *Yage Letters Redux*, ix–lii.

———. "Not Burroughs's Final Fix: Materializing *The Yage Letters*." *Postmodern Culture* 16, no. 2 (2006).

————. *William Burroughs and the Secret of Fascination*. Carbondale: Southern Illinois University Press, 2006.

Harris, Oliver, and Ian MacFayden, eds. *Naked Lunch@50: Anniversary Essays*. Carbondale: Southern Illinois University Press, 2009.

Harris, William J. Introduction to Baraka, *Reader*, xvii–xxx.

Hemmer, Kurt. "Aestheticizing the Revolution: William S. Burroughs in Tangier." In Hibbard and Tharaud, *Bowles/Beats/Tangier*, 99–106.

————. "The Natives Are Getting Uppity: Tangier and *Naked Lunch*." In Harris and MacFayden, *Naked Lunch@50*, 65–72.

Hemmer, Kurt, and Tom Knoff. *Wow! Ted Joans Lives!* Palatine, IL: Harper College, 2010.

Hibbard, Allen. "Tangier and the Making of *Naked Lunch*." In Harris and Mac-Fayden, *Naked Lunch@50*, 56–64.

Hibbard, Allen, and Barry Tharaud, eds. *Bowles/Beats/Tangier*. Denver: International Centre for Performance Studies, 2010.

Holmes, John Clellon. *Nothing More to Declare*. New York: Dutton, 1967.

————. "This Is the Beat Generation." *New York Times Magazine*, November 16, 1952.

Howls, Raps, and Roars: Recordings from the San Francisco Poetry Renaissance. San Francisco: Fantasy, 1993.

Huerta, Javier O. *American Copia: An Immigrant Epic*. Houston: Arte Público, 2012.

————. *Some Clarifications y otros poemas*. Houston: Arte Público, 2007.

Joans, Ted. "Bird and the Beats." *Coda: The Jazz Magazine*, no. 181 (1981): 14–15.

————. *A Black Manifesto in Jazz Poetry and Prose*. London: Calder and Boyars, 1971.

————. "Ted Joans: Tri-Continental Poet." Interview by Henry Louis Gates Jr. *Transition*, no. 48 (1975): 4–12.

————. *Teducation: Selected Poems, 1949–1999*. Edited by Gerald Nicosia. Saint Paul, MN: Coffee House, 1999.

Johnson, Ronna C., and Nancy M. Grace, eds. *Girls Who Wore Black: Women Writing the Beat Generation*. New Brunswick, NJ: Rutgers University Press, 2002.

Jones, James T. *Map of Mexico City Blues: Jack Kerouac as Poet*. Carbondale: Southern Illinois University Press, 1992.

Kaplan, Amy. *The Anarchy of Empire in the Making of U.S. Culture*. Cambridge, MA: Harvard University Press, 2005.

Kaplan, Amy, and Donald E. Pease, eds. *Cultures of United States Imperialism*. Durham, NC: Duke University Press, 1994.

Kaufman, Bob. *The Ancient Rain: Poems, 1956–1978*. New York: New Directions, 1981.

————. *Solitudes Crowded with Loneliness*. New York: New Directions, 1965.

Kerouac, Jack. *Big Sur*. New York: Penguin, 1992.

————. *Desolation Angels*. New York: Riverhead, 1995.

————. *Good Blonde and Others*. Edited by Donald Allen. San Francisco: City Lights, 1994.

————. *Lonesome Traveler*. New York: Grove, 1988.

————. *Mexico City Blues*. New York: Grove, 1994.

————. *On the Road*. New York: Penguin, 1976.

———. *On the Road: The Original Scroll*. Edited by Howard Cunnell. New York: Viking, 2007.

———. *Road Novels, 1957–1960*. New York: Library of America, 2007.

———. *Selected Letters*. Vol. 2, *1957–1969*. Edited by Ann Charters. New York: Penguin, 2000.

———. *The Subterraneans*. New York: Grove, 1958.

———. *Tristessa*. New York: Penguin, 1992.

———. *Visions of Cody*. New York: Penguin, 1993.

Kingston, Maxine Hong. *Tripmaster Monkey: His Fake Book*. New York: Vintage, 1990.

———. *The Woman Warrior: Memoirs of a Girlhood among Ghosts*. New York: Vintage, 1989.

Kipling, Rudyard. *Kim*. New York: Dover, 2005.

Knabb, Ken, ed. *Situationist International Anthology*. Berkeley: Bureau of Public Secrets, 2006.

Knight, Brenda, ed. *Women of the Beat Generation: The Writers, Artists, and Muses at the Heart of a Revolution*. 2nd ed. Berkeley: Conari, 1998.

Kuri, José Férez. *Brion Gysin: Tuning in to the Multimedia Age*. London: Thames and Hudson, 2003.

Kyger, Joanne. *Strange Big Moon: The Japan and India Journals, 1961–1964*. Berkeley: North Atlantic, 2000.

Lamantia, Philip. *The Collected Poems*. Edited by Garrett Caples, Andrew Joron, and Nancy Joyce Peters. Berkeley: University of California Press, 2013.

———. "Philip Lamantia: Shaman of the Surreal." Interview by Thomas Rain Crowe. *Rain Taxi* 10, no. 2 (Summer 2015).

———. *"Tau" by Philip Lamantia and "Journey to the End" by John Hoffman*. Edited by Garrett Caples. San Francisco: City Lights, 2008.

Lawrence, D. H. *Studies in Classic American Literature*. New York: Penguin, 1977.

Lee, A. Robert. "Black Beats: The Signifying Poetry of LeRoi Jones/Amiri Baraka, Ted Joans and Bob Kaufman." In *The Beat Generation Writers*, edited by A. Robert Lee, 158–77. London: Pluto, 1996.

Leibniz, Gottfried Wilhelm. "The Principles of Philosophy; or, the Monadology." In *Philosophical Essays*, translated by Roger Ariew and Daniel Garber, 213–25. Indianapolis: Hackett, 1989.

Lesser, Wendy. *The Life below the Ground: A Study of the Subterranean in Literature and History*. London: Faber and Faber, 1986.

Lewis, Wyndham, ed. *Blast: The Review of the Great English Vortex*. New York: Kraus Reprint, 1967.

Lyon, Janet. *Manifestoes: Provocations of the Modern*. Ithaca, NY: Cornell University Press, 1999.

MacFayden, Ian. "Dossier One." In Harris and MacFayden, *Naked Lunch@50*, 4–13.

Macías, Anthony. *Mexican Mojo: Popular Music, Dance, and Urban Culture in Los Angeles, 1935–1968*. Durham, NC: Duke University Press, 2008.

Marcus, Greil. *Lipstick Traces: A Secret History of the Twentieth Century*. Cambridge, MA: Harvard University Press, 1990.

———. *The Old, Weird America: The World of Bob Dylan's Basement Tapes*. New York: Picador, 2001.

Marinetti, Filippo Tommaso. "Founding and Manifesto of Futurism." In *Let's Murder the Moonshine: Selected Writings*, edited by R. W. Flint, translated by R. W. Flint and Arthur A. Coppotelli, 47–52. Los Angeles: Sun and Moon, 1991.

Martínez, Manuel Luis. *Countering the Counterculture: Rereading Postwar American Dissent from Jack Kerouac to Tomás Rivera*. Madison: University of Wisconsin Press, 2003.

Marx, Karl. *Selected Writings*. Edited by David McLellan. Oxford: Oxford University Press, 2000.

Matthiessen, F. O. *American Renaissance: Art and Expression in the Age of Emerson and Whitman*. London: Oxford University Press, 1941.

Maynard, John A. *Venice West: The Beat Generation in Southern California*. New Brunswick, NJ: Rutgers University Press, 1993.

Mazón, Mauricio. *The Zoot-Suit Riots: The Psychology of Symbolic Annihilation*. Austin: University of Texas Press, 1984.

Melehy, Hassan. "Jack Kerouac and the Nomadic Cartographies of Exile." In Grace and Skerl, *Transnational Beat Generation*, 31–50.

———. "Literatures of Exile and Return: Jack Kerouac and Quebec." *American Literature* 84, no. 3 (2012): 589–615.

Meltzer, David. "The Revolution Is Dead." In Finson, *Rolling Renaissance*, 32–34.

———. *San Francisco Beat: Talking with the Poets*. San Francisco: City Lights, 2001.

Miles, Barry. *The Beat Hotel: Ginsberg, Burroughs, and Corso in Paris, 1957–1963*. New York: Grove, 2001.

———. *Call Me Burroughs: A Life*. New York: Twelve, 2014.

Miller, Henry. *Black Spring*. New York: Grove, 1963.

———. *Hamlet Letters*. Edited by Michael Hargraves. Santa Barbara, CA: Capra, 1988.

Miller, Tyrus, ed. *Given World and Time: Temporalities in Context*. Budapest: Central European University Press, 2008.

———. *Time-Images: Alternative Temporalities in Twentieth-Century Theory, History, and Art*. Newcastle upon Tyne, UK: Cambridge Scholars, 2009.

Morgan, Bill. *Beat Atlas: A State by State Guide to the Beat Generation in America*. San Francisco: City Lights, 2011.

Morgan, Ted. *Literary Outlaw: The Life and Times of William Burroughs*. New York: Norton, 2012.

Murphy, Gretchen. *Hemispheric Imaginings: The Monroe Doctrine and Narrative of U.S. Empire*. Durham, NC: Duke University Press, 2005.

Murphy, Timothy S. *Wising Up the Marks: The Amodern William Burroughs*. Berkeley: University of California Press, 1998.

Muthyala, John. *Dwelling in American: Dissent, Empire, and Globalization*. Hanover, NH: Dartmouth College Press, 2012.

———. *Reworlding America: Myth, History, and Narrative*. Athens: Ohio University Press, 2006.

Nicosia, Gerald. "A Lifelong Commitment to Change: The Literary Non-Career of Ted Joans." Introduction to Joans, *Teducation*, i–vii.

Nielsen, Aldon. *Black Chant: Languages of African American Postmodernism*. Cambridge: Cambridge University Press, 1997.

———. "'A Hard Rain': Looking to Bob Kaufman." *Callaloo* 25, no. 1 (2002): 135–45.

Nietzsche, Friedrich. *Thus Spake Zarathustra*. Translated by Thomas Common. New York: Dover, 1999.

Oren, Michel. "The Umbra Poets Workshop, 1962–1965: Some Socio-Literary Puzzles." In *Studies in Black American Literature*. Vol. 2, *Belief vs. Theory in Black American Literary Criticism*, edited by Joe Weixlmann and Charles J. Fontenot, 177–223. Greenwood, FL: Penkevill, 1986.

Orwell, George. *Homage to Catalonia and Down and Out in Paris and London*. Boston: Houghton Mifflin Harcourt, 2010.

———. *Inside the Whale and Other Essays*. London: Penguin, 1969.

Pease, Donald E. "Introduction: Re-mapping the Transnational Turn." In Fluck, Pease, and Rowe, *Re-framing the Transnational Turn*, 1–46.

———. *The New American Exceptionalism*. Minneapolis: University of Minnesota Press, 2009.

Perloff, Marjorie. *The Futurist Moment: Avant-Garde, Avant Guerre, and the Language of Rupture*. Chicago: University of Chicago Press, 1986.

Perse, Saint-John. *Selected Poems*. Edited by Mary Ann Caws. New York: New Directions, 1982.

Pike, David. *Passage through Hell: Modernist Descents, Medieval Underworlds*. Ithaca, NY: Cornell University Press, 1997.

———. *Subterranean Cities: The World beneath Paris and London, 1800–1945*. Ithaca, NY: Cornell University Press, 2005.

Puchner, Martin. *Poetry of the Revolution: Marx, Manifestos, and the Avant-Gardes*. Princeton, NJ: Princeton University Press, 2005.

Ramazani, Jahan. *A Transnational Poetics*. Chicago: University of Chicago Press, 2009.

Raskin, Jonah. *American Scream: Allen Ginsberg's "Howl" and the Making of the Beat Generation*. Berkeley: University of California Press, 2004.

Reyes, Barbara Jane. "Indie Publishing: Some Thoughts." February 13, 2008. *Barbara Jane Reyes, Poeta y Diwata*. WordPress.org.

———. *Poeta en San Francisco*. Kaneohe, HI: Tinfish, 2005.

Rigney, Francis J. "Creativity in Bohemia." In Finson, *Rolling Renaissance*, 12–14.

Rigney, Francis J., and L. Douglas Smith. *The Real Bohemia: A Sociological and Psychological Study of the Beats*. New York: Basic, 1961.

Ross, Kristin. *The Emergence of Social Space: Rimbaud and the Paris Commune*. London: Verso, 2008.

———. *May '68 and Its Afterlives*. Chicago: University of Chicago Press, 2002.

Said, Edward. *Culture and Imperialism*. New York: Vintage, 1994.

———. *Orientalism*. New York: Vintage, 1979.

Saldívar, José David. *Border Matters: Remapping American Cultural Studies*. Berkeley: University of California Press, 1997.

———. *Trans-Americanity: Subaltern Modernities, Global Coloniality, and the Cultures of Greater Mexico*. Durham, NC: Duke University Press, 2011.

Sawyer-Lauçanno, Christopher. *An Invisible Spectator: A Biography of Paul Bowles*. New York: Weidenfeld and Nicolson, 1989.

Scorsese, Martin. *No Direction Home: Bob Dylan*. Hollywood, CA: Paramount, 2005.

Seigel, Micol. "Beyond Compare: Comparative Method after the Transnational Turn." *Radical History Review* 91 (Winter 2005): 62–90.

Skerl, Jennie. "Freedom through Fantasy in the Recent Novels of William S. Burroughs." In *William S. Burroughs at the Front: Critical Reception, 1959–1989*, edited by Jennie Skerl and Robin Lydenberg, 189–96. Carbondale: Southern Illinois University Press, 1991.

———. Introduction to Skerl, *Reconstructing the Beats*, 1–7.

———, ed. *Reconstructing the Beats*. New York: Palgrave, 2004.

———. *William S. Burroughs*. Boston: Hall, 1985.

Situationist International. "The Sound and the Fury." In Knabb, *Situationist International Anthology*, 47–49.

Smethurst, James. "Remembering When Indians Were Red: Bob Kaufman, the Popular Front, and the Black Arts Movement." *Callaloo* 25, no. 1 (2002): 146–64.

Smith, Richard Cándida. *Utopia and Dissent: Art, Poetry, and Politics in California*. Berkeley: University of California Press, 1995.

Snyder, Gary. *Earth House Hold: Technical Notes and Queries to Fellow Dharma Revolutionaries*. New York: New Directions, 1969.

———. *Passage through India*. San Francisco: Fox, 2001.

Sobredo, James. "From Manila Bay to Daly City: Filipinos in San Francisco." In *Reclaiming San Francisco*, edited by Peter Brook, Chris Carlsson, and Nancy Joyce Peters, 273–86. San Francisco: City Lights, 1998.

Sollors, Werner. *Amiri Baraka/LeRoi Jones: The Quest for a "Populist Modernism."* New York: Columbia University Press, 1978.

Solnit, Rebecca. *A Field Guide to Getting Lost*. New York: Penguin, 2005.

———. *Infinite City: A San Francisco Atlas*. Berkeley: University of California Press, 2010.

———. *Storming the Gates of Paradise: Landscapes for Politics*. Berkeley: University of California Press, 2008.

———. *Wanderlust: A Brief History of Walking*. New York: Penguin, 2001.

Solnit, Rebecca, and Susan Schwartzenberg. *Hollow City: Gentrification and the Eviction of Urban Culture*. London: Verso, 2001.

Sommer, Doris. *Proceed with Caution, When Engaged with Minority Writing in the Americas*. Cambridge, MA: Harvard University Press, 1999.

Spahr, Juliana. *Fuck You–Aloha–I Love You*. Middletown, CT: Wesleyan University Press, 2001.

———. *This Connection of Everyone with Lungs*. Berkeley: University of California Press, 2005.

Spengler, Oswald. *The Decline of the West*. 2 vols. New York: Random House, 1945.

Spicer, Jack. *The House That Jack Built: The Collected Lectures of Jack Spicer*. Edited by Peter Gizzi. Hanover, NH: University Press of New England, 1998.

Spivak, Gayatri. *Death of a Discipline*. New York: Columbia University Press, 2005.

———. "Rethinking Comparativism." *New Literary History* 40, no. 3 (2009): 609–26.

Suiter, John. *Poets on the Peaks: Gary Snyder, Philip Whalen, and Jack Kerouac in the North Cascades*. Washington, DC: Counterpoint, 2002.

Tharaud, Barry. "Language, Noise, Silence: Communication and Community in Bowles's *Let It Come Down*." In Hibbard and Tharaud, *Bowles/Beats/Tangier*, 21–34.

Thoreau, Henry David. *The Portable Thoreau*. Edited by Carl Bode. New York: Penguin, 1982.

———. *A Week on the Concord and Merrimack Rivers*. New York: Dover, 2001.

Tietchen, Todd. *The Cubalogues: Beat Writers in Revolutionary Havana*. Gainesville: University Press of Florida, 2010.

Trotter, David. "Techno-Primitivism: À Propos of *Lady Chatterley's Lover*." *Modernism/Modernity* 18, no. 1 (2011): 149–66.

Tzara, Tristan. "Dada Manifesto 1918." In *Approximate Man and Other Writings*, edited and translated by Mary Ann Caws, 149–57. Detroit: Wayne State University Press, 1973.

Uexküll, Jakob von. *A Foray into the Worlds of Animals and Humans*. Translated by Joseph D. O'Neil. Minneapolis: University of Minnesota Press, 2010.

Van der Bent, Jaap. "Beating Them to It? The Vienna Group and the Beat Generation." In Grace and Skerl, *Transnational Beat Generation*, 165–78.

Vrbančić, Mario, "Burroughs's Phantasmic Maps." *New Literary History* 36, no. 2 (2005): 313–26.

Waldman, Anne. "Outrider: The Pedagogy." In *Outrider: Essays, Poems, Interviews*. Albuquerque: La Alameda, 2006.

Waldman, Anne, and Mary Kite. *Fleuve Flâneur*. Boulder, CO: Smokeproof, 2006.

Wallerstein, Immanuel. *World-Systems Analysis: An Introduction*. Durham, NC: Duke University Press, 2004.

Wark, McKenzie. *The Beach beneath the Street: The Everyday Life and Glorious Times of the Situationist International*. London: Verso, 2011.

Weiss, Jason. Introduction to Gysin, *Back in No Time*, ix–xiv.

Wheatland, Thomas. *The Frankfurt School in Exile*. Minneapolis: University of Minnesota Press, 2009.

Whitman, Walt. *Poetry and Prose*. Edited by Justin Kaplan. New York: Library of America, 1996.

———. *The Uncollected Poetry and Prose*. Edited by Emory Holloway. 2 vols. Garden City, NY: Doubleday, 1921.

Wild, Paul. "William S. Burroughs and the Maya Gods of Death." *College Literature* 35, no. 1 (2008): 38–57.

Williams, William Carlos. *Paterson*. Edited by Christopher MacGowan. New York: New Directions, 1995.

Wilson, Rob. *Be Always Converting, Be Always Converted: An American Poetics*. Cambridge, MA: Harvard University Press, 2009.

———. "Masters of Adaptation: Paul Bowles, the Beats, and 'Fellaheen Orientalism.'" *Cultural Politics* 8, no. 2 (2012): 193–206.

———. *Reimagining the American Pacific: From South Pacific to Bamboo Ridge and Beyond*. Durham, NC: Duke University Press, 2000.

———. "*Worlding* as Future Tactic." Afterword to Connery and Wilson, *Worlding Project*, 209–23.

Wilson, Rob, and Wimal Dissanayake, eds. *Global/Local: Cultural Production and the Transnational Imaginary*. Durham, NC: Duke University Press, 1996.

Winkiel, Laura. *Modernism, Race, and Manifestoes*. Cambridge: Cambridge University Press, 2008.

Worden, Curt. *One Fast Move or I'm Gone: Kerouac's Big Sur*. Providence, RI: Tango, 2008.

"World Economic Outlook Database." *International Monetary Fund*. April 2015. www.imf.org.

Yamashita, Karen Tei. *I Hotel*. Saint Paul, MN: Coffee House, 2010.

Yu, Timothy. *Race and the Avant-Garde: Experimental and Asian American Poetics since 1965*. Stanford, CA: Stanford University Press, 2009.

Žižek, Slavoj. *The Sublime Object of Ideology*. London: Verso, 1989.

CREDITS

INDEX